MODERN EUROPEAN SOCIALISM

To my friends from Merseyside

Modern European Socialism

LAWRENCE WILDE
Reader in Politics
The Nottingham Trent University

Dartmouth

Aldershot . Brookfield USA . Hong Kong . Singapore . Sydney

Published by
Dartmouth Publishing Company Limited
Gower House
Croft Road
Aldershot
Hants GU11 3HR
England

Dartmouth Publishing Company
Old Post Road
Brookfield
Vermont 05036
USA

British Library Cataloguing in Publication Data
Wilde, Lawrence
    Modern European Socialism
    I. Title
    320.531094

Library of Congress Cataloging-in-Publication Data
Wilde, Lawrence.
    Modern European socialism / Lawrence Wilde.
        p.   cm.
    Includes bibliographical references and index.
    ISBN 1-85521-446-6 (hbk.) - ISBN 1-85521-539-X (pbk.)
    1. Socialism--Europe. 2. Communism--Europe. 3. Europe--Politics
and government--20th century.   I. Title.
    HX238.5.W53   1994
    335'.0094--dc20   93-40046
                                                                              CIP

ISBN 1 85521 446 6 hbk
ISBN 1 85521 539 X pbk

Printed in Great Britain at the University Press, Cambridge

Contents

Preface

This book was conceived early in 1989, at a time when Europe was politically divided into the liberal democracies of the West and the communist dictatorships of the East. The postwar settlement had been in place for more than 40 years and the sundering of European socialism into communist and social democratic camps appeared to be permanent. It was clear at that time that both major forms of socialism were facing severe strategic problems in dealing with the economic environment which had changed so dramatically since the mid-1970s. These problems formed the subject matter of two courses at Nottingham Polytechnic, now The Nottingham Trent University, a final year undergraduate course, *Modern European Socialism*, and a postgraduate course, *Marxism and the State*. I am grateful to all the students who contributed to the discussion of these issues.

I am indebted to the following friends and colleagues who commented on a part or the whole of earlier drafts; Terrell Carver, Vince Geoghegan, Neil Harding, Stephen Heasell, Jill Krause, Joan Melia, Jill Murdoch, Rick Simon, Peter Thompson, Malcolm Vout, Immanuel Wallerstein, and Gordon Wightman. I am grateful to my colleagues in the Department of Economics and Public Administration for their support and encouragement, to Sandra Odell for preparing the manuscript, and Tim Walton for compiling the index. The Nottingham Trent University facilitated research visits to Prague and Warsaw, and my thanks go to the people in those cities who gave me such generous cooperation.

Lawrence Wilde
Nottingham, November 1993

1 Introduction

Is there a future for socialism? Since 1989 the communist dictatorships of Eastern Europe have fallen, Germany has been reunited, and the Soviet Union and Yugoslavia have disintegrated. There have been major advances towards a federal Europe, with the creation of the single market within the European Community and preparations in hand for its further integration and expansion. For democratic socialists who shared the popular exhilaration when the Berlin Wall was breached and when Havel and Dubček waved to a jubilant crowd in Wenceslas Square, the joy has been tempered by subsequent developments. Wars have erupted in the territories of the former Yugoslavia and the Soviet Union, and in many parts of Eastern Europe the common experience has been one of falling living standards, rising unemployment, and ethnic enmity. The ignominious collapse of communism has presented the opportunity for liberal and conservative critics to brand socialism as an anachronism, tainted with tyranny and inefficiency. Despite more than a decade of low growth and mass unemployment in Western Europe, socialist parties have failed to persuade their electorates that they can produce viable alternatives to the rule of the free market and the creation of a poverty–stricken sub–class. It is no exaggeration to speak of a crisis of socialism.

The wide variety of movements and ideas espousing the name 'socialist' places considerable strain on attempts to elucidate its meaning, but as Berki argued, the diversity within socialism does not justify attempts to deny it an identity (Berki, 1975: 15). Much light has been thrown on the meaning of socialism by looking at the history of its movements and influential ideas, and by theoretical analysis of the important concepts such as equality, solidarity, and social justice. The approach favoured here begins with the generalisation that the movements and ideas of socialism developed in response to the emergence of industrial capitalism and as a protest against its social consequences. As Dunn has claimed, 'the centre of socialist political theory – and by far its most robust, enduring and cogent component – has been its understanding of the intrinsic defects of the capitalist mode of production' (Dunn, 1984: 37). In similar vein, the notable English socialist G. D. H. Cole argued that the common thread of socialism was 'hostility to laissez–faire and economic competition, and belief in some sort of collective or cooperative action as a means of improving the condition of the many poor' (Cole, 1978: 79–80). These characterisations are sufficiently broad to cover a wide range of ideas and movements, but they imply the shared conviction that it is possible to organise society on the basis of cooperation in such a way as to dispense with extremes of vast wealth and dire poverty.

The word 'socialism' entered the language in the 1830s, but it was an ideal espoused by a variety of groups with sharply differing views on the society in which they lived (Williams, 1976: 238–9). Some thought it capable of reform and were willing to support liberal reformers against the conservative hierarchy. Others considered that liberalism was a sham and that the existing political and economic power structures had to be abolished through revolutionary action. Some even thought that they could create their own alternative communities in isolation from the state. One of the first points of strategic difference between socialist movements arose over the question of participation in the prevailing socio–political system. The anarchists opposed constitutional politics, and many of them opposed trade union organisation on the grounds that it collaborated with the very system which oppressed the workers. However, as participation in constitutional politics and economic struggles delivered significant gains for working people, anarchism was gradually eclipsed. In the leading capitalist country, Britain, reformist socialism predominated and Marx's revolutionary doctrines played only a marginal role. Elsewhere in Europe, however, Marxism became the predominant refrain of the socialist parties (Lichtheim, 1985; Lindemann, 1983; Landauer, 1976).

Marx (1818–83) left behind an ambiguous political legacy. He endorsed the revolutionary action which had set up the abortive Paris Commune of 1871, but also encouraged the idea that socialists could achieve their goals through peaceful means. In addition there was an apparent tension between his emancipatory and radical–democratic political views and the centralising logic of his commitment to the planned coordination of production (Selucky, 1979: 86–7). Within the Marxist movement there were a number of tendencies which reflected these ambiguities. In Germany, the home of the largest workers' movement, Eduard Bernstein's revision of Marx's ideas encouraged a form of evolutionary state socialism in the Social Democratic Party (Fletcher, 1987). Although his 'revisionist' position was rejected at SPD Congresses in 1899 and 1903, it was clear that reformism was a very important element in the party, and it contributed to the caution displayed by the majority of its leaders in the

1914–20 period. Karl Kautsky, the principal theorist of the SPD, advocated a 'strong reformism' which would lead to the gradual termination of capitalism and the transformation of society. Insurrection was ruled out, reserving the possibility of armed action only for purposes of defence against illegal reactionary interventions (Kautsky, 1983: ch. 7). Despite the more militant views of leaders such as Rosa Luxemburg and Karl Liebknecht, caution held sway in the German labour movement (Moses, 1987; Tegel, 1987). However, there was at least one revolutionary Marxist organisation which was not afraid to contemplate insurrection, the Bolsheviks in the Russian empire. Here the problem of being drawn into liberal political processes was less pronounced, since Russia was ruled by a Czarist autocracy and socialist politics was a hazardous, clandestine endeavour. V. I. Lenin engineered a split in the Social Democratic Party in 1903 to fashion a dedicated band of highly disciplined revolutionaries, although their strategy until 1917 was to support a liberal democratic revolution rather than a socialist one (Harding, 1971: ch. 7; Lane, 1982: ch. 2).

The differences between the various strands of socialism were accommodated within the institutional frameworks of the short–lived First International (1864–76) and the more powerful Second International (1889–1914). However, the superficial nature of this unity was exposed by the failure of the socialist parties to mount effective protests to the war efforts of their governments in 1914. Taking advantage of Russia's position as the 'weak link' in the capitalist world economy and its catastrophic war performance, the Bolshevik leaders seized power in 1917 in the hope of inspiring socialist revolutions elsewhere, in particular in Germany. Following the defeat of revolutions in Germany and Hungary, the Bolsheviks were left in isolation, in command of a huge agrarian country with a tiny industrial working class. In order to maximise international support, the Bolsheviks, renaming themselves the Communist Party, set up the Third International in Moscow in 1919 (Hulse, 1964). Its affiliates set up communist parties throughout Europe, and the great institutional and ideological schism within socialism between social democracy and communism had begun.

SOCIAL DEMOCRACY

'Social democracy' refers to those movements which have claimed to be socialist and have consistently adhered to parliamentary democracy as the ideal political process to pursue their goals. Distinctions have sometimes been made between social democrats and socialists on the basis that the former have accepted the permanence of the mixed economy and have abandoned the idea of replacing the capitalist system with a qualitatively different socialist society. For example, the French Socialist Party (PS) in the run up to the elections of 1981 spoke boldy of making a break from capitalism, and many PS members were keen to distinguish their 'socialism' from the cautious policies of the German Social Democrats (SPD). In practice, the PS in government, confronted with the same constraints on its reforming zeal which had faced the German SPD and the British Labour Party, responded in a similar way, much to the disappointment of many of its left–wing supporters. The Greek Socialist Party (PASOK) also sought to distinguish itself from the more moderate social democratic parties which had consistently and uncritically supported the American–led Atlantic Alliance, but when it achieved governmental power in 1981 its policies remained within the parameters of the social democratic model outlined below. It does not appear to be analytically useful to distinguish 'socialist' from 'social democratic' on the basis of intentions, rhetoric, or particular programmes adopted for specific historical reasons. In organisational terms there are important differences between the various parties, particularly in their relationships with the trades unions, but these can be viewed as differences within the social democratic family (Merkl, 1992). The majority of these parties are members of the Socialist International.

To describe a model of social democracy poses problems in encompassing considerable differences in organisation, tactics and rhetoric, but it is possible to discern some features which the various parties have shared. Perhaps the strongest and most consistent feature of social democracy has been its allegiance to parliamentary democracy as the *sine qua non* of legitimate political action. On the twin assumptions that wage earners would eventually form a majority of the population in most European countries and that universal franchise would be won, social democrats viewed parliament as the main focus of their efforts. However, the split in the European socialist movement occurred at the very moment when universal franchise was won in Germany, Austria, Denmark, Sweden, and Britain (Therborn, 1977; DuBois, 1991). In the inter–war period social democratic parties commanded more votes than their communist rivals, but only in Sweden, Norway and Austria were the social democratic parties able to secure more than 40 per cent of the votes. Elsewhere, social democracy lacked the electoral support, potential allies, or economic strategy to effect major reforms in difficult economic circumstances. In most of the countries of East and Central Europe the social democrats were limited to a clandestine existence under right–wing dictatorships. After the Second World War the vote was extended to women in France, Italy, and Belgium, and social democratic parties scored notable successes in Britain and Sweden. The peak of support for social democratic parties came in the 1960s and early 1970s, but only in Sweden and Austria did they achieve an overall majority support from the electorate (Padgett & Paterson, 1991b: ch. 3).

Many writers have noted the moderating effects of focusing political activity on parliament. Perhaps the most enduring theory related to this institutionalised conservatism is the 'iron law of oligarchy', formulated by Robert Michels in his study of the German Social Democratic Party before the First World War. Organisation was the weapon of the weak, he argued, but organisations inevitably adopted hierarchical and bureaucratic structures which concentrated power in the hands of an elite group of leaders. Those who achieved power within the organisation developed a vested interest in preserving the conditions on which their power had developed, even if it meant manipulating the decision–making process and compromising the party's initial revolutionary thrust (Michels, 1959: 21–2 & part 6). It might be argued that the revolutionary elements were always in the minority in most of the socialist parties, but it can hardly be doubted that the professionalisation of the parties produced strong moderating pressures on leaders. The 'iron law' appeared to be confirmed by the failure of the member parties of the Second International to try to use their power to prevent hostilities in 1914. At this moment it was clear that socialist parties risked suspension or even suppression, and that they had much to lose in terms of funds and property. The Bolsheviks took a firm anti–war stance, but as a banned group they had nothing to lose (Wallerstein, 1984: 114–5). The social democratic parties also saw that support for the war effort might bring rewards such as the extension of the franchise and popular support for their patriotism (Eley, 1987: 65–6).

The electoral focus tempts social democratic parties to tailor policies to accord with what is considered popular with the majority, even though this may be based on narrowly perceived self–interest or reactionary sentiments such as national chauvinism. Faced with the domination of the means of communication by anti–socialist interests, social democratic parties might consider that the task of educating or persuading the electorate to support radical policies is simply too great. For example, in recent years the low taxation policies suggested by neo–liberal economists were accepted by many social democratic parties for fear of losing the support of those on middle incomes, even though this excluded the possibility of using increased public expenditure to tackle unemployment and poverty. Social democratic parties have sometimes appeared to take a 'tough' stand against immigration to assuage reactionary popular sentiment, as for example when the French Socialist Government under Prime Minister Edith Cresson organised a public deportation of illegal immigrants in 1991.

For decades social democratic parties combined their focus on elections and parliament with a mass grassroots movement. However, in the face of a hostile media anxious to magnify disagreements or expose 'extremists', social democratic leaders may prefer a party of followers rather than activists. Lacking the communist–style discipline of democratic centralism, the leaders of social democratic parties may be embarrassed by the radicalism of certain sections of the membership. The electoral drive to present a united image may well encourage leaders to demobilise the party by expelling 'extreme' members, dissolving youth organisations, or 'managing' decision–making processes using the range of techniques described by Michels. Certainly there has been a sharp decline in party membership in recent years.

The second feature of social democracy has been its commitment to guaranteed minimum levels of social welfare for all citizens, so that health, education, housing, pensions, unemployment and disability benefits would be provided as a legal entitlement. In Germany in the 1920s, the SPD, either as coalition partners or as a powerful opposition, helped to establish the basis of a welfare state. In Sweden, the electoral successes of the Social Democratic Party in the 1930s led to welfare reforms rather than nationalisation of key industries. After the Second World War, the Labour Government in Britain established the major institutions of the welfare state, including a comprehensive free national health service, and, for the first time, involved trade unions on state bodies. In France, important developments in welfare provision occurred in the immediate postwar years under the coalition government which contained socialists and communists. Since the mid–1970s there has been considerable pressure on governments to limit public expenditure. The rise in unemployment led to a large increase in transfer payments, but there has been a tendency to shorten or reduce benefits, and to target them rather than make them 'universal'. Attacks on the welfare state from the Right have not destroyed its basic elements. They have, however, pressured social democrats into re–examining some of the excessively bureaucratic and patriarchal aspects of the old system, and to examine new ideas such as basic income schemes (Van Parijs, 1992).

Social democracy strove to secure its welfare goals by controlling the national economy. Many social democrats believed that this control would be gained by progressive nationalisation of the means of production, as a logical outcome of the monopolistic tendencies of capitalism. However, there have been a number of different strategies employed to try to achieve 'control'. In Sweden, for example, the Social Democratic Workers Party (SAP) in government was highly successful in maintaining full employment and high levels of welfare provision, but it chose not to embark on the widespread nationalisation of industry. In Britain the postwar Labour government nationalised many industries but did not inaugurate a planning system. In France in 1981 a sweeping nationalisation programme was undertaken by the socialist–communist government, but after 1983 these industries were compelled to behave on a strict profit and loss basis in the same way as private industries. As we shall see, this created a large public sector, but with less central planning than at any time in the postwar period. During the long period of prosperity in the 1950s and 1960s many social democratic leaders became convinced that they could exert sufficient control over the national economy to sustain exponential growth and redistributive policies. They assumed that the advent of the welfare state/mixed economy had changed capitalism fundamentally, so that the problem of major cyclical crises had been resolved through Keynesian economic management. Social democracy moved away from images of class struggle led by the organised industrial working class and sought to build a broad consensus around the goal of a society of equal opportunity. This was marked by major programmatic changes. The 1958 Bad Godesberg programme of the German SPD, with its slogan of 'as much competition as possible, as much planning as necessary', expressed its acceptance of the permanence of the mixed economy (Graf, 1976: ch. 7). The British Labour Party leaders, known as 'revisionists', attempted unsuccessfully to remove the socialist clause four from its constitution in 1959, but the party adopted a statement of aims which acknowledged the permanence of the mixed economy (Haseler, 1969). The two largest social democratic parties in the world thereby abandoned the vision of a socialist society qualitatively different from the full–employment welfare state.

The assumptions on which this redistributive strategy was based were shredded by the collapse of the postwar boom and the development of a cyclical depression comparable on a world scale to that of the 1930s. The experiences of the British Labour Governments of 1974–9 and the French Socialist Government of 1981–6 demonstrated the limits of the power left to social democratic governments in pursuing Keynesian policies when the major players in the world economy reacted to the inflationary crisis with deflationary policies. It became more difficult than ever before to resist the trend towards lower growth, cuts in welfare expenditure, and the return of mass unemployment. The crucial factors here were the increased openness of the world economy and the 'transnationalisation' of production. Between 1963 and 1980 the propensity to trade of the developed countries doubled (Gill & Law, 1988: 145–6), increasing pressure on governments to ensure the most favourable conditions for capital accumulation. Production became increasingly dominated by large multinational corporations which were in a strong bargaining position *vis a vis* national governments.

The rapid expansion of the world economy and its domination by huge multinational corporations developed under the hegemony of the United States. Hegemony can be defined as 'a situation in which a single core power has demonstrable advantages of efficiency simultaneously in production, commerce, and finance', and in which 'one power can impose its rules and wishes (at the very least by effective veto power) in the economic, political, military, diplomatic, and even cultural arenas' (Wallerstein, 1984: 5 & 38; Chase–Dunn, 1989: 169–71). The USA dramatically increased its output and productivity during the Second World War, and its capacity was completely intact at the end of hostilities. As its potential economic rivals were either defeated or greatly weakened by the physical and financial cost of the conflict, the stage was clear for its domination of the world market (Kennedy, 1988: 459–80). Its two potential rivals were in no position to match it; Britain was exhausted by its war effort and unable to maintain the global commitments which it had inherited from the previous century, while the Soviet Union was devastated by a war which had claimed the lives of over 20 million of its people.

Every hegemonic power favours free trade, since it is in the best position to benefit from it, as Britain had done in the mid–nineteenth century. The USA elected to revive world trade in a series of bold measures. The Bretton Woods agreement of 1944 secured the pre–eminence of the dollar as the international currency, initiating fixed exchange rate mechanisms which remained in place until 1971. The International Monetary Fund and the World Bank were set up to promote development and trade and their policies were dominated by the chief financier, the United States. The General Agreement on Tariffs and Trade was a flexible agreement to progressively reduce tariffs, initiated in 1947, since when it has greatly assisted the internationalisation of capital (Brett, 1985: ch. 3). The most spectacular American intervention was the plan for massive economic aid for Europe advocated by US Secretary of State George Marshall in a speech at Harvard University in June 1947 (Hogan, 1989: ch. 1). Faced with the sudden contraction of the war economy, the United States was threatened by the likelihood of massive over–capacity and the return of the depression unless new markets could be found. The potential demand existed in hungry Europe, but everywhere there was a dollar shortage; the Marshall plan solved the problem at a stroke, by giving the European nations the dollars with which to buy American products. At the same time it secured long–term trading advantages for the United States (Van der Pijl, 1984: 143–50; Loth, 1988: 184–5).

More was produced in the postwar boom than in the previous three quarters of a century, and the world economy became highly interdependent and increasingly dominated by a relatively small number of huge multinational corporations. The process of capital 'concentration' has greatly increased through mergers and takeovers since 1974. The power of these corporations to 'play off' nation against nation by demanding low taxes and investment incentives was increased by the advent of unemployment, for governments became desperate to protect jobs and attract investment. The power of the multinationals to move operations to other countries was formidable. The threat of unemployment made workforces more compliant and greatly weakened the influence previously exerted by trade unions, whose organisational power and resources had been a pillar of strength of social democracy in the postwar period, particularly in Britain, Germany, and the Scandinavian countries. The effects of changes in the production process have undermined the strength of communities and institutions which have traditionally nourished the socialist movements. In the most advanced capitalist countries the number of industrial workers began to decline in relative terms. Communities based on old industries began to shrink, the old craft unions rapidly lost members and influence, and social solidarity was weakened by the ideological onslaught of competitiveness and individualism. As the industrial workforce formed the bedrock of support and recruitment for the social democratic and communist parties, the shrinking of this natural constituency has presented a serious challenge for socialists.

The final strand of the social democratic model is its internationalism, its greatest potential strength and perhaps its biggest historical weakness. As the early formation of the First and Second Internationals indicates, socialists of different hues recognised the importance of moving beyond the politics of the nation state. However, the logic of parliamentary competition meant that they had to compete with other parties to demonstrate that they were responsible custodians of the 'national interest', even though that national interest was largely defined by the interests of national capital. The commitment to parliamentary democracy and civil liberties meant that social democracy could not make common cause with communism, but in the immediate postwar period most of its leaders saw the possibility of creating a 'third way' between the American model of *laissez–faire* capitalism and Soviet communism. This was explicit in the speeches of British Labour leaders Attlee and Bevin. But the European countries were caught up in the polarised reality of the Cold War, and social democracy elected for the American camp. It received a great deal of encouragement and covert assistance from the American Government, and it played a very active part in welcoming the American intervention in Europe (van der Pijl, 1984: 150–6; Carew, 1987: 244–5). The social democratic parties in the West, many faced with the responsibilities of government and the dreadfully low living standards of their constituents, saw little option but to accept Marshall Aid, despite communist accusations of selling out to the Americans. Not only did this mean that 'broad Left' coalitions were ruled out after 1947, but from 1949 it also meant the division of international trade unionism into the communist World Confederation of Trade Unions and the social democratic International Confederation of Free Trade Unions. The Atlantic Alliance was sealed by the coordination of military power through the North Atlantic Treaty Organisation (NATO), founded in 1949.

The Socialist International was not reconstituted until 1951. The one conceivable way in which social democratic forces might have been able to exert some independence from the super powers was to support moves for a European federation. Indeed the inaugural declaration of the International stated that no nation could resolve its problems in isolation, and that national sovereignty had to be transcended (Featherstone, 1988: 1). In practice the British and Scandinavian parties, the strongest in Europe, showed little interest in a strong international or a federal Europe. The USA, however, anxious to strengthen Western Europe as a bulwark against the Soviet Union, required a measure of co–operation from the countries accepting Marshall Aid, and in this way encouraged the development of trans–European institutions, starting with the European Coal and Steel Community in 1951 and then developing significantly with the formation of the European Economic Community in 1957. It has taken decades for social democracy to move from rhetorical acknowledgement of the need to transcend national sovereignty to serious consideration of the potential for the development of social democratic politics at the level of a federal European state. In helping to rebuild the war–ravaged economies of Japan and Europe, the USA undermined its own economic supremacy (Kennedy, 1989: 665–92; Chase–Dunn, 1989: 185–8). Social forces from across the political spectrum began to appreciate the potential power of a more integrated Europe, and the boldest steps in this direction were initiated by the President of the European Commission, Jacques Delors, formerly a Minister in the French Socialist Government of 1981. The Socialist Group in the European Parliament formed the largest group following the 1989 elections, and it was strengthened by the addition of the Italian Party of the Democratic Left (PDS), formerly the Communist Party, which joined the Socialist International in 1992. During the Presidency of the former German Chancellor Willy Brandt (1976–92) the International has taken on a less Eurocentric appearance. By 1992 it embraced 88 parties attracting worldwide electoral support of over two hundred million. Although it is largely a consultative body, it has produced highly influential reports on the North–South economic divide and the perilous state of the world environment.

COMMUNISM

'Communism' began life as an alternative term to 'socialism', and was popularised by Marx and Engels in *The Manifesto of the Communist Party* in 1848. It referred to the goal of a co–operative stateless society in which production for profit was replaced by production for use (Carver, 1987: 65–70). The adoption of the name by the Bolsheviks and their supporters in the rest of Europe symbolised a complete break from those parliamentary socialists who had either supported the participation of their countries in the war, or who had acquiesced to it. The opposition of many western socialists to the Bolshevik revolution sharpened the division between communists and social democrats. Differences which at first appeared to be largely strategic or tactical developed into ideological confrontations on the nature of democracy and freedom (see ch.8).

Some may object to the use of the word 'communist' to describe the practices of communist parties and the postwar regimes in Eastern Europe. It is true that the Soviet and East European regimes did not claim that their societies were communist. Following Marx's distinction between the dictatorship of the proletariat and communism, they recognised that communism involved a self–regulated stateless society, and this was some distance away. Nevertheless, the achievement of this ideal was their stated goal, even though there was little in the life of these states that suggested they were getting closer to it. It could be argued that the practice of Soviet communism under Stalin and his followers was a betrayal of the original ideal, and that the emancipatory force of pre–Stalinist communism should not be discarded. However, the historical experience of communist party politics has surely doomed attempts to retrieve the original emancipatory meaning. Alternative designations of societies of the Soviet type such as 'state socialism' or 'actually existing socialism' are less satisfactory. While it is true that in abolishing private productive property they fulfilled one of the most important aspects of socialist thought, the abandonment of political liberty under communism ran counter to just about every other strand of socialist thought, including that of Marx.

Let us now try to sketch the principal features of the communist model. The first relates to the question of party organisation, which operated according to the principle of 'democratic centralism' (Waller, 1981). In theory this implied full discussion of an issue before a vote was taken, followed by iron discipline in supporting and acting on the outcome. By the mid–1920s open discussion had been virtually eliminated within the Soviet Communist Party, so that what was left was centralism without democracy, requiring unquestioning obedience by subordinate bodies to the decisions taken by the leadership. The leadership itself ceased to be chosen democratically once Stalin achieved dictatorial power. This authoritarian system also operated within the International (Claudin, 1975). The executive committee (Comintern), directed by Stalin, imposed its 'line', and all communists spoke as with one voice. As such it was very difficult to gauge the sincerity of a communist, as the line was altered in startling fashion, according to what was deemed efficacious to the defence of the Soviet Union. For example, communists were instructed to denounce social democrats as 'social fascists' between 1928 and 1934, and in Germany this had the disastrous effect of allowing the Nazis to assume power and destroy the entire Left. Between 1935 and 1939 the communists belatedly advocated 'popular front' movements embracing all 'democrats' against the fascist menace, but this phase ended with the signing of a pact between the Soviet Union and Nazi Germany. Communists everywhere who had been calling for war against fascism now denounced the idea of such a war as an inter–imperialist conflict in which communists should play no part. When the Soviet Union was invaded in 1941 the communists reverted to their pre–1939 position and threw themselves into the fight against fascism. This discipline continued after the war, and although Yugoslavia, China and Albania chose independent paths, the invasion of Czechoslovakia in 1968 showed that there were strict limits to the autonomy enjoyed by the regimes within the Soviet sphere. For western communists, democratic centralism also applied, although without the use of state coercion to back it up differences of opinion sometimes spilled out.

Another feature of the model was contempt for parliamentary or 'bourgeois' democracy, which was viewed as a sham which masked the real locus of power in capitalist society. Against this was posited the superiority of 'soviet democracy', based on the spontaneous bodies which developed in the Paris Commune of 1871 and the Russian Revolutions of 1905 and 1917 (Liebman, 1985). These bodies worked on a delegate system whereby the representatives could be recalled at any time. They were supposed to exercise power directly and be much more sensitive to the needs of the people. In practice the soviets in the Soviet Union were quickly controlled by the Communist Party and all other parties were abolished. Elections to the soviets were a sham, and not until the late 1980s were elections open to more than a single candidate. In some of the other communist states a plurality of candidates was permitted, but they were also approved by the communist authorities. Other parties had a nominal existence in some of the communist states, but they operated only as transmission belts for communist policies to be explained and applied to specific interests, such as the peasantry (Lovenduski & Woodall, 1987: 288–92). Independent political activity, including that of the socialist parties, was banned in all of the communist states. Parliaments in communist states had no democratic credentials; they passed laws unanimously at the behest of the communist leadership which did not deem it necessary to seek a mandate through free elections. For the communists operating in liberal democracies the advent of 'Eurocommunism' in the 1970s signalled a more positive acceptance of political pluralism and the civil liberties which were all too obviously lacking in the communist countries. However, those parties were slow to democratise their own organisations, and they had difficulty in convincing sceptical voters that this was not simply another 'tactical' turn.

A major feature of the communist model in those countries where the communists held power was the abolition of private productive property and the organisation of the system of production by a central planning apparatus (the system of 'material balances') rather than by market mechanisms (Mandel, 1974: ch. 15). This system was imposed on the countries which became communist as a result of the postwar settlement, although there were national variations, such as the retention of private farms in Poland. Control of the 'command economy' provided the material basis of communist power and also presented a powerful institutional obstacle to reform of the system. All major appointments within the huge administrative apparatus of planning bodies, ministries, enterprises and public bodies were made with approval of the party, through a system known as the *nomenklatura*. The system of production was never self–sufficient, even when the communists held power only in the Soviet Union, but it held a considerable degree of autonomy within the world economy until the late 1970s. In the postwar period the communist economies traded between themselves within the Council of Mutual Economic Assistance, better known as COMECON. They were increasingly drawn into trade within the world economy, importing technology from the advanced capitalist countries and exporting cheap manufactures, fuel and raw materials to the West and the third world (Frank, 1980: 315–6). This involvement in the world economy created enormous difficulties which were beyond the capacity of the communist authorities to resolve. Ultimately it exploded the basic assumption on which the success of the communist model was always based, that the communist countries could catch up and surpass the productivity of the capitalist countries, something the Soviet Prime Minister was promising as late as 1986 (Sakwa, 1990: 270).

The question of the relationship between the Soviet bloc and the rest of the world moves us on to consider the global dimension of the communist model. In the inter–war years the Soviet Union was isolated and fearful of invasion, which eventually came in 1941. The defeat of Germany led to a consolidation of Soviet power, with territorial gains including the Baltic republics of Latvia, Lithuania, and Estonia. The 'spheres of influence' agreements which Stalin made with Churchill in 1944 (Churchill, 1988a: ch. 16; Churchill, 1988b, chs. 14, 15) had developed into the effective division of Europe by 1948, with the communist model extended to Poland, Czechoslovakia, Bulgaria, Romania, Hungary and Albania. In 1955 these countries joined with the Soviet Union in a military alliance sealed by the Warsaw Pact, and they were joined by East Germany the following year. The political division of Germany created the front line of the bitter rivalry between the two great power blocs led by the Soviet Union and the United States. The prospect of mutual destruction through nuclear warfare ensured that war did not break out in Europe, but communists came to power through armed struggle in China, Korea, Cuba, South–East Asia, and parts of Africa, and these movements received considerable assistance from the European communist states.

The Soviet influence on the communist parties of the world changed after Stalin's death. It had been flouted by the defection of Yugoslavia from the 'family' in 1948, but it was impaired more seriously after 1961 by the rift between China and the Soviet Union. Togliatti, the leader of the Italian Communists, argued in the late 1950s and early 1960s that national parties had to have autonomy to deal with their specific conditions, and he claimed that there was 'polycentrism' in the relationship between the various parties (Daniels, 1985: 227–9). However, the Soviet invasion of Hungary in 1956 and the Warsaw Pact invasion of Czechoslovakia in 1968 demonstrated the limits of Soviet tolerance of dissent in its 'zone' (Dawisha, 1988: part 1). The 1968 invasion provoked open protests by several communist parties in Western Europe, and the Eurocommunist strategy which developed in its wake began to suggest that communism was becoming 'polymorphic', adopting different forms for different circumstances (Waller & Szajkowski, 1986). In fact the communist model was crumbling, but an extensive network of political and cultural contacts was maintained: The 'family' continued to share the emotional bonds of Lenin and the Russian Revolution, still regarded by all communists as the harbinger of world socialist revolution.

PERSPECTIVES AND STRUCTURE

The rest of this book will look at the responses of social democratic and communist parties to the conditions created by changes in the world economy since the collapse of the postwar boom in the early 1970s. It is an attempt to flesh out the implications for particular socialist movements in Europe of the daunting insights provided by global political economy (e.g. Lipietz, 1987; Palan & Gills, 1993; Strange, 1988). If it is true that the progressive globalisation of production and trade has greatly reduced the capacity of socialist movements to devise viable egalitarian programmes at the level of the nation–state, has socialism lost its relevance? As Chase–Dunn has admitted, some radical critics of 'world–system' approaches have argued that 'emphasis on the structural importance of global relations leads to political do–nothingism while we wait for socialism to emerge at the world level' (Chase–Dunn, 1989: 343). In order to retain the insights of the global approach while resisting the tendency to skate over particular political and social conditions, the need to 'transcend the global–state divide' has been identified (Palan & Gills, 1993). This is imperative when dealing with Europe, for the continent is in the process of reconstituting itself and the political, economic and social outcomes are highly contestable.

The early chapters comprise of a number of case studies of social democratic parties in government which will examine not only the policies which they attempted to implement but also the alternatives which were urged on them by others in the socialist camp. The recent electoral failures of these movements poses the crucial question of how they can devise viable egalitarian strategies which will attract broad popular support. The chapter on Germany includes a discussion of the Social Democrats in government in the Federal Republic, but is extended to examine communism in the former Democratic Republic. The two Germanies provided the site of the clash between social democracy and communism, and Germany has also witnessed left–wing attempts to promote a new form of radical politics, the 'new' politics of new social movements. At the heart of the emerging European state, the progress of the Left in Germany is of crucial significance. The middle chapters deal with the experience of communism in Western Europe and the relationship between socialism and the politics of new social movements. The latter is particularly important, since it will be argued that if socialism is to recover its energy to challenge the power of global capitalism, an articulation of the new and the old 'antisystemic' movements is required (Arrighi, Hopkins & Wallerstein, 1989: ch. 4). Three chapters deal with Soviet–type communism and its aftermath. In view of the collapse of communist state power and the disintegration of the Soviet Union, it is timely to appraise the premises of communist politics as they developed in their heartland, and to examine the frailty beneath the surface strength of 'socialism in one zone'. The chapter on the failure of major political or economic reform movements in communist states again shows the decisive importance of the international political and economic context. Chapter ten examines the demise of communism in Poland and Czechoslovakia and the regrouping of the Left there following the collapse of the dictatorships. The conclusion explores the possibility of developing a new socialist internationalism capable of providing solutions to the most pressing problems facing Europe, and at the same time offering the hope of a more egalitarian world order.

2 The Travails of Labour in Britain

When Harold Wilson formed a Labour Government following the election of February 1974 he presided over a party which had recently adopted one of the most radical programmes in its history. It coincided with the onset of a global crisis of capitalism which defied the expectations of professional economists throughout the western world, with the notable exceptions of Ernest Mandel (1987, ch. 17) and André Gunder Frank (1980: 68). The 'trigger' which precipitated the cyclical crisis was the quadrupling of oil price rises in the winter of 1973–4, and economic growth faltered alarmingly throughout the world from the summer of 1974 (Armstrong, Glyn & Harrison, 1984: ch. 13). These were the daunting conditions which faced Labour. This chapter will examine the Labour Government's responses to the pressures imposed by the international economic crisis, and the critical reaction of the Labour Left to those responses. The experience dramatically revealed the limitations of political power at the level of the medium–sized nation state in coping with pressures exerted by changes in the world economy. The issues dealt with here – economic management, the role of the state as a mediator between capital and labour, and the future of the European community – have a wider relevance, for Labour's battles foreshadowed similar problems which continue to beset social democracy throughout Europe.

First let us briefly review the development of socialist politics in Britain prior to the period in question. As befits the first fully industrialised nation, Britain has had one of the strongest labour movements in the world, with one of the highest levels of trade union membership. Its socialist origins predate Marx, and Marxism has played only a marginal role in its history (Webb, 1987). The Labour Party adopted a socialist constitution in 1918 (Miliband, 1973: 60–1), but in two short–lived minority governments in the interwar years it attempted no radical reforms. Unlike most of the other European countries, Britain did not have a large Communist Party to take votes and members from Labour, and in 1945 it swept to power under Clement Attlee. It nationalised many of the major industries and launched the welfare state, and even when losing the election of 1951 it commanded almost half the popular vote. When Attlee resigned in 1955, the new leader, Hugh Gaitskell, set about refashioning the party's image with an approach which came to be known as 'revisionism'. What was to be revised in this approach was the centrality of the goal of the public ownership of the means of production, common to virtually all forms of socialism until that time, subject only to disagreements about the pace and form that public ownership would take. The party was formally committed to it in clause four of the constitution, reproduced on party membership cards; 'to secure for the workers by hand or by brain the full fruits of their industry and the most equitable distribution thereof that may be possible, upon the basis of the common ownership of the means of production, distribution and exchange, and the best obtainable system of popular administration and control of each industry and service.' The revisionists considered that the changes which had been effected by the postwar Labour Governments had established effective state control over the economy, and calls for further nationalisation were destabilising and unnecessary (Haseler, 1969).

The most comprehensive revisionist text was Tony Crosland's *The Future of Socialism*, first published in 1956, in which he argued that the emergence of the welfare state and the mixed economy meant that it was 'misleading to continue talking about "capitalism" in Britain' (Crosland, 1968: 67). The adoption of Keynesian economic policy, with management of effective demand through fiscal measures and deficit budgets, appeared to have resolved the problem of the deep cyclical depression, and Marx's analysis of the inherent instability of capitalism was peremptorily dismissed. What was left for socialists was to use the benefits of exponential growth and full employment to attack the remaining inequalities. Election defeats in 1955 and 1959 were used by the revisionists as evidence that calls for more nationalisation were falling on deaf ears as the working class shared in growing prosperity. The revisionists controlled the party because they had the support of the leadership of the largest trade unions. In a full employment economy the union leaders were in a strong bargaining position with employers, and politically their chief interests were in extending and improving social welfare and in controlling their own rank and file, in which many Communist Party members were active. At Conference, the policy–making body of the party, the union block votes accounted for 80 per cent of all votes. One half of the National Executive Committee, which suggests and formulates policy, was elected by the trade unions. In the 1950s the unions sponsored about one third of the Parliamentary Labour Party. The overwhelming amount of party income came from the unions, particularly the funds for fighting elections. One of the few occasions in which the unions did not support Gaitskell was in his abortive attempt to persuade the Party to drop clause four from its constitution in 1959, but he succeeded in persuading Conference to accept a declaration of aims which explicitly recognised the desirability of private enterprise and declared that any nationalisation should take place only on a piecemeal and gradual basis. This move to the right was also taking place in most of the social democratic parties of northern Europe (Padgett & Paterson, 1991: ch. 1), in response to the twin 'pressures' of economic prosperity and anti–communist propaganda.

The hopes of the Left rose considerably when Harold Wilson became leader following Gaitskell's death in 1963, for he was a member of the left–wing Tribune Group of MPs. However, in an article for The New York Times in 1963 Wilson made it clear that he supported the declaration of aims adopted by the Conference in 1959 (Wilson, 1964: 263–70). The idea of socialism outlined in the article was described as 'pragmatic', one of the key words of Wilson's rhetoric, and his aim was clearly to establish a planned control over the economy which would demonstrate the superior efficiency of social democratic interventionism by promoting technological change. The institutional centrepiece of the modernising experiment was to be the National Plan operated by the Department of Economic Affairs, headed by his Deputy, George Brown. There was no anticipation of antagonism between Labour's aims and the capitalism it was preparing to manage. One thing that was acknowledged, however, was Britain's economic decline relative to its industrial rivals, and Labour aimed to halt the slide.

Labour won the 1964 election with 44 per cent of the popular vote and an overall majority of only three. The Government was faced with a large balance–of–payments deficit and was immediately placed under considerable pressure from financial institutions to take deflationary measures and effectively abandon the social reforms which formed such an important part of the revisionist programme (Wilson, 1971: 37–8). In the short term the Government's tactic was to blame the Conservatives for the previous 'thirteen wasted years' and to complain against the powers of 'foreign' financial speculators to weaken sterling. Allied to the communicative skills of the Prime Minister and the disarray of the opposition, the election of March 1966 brought a decisive majority of seats for Labour and a 48 per cent share of the vote. However, the Government struggled to conquer its economic difficulties and provided few radical reforms. The promise to make planning central to Labour's idea of socialism in the technological age was not met. In the heat of a series of 'emergency' measures to try to bring the economy under control, the national plan and the Department of Economic Affairs were marginalised and finally abandoned (Sked & Cook, 1979: chs. 8, 9; Coates, 1975: ch. 5). Wilson's own judgement on the Government acknowledged the overwhelming constraints imposed by the world economy. He claimed that for all but a year the life of the Government 'was dominated by an inherited balance of payments problem which was nearing a crisis at the moment we took office; we lived and governed during a period when that problem made frenetic speculative attack on Britain both easy and profitable' (Wilson, 1971: xvii).

The moderation of the Government contrasted starkly with the wave of radicalism among millions of young people in advanced capitalist societies. The biggest issue which upset the Left was the Government's tacit support for the American war effort in Vietnam. The pro–American stance of postwar Labour leaders dated back to Bevin's successful attempts to draw the United States into the defence of Western Europe against the Soviet Union. Britain was treated as a very junior partner by the US administration, which put heavy pressure on Wilson and Healey to maintain their defence commitments (Ponting, 1989: 392).

As early as 1964 Wilson had acknowledged that Britain's defences were 'over–stretched almost to breaking point' (Wilson, 1971: 42), but cuts were applied very slowly and with apparent reluctance. The American influence, founded on its economic and military power, had a profound impact on Labour. Gaitskell had been firmly committed to the 'special relationship' and it was an important factor in his opposition to British membership of the European Economic Community (Williams, 1979: 511–4; Callaghan, 1988: 297). The American connection was still powerful during the 1974–9 period, but it was to prove less than helpful to Labour.

The Labour Party in opposition moved sharply to the Left. There was a tremendous sense of disappointment among the grassroots membership, and trade unionists were affronted by the Labour Government's abortive attempt to impose restrictions on the legal powers of trade unions set out in the 1969 White Paper, *In Place of Strife*. The move to the Left was accelerated by the confrontational attitude of the Conservative Government which had been elected to power in 1970. It was marked by social and industrial struggles on a scale which had not been seen in Britain since the 1930s. The Fair Rents Act and the Industrial Relations Act provoked a series of clashes which culminated in a strike by mineworkers against the statutory pay policy. Against a background of a three–day working week brought on by fuel shortages, television broadcasts ending early to save power, and frequent power cuts, the Conservatives failed to win a majority in the election of February 1974.

CRISES AND CONFLICT

Labour could hardly claim a great victory, polling only 37 per cent of the vote, with both major parties losing considerable support to the Liberals. Wilson called an election for October in order to improve the position of his

Government, but the improvement – 39 per cent of the vote and a majority of only three over all other parties – was much smaller than he had hoped. It is worth pausing to consider these electoral statistics. Labour's move to the Left was reflected in its 1973 Programme and the subsequent manifestos. The party was committed to securing a 'fundamental and irreversible shift in the balance of power and wealth in favour of working people and their families' (Butler & Kavanagh, 1974: 50–1). The manifesto also promised the 'elimination of poverty', as well as measures to 'make power in industry genuinely accountable to the workers and community' (Craig, 1975: 398–405, 451–66). However much the supporters of the Left were determined to implement their programme, the fact remained that Britain's 'first–past–the–post' electoral system helped to obscure the limited popular support for it. A more proportional electoral system would have obliged Labour to negotiate a coalition. It may be argued that the Conservatives later pursued radical right–wing measures with electoral support hovering on the 43 per cent mark in four elections, but the resources available to parties of the Right are much greater than those available to parties seeking to challenge fundamental power relationships which have developed over centuries. In such a position it is likely that the socialists will face the hostility of international and national capital, the institutions of the state which have developed out of those social relationships, and the media.

It would be a mistake to assume that the Labour Government was determined to achieve its stated goals. In this case the radicalism of the manifesto was not reflected in the composition of the Parliamentary Labour Party, and the leadership remained in the hands of those who had been so cautious in 1964–70. Wilson commented that the February election indicated that 'they had voted against Mr. Heath and confrontation, rather than for Labour, still less for Labour legislation which had not even been clearly formulated' (Wilson, 1979: 14). The ground was therefore prepared for retreat from the outset. However, it was not true that Labour's programme was unclear. Indeed, the prominent American economist J. K. Galbraith had commented that Labour's programme 'improves on the past discussion of corporate power in Britain and vastly on the perception of the problem by parties of the Left in other countries' (Labour Weekly, 25 January 1974).

Labour's programme of 1973 was consciously designed to avoid the abandonment of strategic thinking which had happened after 1964, and to address the central problem of deficient investment. Like the 1964 Government, it aimed to tackle Britain's relative economic decline. Britain had shared in the postwar boom which had yielded an average annual growth rate for the advanced capitalist countries of 4.9 per cent between 1950 and 1973, compared with 1.9 per cent between 1913 and 1950 (Armstrong, Glyn & Harrison, 1984: 167). This brought a considerable expansion of consumer durable goods to the working class, yet Britain's average annual growth of 2.8 per cent in the

1951–73 period was much slower than that of her major rivals in Western Europe and Japan (Smith, 1989: 81). Class divisions remained wide, reinforced by a divisive education system and a rigid split between private and public housing, and access to the principal positions of power in society remained to a great extent the preserve of the propertied classes (Cronin, 1979; Miliband, 1969). Much has been written on Britain's comparative economic decline, but the most compelling argument, advanced by Pollard and others, centres on the long–term inadequacy of investment and the consequent failure to achieve the productivity rates of her rivals (Pollard, 1982; Brett, 1985: 171–3). Between 1950 and 1976 Britain's annual growth in productivity was 2.8 per cent, compared with Germany's 5.8 per cent, Japan's 7.5 per cent, and France's 4.9 per cent, while between 1950 and 1970 Britain's share of manufactured goods in world exports declined from 25.5 per cent to under 11 per cent (Gamble, 1985: 16–7).

One of the chief architects of Labour's industrial programme was Stuart Holland, who had acted as economic adviser to Harold Wilson for two years during his previous administration. Holland was particularly concerned that the increased power which multinational firms exerted in Britain made it very difficult for government to exert the sort of control over the economy assumed by Crosland in 1956. This autonomy of what he termed the mesoeconomic sector made it necessary to reverse the priorities set by Crosland's revisionism. Rather than intervening when the private sector was weak, the state should intervene where it was strong in order to ensure that it operated in the public interest (Holland, 1975: 29). The twin supports for this strategy were to be the National Enterprise Board (NEB) and compulsory planning agreements (see Hodgson, 1981). The NEB was to receive massive public funding which it could use to take control of key industries in each sector of the economy and direct investment in accordance with agreed objectives. Planning agreements would ensure that objectives were clearly specified and coordinated, and would bring a level of state control over the economy which had been witnessed only during the Second World War. In addition there was a commitment to some form of workers' participation in management, which would ensure full information and an element of control from below. One decisive retreat was made from the 1973 Programme, for Wilson made it clear that he would not fight the election committed to the nationalisation of 25 of the largest firms in the country. But even so, the two manifestos of 1974 were probably the most left–wing in Labour's history.

The arguments for the new strategy were based on a sound analysis of Britain's economic position. Trade was a more important component of its economic activity than most of its rivals, and trade within firms formed a high proportion of all trade – Barrett Brown maintained that over half of Britain's trade in the 1970s was within multinational companies (Barrett Brown, 1979:

50). Investment in manufacturing had for a long time trailed its competitors, and it had also been badly allocated (Meacher, 1982: 1–5). In addition, the state had greatly increased its expenditure to private industry in the form of regional grants and export credits, to the tune of £3 billion from 1970–4 (Forester, 1979: 82), and this was a lever which the Government could use to demand cooperation in planning agreements. The Left were in no mood to accept the argument that conditions were not right for the implementation of the new policy. But this time the conditions were indeed extraordinarily inauspicious. Wilson was justified in stating that 'Britain was facing an unparalleled economic crisis, the worse in that we were confronted by fourfold oil–price increases and by balance–of–payments problems unprecedented in our history' (Wilson, 1979: 13). Yet in supporting the Industry proposals at the 1973 Labour Party Conference he had stressed the importance of planning agreements and affirmed that the National Enterprise Board would not be merely 'a public holding and management agency' (Benn, 1979: 48). He put the rhetorical question: 'We have to ask ourselves, do the British people really want a society in which industrialists and bankers have more power over Britain's economic future than the governments they elect?' The man to be in charge of steering the industrial policy, Tony Benn, argued at the same Conference that the poor economic situation should not deter them – 'the crisis that we inherit when we come to power will be the occasion for fundamental change and not the excuse for postponing it' (in Hodgson, 1981: 95). Nevertheless, Benn knew that he would face resistance from his fellow ministers. When he was told that Wilson was to present the industrial policy to Conference in 1973, he wrote in his diary – 'here was the man who had been trying to stop the industrial policy all summer, who threatened to veto it and now wants to present it' (Benn, 1989: 58).

Benn had been a member of the 1964–70 Government, and the experience of a cowed and timid administration had moved him to the Left. In the year leading up to 1974 he had delivered a succession of speeches emphasising the need for industrial democracy, greater control over the economy, and more open government (Benn, 1974). The vigour of his rhetoric did not diminish with ministerial responsibility, despite the vitriolic hostility of the media, the leaders of British industry, the leading civil servants, and many of his own colleagues. Shortly after the February election he wrote in his diary that he felt 'totally isolated' (Benn, 1989: 118). His Permanent Secretary at the Department of Industry, Sir Anthony Part, tried to persuade him to drop the whole strategy, and warned him that he would face hostility from management as great as the Conservatives had faced from the trade unions over the Industrial Relations Act. Benn considered his own Department to be 'a mouthpiece of the Confederation of British Industry' (Benn, 1989: 138–9).

Wilson appointed himself to chair of the cabinet sub–committee which eventually produced the White Paper 'The Regeneration of British Industry'. The

White Paper dropped the commitment to compulsory planning agreements, there was no further talk of an 'official Trustee' to be appointed to run weak firms, and the National Enterprise Board was to be less powerful than had originally been planned (Hamilton, 1989: 135). The White Paper had been rewritten by the Policy Unit, headed by Bernard Donoghue, which monitored it through Parliament to ensure that 'extreme' amendments were not passed. Nevertheless, the White Paper created a 'major crisis' in Whitehall, according to Donoghue's own account (Donoghue, 1987: 52). Wilson has recorded that he had decided against compulsory planning agreements because it would run against the need for secrecy in innovation, and when his book appeared in 1979 he noted with satisfaction that 'more than three years after the second reading of the Bill, not a single planning agreement has been negotiated in respect of a privately owned venture (Wilson, 1979: 141). In fact there was one agreement, reached with Chrysler following the Government's humiliating donation of £184 million to them in December 1975 in the face of Chrysler's threat to close down its Scottish plant (Donoghue, 1987: 53). The planning agreement dissolved when the plant was sold to Peugeot–Citroen in 1978, a deal done without the Government's knowledge (Armstrong, Glyn & Harrison, 1984: 442). The NEB was restricted in its scope by financial limits, despite the original intentions and Benn's plea for increased funding of £1 billion a year (Forester, 1979: 84). James Callaghan, who became Prime Minister when Wilson resigned in 1976, accepted that it was saddled with the costs of keeping British Leyland and Rolls Royce afloat (Callaghan, 1988: 513), but throughout his term of office the Government was concerned with cutting expenditure rather than increasing it. Benn's central role in the industrial policy ended in the summer of 1975 when he was moved to the Department of Energy following the referendum on whether or not Britain should stay in the European Community. He was disappointed at the lack of top–level trade union support for him when he was demoted, but this was the very moment when the union leaders were involved in hammering out a voluntary pay agreement against the threat of a statutory one which was being pushed strongly by the civil service. His deputy, Eric Heffer, had already resigned because of the dilution of the Industry Bill in Commons Committees.

The handling of the industrial policy has to be seen in the broader context of economic policy as a whole. The fourfold increase in the price of oil which took place after the Arab – Israeli war triggered a deflationary response from the other governments of the advanced capitalist world. Labour's immediate settlement of the miners' strike which had brought down the Heath Government set the trend for a series of high wage increases throughout 1974, at a time when world trade was contracting. The rate of inflation reached 25 per cent in the spring of 1975, and it was at this time that leading trade unionists began to realise that this would quickly create an economic crisis which would bring the

Conservatives to power. As early as March 1975 the Government agreed to cut public expenditure for 1976–77 by 2 per cent, although the Ministry of Defence 'refused to accept or even discuss half the proposed cuts' (Donoghue, 1987: 61–2). Chancellor Healey proposed £3 billion cuts over 1975–9 in May 1975, and although this was rejected by Cabinet, it was now accepted that wage restraint would be necessary. The Treasury civil servants then did their utmost to foist a statutory policy on the Government, despite the fact that the previous attempt under the Conservative Government had ended in disaster. Wilson was on the verge of accepting this advice before being convinced by the Policy Unit that a voluntary policy could work (Haines, 1977: ch. 4). The first version of the 'social contract' between Labour and the unions had failed, but a revised version was agreed; the unions would restrain pay claims in return for a sympathetic attitude to working people from the Government (Taylor, 1976). In order to ensure that employers in the private sector did not offer higher wages, the Government warned that they would be subject to a range of sanctions, including the loss of Government contracts, regional subsidies and investment allowances.

Although the strikes which marked the winter of 1978–9 were decisive in ensuring the defeat of Labour, for four years trades union leaders and rank–and–file members kept their part of the social contract despite getting very little in return. Between 1974 and 1977 real disposable income actually declined, although it rose by two per cent over the whole period of Government, while the 'social wage' (benefits, health care and education) was hit by the successive deep spending cuts (Hodgson, 1981: 119) This was despite Wilson's pledge that although living standards would fall there would be a 'marked improvement in the provision of the social service "family bonus"' (Wilson, 1979: 111). Unemployment rose from just over half a million in 1974 to 1.6 million in 1977, falling to 1.3 million by 1979. Although this was no higher than in France, Germany, or the USA, it was a shocking departure from everything that social democrats had cherished. Although there was much worse to come after 1979, the passing of the one million mark brought back memories of the depression years of the 1930s, and the Conservatives were able to make good use of this in their propaganda.

When Wilson retired in March 1976, cuts of £3.5 billion in public expenditure had already been secured by the Treasury, but the Treasury then started – without any political authorisation – to sell sterling in order to achieve a *de facto* devaluation of the pound. This resulted in a crisis of confidence in the economy, manifested by a run on sterling which continued through the summer of 1976 and culminated in the political crisis which centred on the acceptance of a loan from the International Monetary Fund (Burk & Cairncross, 1992). A short term loan of $5 billion was granted in June 1976 by the group of ten industrial countries, but it was due to be repaid by December of the same year and therefore did nothing to relieve the pressure on the pound. The new Prime Minister, James Callaghan, failed in his attempts to convert this loan into a long term arrangement, and later recorded his dissatisfaction at the efforts of the Treasury and the Bank of England to achieve this (Callaghan, 1988: 420). This short term loan was the decisive lever used by the United States government, via the IMF, to break the residual radicalism of the Labour Government and to bring Britain into line with the deflationary monetarism being adopted elsewhere (Holmes, 1985: 87-8; Healey, 1989: 435-6). The decision to apply to the IMF for a loan had been taken in September 1976 by Callaghan, and a few weeks later at the Party Conference he bade farewell to Keynesian social democratic orthodoxy:

> The cosy world we were told would go on for ever, where full employment would be guaranteed by a stroke of the Chancellor's pen, cutting taxes, deficit spending – that cosy world is gone...We used to think that you could just spend your way out of a recession to increase employment by cutting taxes and boosting government spending. I tell you in all candour that that option no longer exists and that in so far as it ever did exist it worked by injecting inflation into the economy (Callaghan, 1988: 426).

However, there were still options open to the Government which were thrashed out at length in cabinet debates. In December it was decided to accept a loan of £2.4 billion in return for the promise of cuts in public expenditure of £2.5 billion over two years and the sale of £500 million worth of shares in British Petroleum (Holmes, 1985: 91). The IMF had originally asked for cuts of £5 billion.

Two groups of opposition to the loan appeared in Cabinet. One was the Keynesian defence led by Tony Crosland, and the other was the alternative economic strategy of the Left, presented in its strongest form by Benn and in a more restrained version by Peter Shore. Crosland considered that the economic situation faced by the Government simply did not warrant taking out a large loan at such a terrible price. He was prepared to countenance cuts of £500 million and the sale of government oil shares for a similar amount, and to tell the IMF, the Americans and the Germans that if they did not extend the loan without the unacceptable conditions, Britain would set up a siege economy and wind down her heavy defence commitments (Crosland, 1982: 378-82). The alternative economic strategy advocated by Benn called for import and exchange controls, nationalisation of the banking sector, the introduction of a wealth tax and higher taxes on petrol, alcohol and tobacco, as well as price controls, cuts in defence expenditure, and a strengthening of the NEB to ensure a high level of investment. Shore supported selective import and exchange controls, and argued that they were perfectly legal under the rules of the EEC and the General Agreement on Tariffs and Trade (GATT). Crosland and his supporters withdrew their opposition to the Healey plan when Callaghan made clear his support for it. Crosland had recently been appointed Foreign Secretary by Callaghan, and felt obliged to stand behind him in this crisis. Benn, in his diary, wrote of the 'total capitulation' of the Croslandites, yet it is conceivable that Crosland's original position might have been adopted if Benn had not undermined it by demanding to know what would be done if the IMF did not respond positively to his 'threats' (Benn, 1989: 661–80).

The divisions on how to deal with the IMF have been reflected in the accounts of the outcome of the deal. Crosland's assessment that no further deflationary measures were needed was proved correct, and Healey later admitted that 'the whole affair was unnecessary' because the Treasury had grossly overestimated the Public Sector Borrowing Requirement, which would have fallen within the IMF's limit 'without any of the measures they prescribed' (Healey, 1989: 432). Donoghue has argued that there was 'no economic justification for further deflation' and that what went on to become known as 'Thatcherism' was 'launched in primitive form at Mr. Callaghan in 1976 from the Treasury, from the Bank [of England], and above all from the IMF and sections of the US Treasury' (Donoghue, 1987: 94). Giles Radice, an orthodox Keynesian Labour MP, has argued that there was no need for the loan and that it delivered a 'severe psychological setback' (Radice & Radice, 1986: 69). Wilson noted 'the intervention of the IMF Cheka in the autumn of 1976 put a stranglehold on the Government's economic policies' (Wilson, 1979: 241), again showing his awareness of the constraining power of international capitalism without indicating how it might be resisted. Tribune, the weekly newspaper of the Party Left, greeted the decision with the headline 'The Last Straw'. Callaghan later defended the deal as a beneficial cheap loan which bought time and helped to bring the economy under control (Callaghan, 1988: 446–7). Healey agreed, arguing that 'despite the fact that we used only half of the IMF loan, and might have managed without it altogether, it marked the turning point in our affairs' (Healey, 1989: 435). This 'technical' judgement pays no attention to the fact that it was widely perceived to be a humiliating surrender.

The public passed judgement on the Government's competence in April 1977, when Labour lost a by-election at Ashfield, where it had enjoyed a 23,000 majority. By this time a string of by-election defeats had seen its electoral majority disappear, and Labour entered a pact with the Liberals to ensure survival. In future all legislation was to be discussed in advance with the Liberal leadership. The results of the 'pragmatic' Wilson–Callaghan–Healey leadership, later supported by the Liberals, did nothing to address the problems which Britain faced in relation to her competitors:

Output per hour in manufacturing rose by only 5 per cent between 1973 and 1978 compared with 15 to 25 per cent in its major competitors... By mid-1979 imports of finished manufactures was 70 per cent higher than in 1973, while domestic production had not risen at all (Armstrong, Glyn & Harrison, 1984: 442).

In a world in which the major economic powers reacted to the collapse of growth in 1974–5 with deflationary policies, the moderate postwar social democratic strategy was blown away. The average annual growth in Gross Domestic Product in Western Europe had been 4.3 per cent between 1960 and 1973, and this reduced to 1.9 per cent between 1973 and 1981 (Armstrong, Glynn & Harrison, 1984: 347). In Germany growth declined from 4.7 per cent between 1960 and 1973 to 3 per cent between 1973 and 1978, but in Britain the decline was much more serious, from 3.2 per cent between 1960 and 1973 to 0.8 per cent between 1974 and 1978 (Gill and Law, 1988: 337). At the same time the volume of trade doubled in dollar terms in the developed capitalist countries (Gill & Law, 1988: 232 & 146). Despite a slowdown in the growth of trade at the height of the crisis in 1979–82, the continued transnationalisation of production greatly constrained the ability of individual nation–states to apply conventional social democratic measures of protection and redistribution. In Britain this was particularly difficult because of the openness of the economy and the unwillingness of private capital to cooperate in corporatist arrangements.

Was there, then, no alternative for Labour to follow? The Government ought to have been better prepared for the effect of the 1973–4 oil price rise. During its first year there was not one sustained discussion of economic policy in cabinet or cabinet committee (Donoghue, 1987: 51). Partially as a result of this lack of strategic planning, inflation rose to 25 per cent in 1975 and little thought was given to infrastructural projects and training programmes to offset job losses. The financial crisis of 1976 which culminated in the IMF loan was certainly fuelled by both the British Treasury officials and the US Treasury. It is now generally acknowledged that the loan was economically unnecessary (Burk & Cairncross, 1992). Either Crosland's 'bluff' option or the left–wing alternative economic strategy was feasible, but both implied standing up to American pressure in a way which the Labour leadership was not prepared to contemplate. Both Healey (Healey, 1989: 111–4, 121, 307) and Callaghan had long been staunch supporters of the Atlantic alliance. When President Ford expressed concern that Labour would respond to the 1976 crisis by imposing import controls, Callaghan reassured him that he opposed the alternative economic strategy because it would 'call into question Britain's role as an Alliance partner which I am anxious to preserve' (Callaghan, 1988: 430). As Foreign Secretary in 1974 Callaghan had made it a priority to strengthen the American alliance, which he considered had been weakened by Britain's entry to the EEC (Callaghan, 1988: 295). This loyalty to the USA was not repaid at the time of the IMF crisis, and Benn records Callaghan as saying that he felt anti–American for the first time in his life (Benn, 1989: 687).

In theory the alternative economic strategy might have succeeded in protecting jobs and arresting cuts in public expenditure, at least in the medium term. However, if it were not to lead to a new surge in inflation, a mixture of enormous cuts in defence expenditure and higher taxes would have been needed. Labour leaders had always been careful to reassure the voters that they were reliable on defence, and they largely accepted the views of the defence establishment when it came to deciding on the safety of the nation. Accordingly, there was a reluctance to seriously reduce the military budget, and throughout the 1970s Britain spent more than 2 per cent more of its Gross National Product on defence than France and Germany (Meacher, 1982: 7). The 1974–9 Government suffered greatly from the anachronistic commitment to Britain's world role, which included a nuclear arsenal and an army of over 50,000 troops in Germany. The Labour leaders spurned the opportunity to use its defence contribution as a bargaining lever in loan negotiations, and given Labour's postwar history this was hardly a surprise.

Ultimately, the alternative strategy did not have sufficient support in Cabinet or in the Parliamentary Labour Party. If it had brought a surprise conversion from the Prime Minister, with the support of the Croslandites, its implementation would have brought outright opposition from the Liberals and probably defections from within Labour. It would have certainly provoked capital flight and an investment strike. Politically, it may have been less harmful to Labour in the long term if it had refused to agree to deep cuts in social expenditure and taken the risk of going into opposition, which was apparently the position of Michael Foot (Benn, 1989: 673). But to go down with flags flying would have been a bold move indeed for a new Prime Minister who had spent a long career hoping for the call to the highest office. The leadership was always going to hang on in the hope of stabilising the economic situation and enjoying the boost of the revenues from North Sea oil, which had not yet come on stream.

THE STILLBIRTH OF CORPORATISM

The hostility of the leaders of industry and finance towards Labour intensified as the economic situation grew worse and a coherent alternative began to emerge from the Conservatives under Margaret Thatcher. Callaghan's attempt to form a tripartite corporatist consensus (Callaghan, 1988: 425) between the state, the unions, and the Confederation of British Industry (CBI), failed to materialise principally because the CBI was in no mood to cooperate. 'Corporatism', in which the state brings together the representatives of capital and labour to coordinate economic steering and to manage industrial relations, is widely regarded with suspicion from the Left because it implies the integration and pacification of the labour movement (Panitch, 1986). But in times of economic crisis it is the Right who become suspicious of any mechanisms which prevent the unfettered pursuit of profitability. Any power given to organised labour is resented. The 'new' Conservatism based its strategy ostensibly on fighting inflation by strict monetary controls, with the clear implication of mass unemployment, the most effective way to break the power of organised labour (Gamble, 1988: ch.2).

One aspect of Labour's industrial policy revealed not only the antagonism between organised labour and the employers, but also a difference of opinion within the labour movement. This was the issue of workers' participation on company boards. The 1973 Labour Programme committed itself to the extension of industrial democracy and favoured 'the provision of direct representation for workers' based upon the unions, to be 'directly accountable to the workers in the company concerned' (Hodgson, 1981: 234). The unions had approved a report on industrial democracy which proposed worker directors in 1974, and the largest union, the Transport and General Workers, led by Jack Jones, was enthusiastic. The issue was put to a Committee of Enquiry on Industrial Democracy chaired by Alan Bullock, the historian, which was unable to reach unanimity and delivered two reports in January 1977. The majority report recommended that all enterprises with more than 2,000 employees should have worker representatives on a single board of directors, providing that one third of the workforce agreed. There were to be equal numbers of worker and shareholder representatives, plus some co-opted directors, and the workers representatives were to come from the trades unions. Three committee members produced a minority report which opposed employee directors, although it said they might be considered in a minority capacity on supervisory boards in a two-tier board system.

The minority report reflected the complete opposition of British management to the proposals. Lord Watkinson, the CBI President, said that his members were in no mood to cooperate with the Government on this issue. The official CBI statement said that it was 'utterly opposed', and that if implemented the proposals 'would fundamentally change our free enterprise system' (Bain Papers: MSS 65). James Prior, the Conservative shadow employment spokesman, told the Industrial Society Conference at the Café Royal in February that if implemented the proposals would hit investment and encourage firms and managers to leave Britain. Jan Hildreth, Director-General of the Institute of Directors, accused the Bullock Committee of doing the TUC's bidding (*The Director*, February 1977). Donoghue has described the attitude of some senior civil servants to the proposals as 'foolish and reactionary', adding that they seemed to be 'totally unaware' that worker participation was already in place in other countries (Donoghue, 1987: 149). Germany had operated such a system (the *Mitbestimmung*) since the early 1950s, while Sweden and Holland followed in 1973, and Denmark in 1974. Healey later argued that the employers were 'typically short–sighted in opposing it root and branch' (Healey, 1989: 459). This misses the point. The employers were feeling the effects of the crisis and desperately needed to break the power of the unions, which is why they were turning to Thatcher's new ideas. For them, industrial democracy was an emblem of a socialist advance which had to be halted.

What is perhaps more surprising is the opposition or indifference to workers participation within the labour movement. The solitary daily newspaper supporting Labour, the Daily Mirror, described the Bullock Report as a battleplan at a time when peace was needed, while it was reported that sections of the left–wing Tribune Group were opposed to the idea (*New Statesman*, 7 January 1977). From over three hundred submissions received by the Committee, there was one from the Trades Union Congress and only five from individual trades unions. Of these, the largest, the Engineers, opposed worker–directors in the private sector but supported them (in a majority position) in the nationalised industries. The Electricians rejected the whole idea as a 'diversion', and another large union, the Construction Workers, also rejected workers participation (Bain Papers). The opposition from many trade unionists reflected a feeling that it was the task of managers to manage and trade unions to negotiate on behalf of the workers; worker directors blurred these distinctions. The worker directors might be persuaded by the majority of the board to recommend moderation in pay demands, asking the workers to share in corporate responsibility while being excluded from real decision–making power. Some sections of the Left believed that workers risked being integrated into capitalist structures which they ought to be challenging, and the demand was made for control rather than participation. While these arguments raised very serious points, the 'all or nothing' approach ran the risk of consolidating unchecked power in the hands of capital while denying workers the opportunity to obtain information and experience of decision–making in firms. With such stern opposition to the idea of industrial democracy and such lukewarm support, it was not surprising that the White Paper came out with less radical proposals in May 1978. It proposed Joint Representation Committees of the trade unions which would have the power to discuss the industrial strategy of a company with the board. The possibility of worker directors was left flexible, as was the issue of unitary of two–tier board systems. No legislation emerged.

If the employers considered that the Labour Government was too close to the unions, many left–wingers considered that the state apparatus was rather too close to the employers. Michael Meacher, a junior minister throughout the period in question, argued that top civil servants were 'steeped in the principles of capitalism, regard their main function as the defence and consolidation of the existing (capitalist) order, and view the boardroom spokesman of the large multinational companies not only as their main source of industrial information .... but as their natural allies in the running of the country' (Meacher, 1982: 199). In the Commons debate on the civil service in January 1979 Brian Sedgemore pointed out that twenty six civil servants of Permanent Secretary rank or the equivalent who retired between 1974 and 1977 had been recruited by firms in the private sector (Meacher, 1979: 181; Meacher, 1982: 37). Holland argued that 'they sought to preserve a framework of unreconstructed class relations in society, with themselves as the ruling elite' (Holland, 1979: 226). Both Bernard Donoghue and Joe Haines have revealed the tremendous battle they had to put up to stop the Treasury from foisting a statutory pay policy on the Government in 1975. The Treasury officials' independent decision to sell sterling in March 1976 triggered the chain of events which culminated in the IMF crisis (Holmes, 1985: 179). Donoghue claimed that important 'concessions' were granted to him by the civil service regarding access to the Whitehall machine, but this implies the right of the state machine to keep information from the Government. Even as chief political advisor he was excluded from the most important meeting of all, the weekly meetings of all the Permanent Secretaries (Donoghue, 1987: 22–3).

Meacher's proposed remedy to the bias of the state apparatus was the 'ruthless' democratisation of decision–making in all the main institutions of society (Meacher, 1982: 200). Making the higher echelons of state power more accountable was a common demand of the Left, but the Labour Party has been slow to move on this or other constitutional issues. The 1974–9 Labour Government failed to abolish the Official Secrets Act or introduce a Freedom of Information Act. It also left the House of Lords alone, despite the fact that its obstructive role led to the 1977 Conference voting for its abolition by a huge majority (Coates, 1979). Little consideration was given to reforms which would have reduced the autonomy of the Whitehall machine. Political advisers were limited to two per ministry, and there was no discussion of the state financing of political parties, which would have provided the resources to counter the informational dominance of the civil service. Perhaps the most disturbing sign of the lack of control over elements of the state machine was the fact that members of the secret service, the most unaccountable of any in the Western world, were actively planning to destabilise the Government by discrediting Labour leaders (Wright, 1987: 269–72; Dorril & Ramsay, 1991).

EUROPE

The debate about Britain's membership of the European Economic Community was one of the most divisive issues for the Labour Party. From its position of national strength in the immediate postwar years, Labour showed little interest in European integration (Newman, 1983). However, Britain's decline and the growing strength of the Community countries persuaded the 1966 Labour Government to apply for membership, which was vetoed by President De Gaulle (Sked & Cook, 1979: 266–8). The Left of the party was opposed then and was still opposed in 1974, by which time Britain was a full member of the EEC. The Left argued that some of the radical economic plans which they supported, such as compulsory planning agreements, were forbidden by Community regulations. In other words, the EEC was a capitalist club which limited Britain's autonomy and obstructed its chances of achieving socialism. More specifically, the Common Agricultural Policy had a considerable inflationary impact on Britain's food prices, and also hit trade with the Commonwealth. Benn later expressed the importance of the EEC issue for the Left by describing it as the 'inevitable focus for the debate as to whether we were to abandon national planning and submerge ourselves in the free movement of capital and goods under the Treaty of Rome' (Benn, 1982: 27).

Wilson seized on Benn's idea of a referendum as possibly the only means to overcome the deep division within the Labour Party. It was to decide whether or not Britain should stay in the EEC after the terms of membership were renegotiated. The 'ground rules' for the debate were that Cabinet ministers could argue for either option, but the Government recommended staying in on the revised terms. The National Executive Committee of the Labour Party campaigned for a 'no' vote. The campaigners for the 'yes' vote had considerably greater resources than their opponents, a point seized upon by the 'no' campaigners when they lost the referendum in June 1975. On a 64.5 per cent turnout, 17.4 million voted for (67 per cent) and 8.5 million voted against. It was estimated by Gallup that 56 per cent of Labour voters voted 'yes'. *Tribune* voiced the disappointment of the anti–marketeers on the Left:

> So, we lost. But the idea that the argument about the Common Market "is over" is bunk. It will keep coming up in socialist arguments because the European Economic Community has been, is, and remains, an effort to salvage West European capitalism from the serious crisis which has been affecting it for some years (*Tribune*, 13 June, 1975).

Wilson took the opportunity to move Benn from Industry to Energy, an important signal that the radicalism of the 1973 programme was not going to be realised. In response to his move from Industry, Benn accused Wilson of 'capitulating to the CBI, to the Tory press and to the Tories themselves, all of whom have demanded my sacking' (Benn, 1989: 394).

The argument that the electorate was swayed decisively by the greater resources at the disposal of the 'yes' campaign smacked of complacency. It was a convenient way of avoiding a searching self–examination of the Left's implicit allegiance to the illusion of 'socialism in one country'. The Left simply refused to consider the possibility of transforming the EEC into a democratic federation with a strong socialist tradition and presence. Nor did it consider that a strong EEC would be in a position to challenge the hegemony of the United States, the only industrial power without a socialist movement. It is hard to escape the conclusion that much of the anti–EEC sentiment was based on a false conception of Britain's ability to develop radical policies from a position of semi–autonomy in the world economy. This argument was levelled at the Left at the time of the campaign, and rejected on the basis that socialist internationalism had nothing to do with a 'rich man's club' and 'rigid anti-democratic institutions' (Joan Lestor in *Labour Weekly*, 25 January, 1974). However, no internationalist alternative was offered, and none was available. Interestingly, Stuart Holland in *The Socialist Challenge* did not dismiss the possibility that Britain could stay in the EEC and use a socialist application of the power of veto, and he also discussed the possibility of 'concerted action' with other socialist governments in Europe, but this view was not widely shared on the Left (Holland, 1975: ch.13). Barbara Castle's view of Britain's relationship to Europe was more typical. As a left–wing member of Cabinet in January 1975 she revealed that only Crosland supported the idea of a Channel Tunnel. She commented that 'an island is an island and should not be violated .... a tunnel would do something profound to the national attitude – and certainly not for the better' (Castle, 1980: 281). She went on to become leader of the Labour Group in the European Parliament. The continued hostility to EEC membership from the Left led to the neglect of economic strategies for working within Europe, even though the likelihood of withdrawal grew more remote with every passing year. The argument that the European Community was a 'capitalist club' conveniently neglected the fact that so too was Britain, and so too were the institutions which increasingly shepherded the world economy. In choosing to make withdrawal from the Community a central element of its strategy even after the people had voted decisively to stay in, the Left operated from the assumption that a British Labour Government could fulfil a socialist programme in isolation, with minority support. Not only was this untenable from a long–term global economic perspective, but it presupposed the compliance of a generation of leaders and members who had largely accepted the revisionist arguments made by Crosland and Gaitskell in the 1950s.

DEFEAT AND DECLINE

The deflationary measures taken by the Government succeeded in reducing inflation to single figures by 1979, but the imposition of a 5 per cent limit on pay increases provoked a wave of strikes in the winter of 1978–9 which sealed the fate of the Government. The manifesto for the 1979 election was a moderate document drawn up by Callaghan and close advisors without consulting the joint NEC–Cabinet committees set up for the purpose. Some policies were excluded. For example, the Conference of 1977 passed a resolution calling for the abolition of the House of Lords by over six million votes, yet Callaghan threatened to resign if abolition of the House of Lords was included in the manifesto (Hamilton, 1989: 145–6), presumably because he thought it would be an unpopular measure. This 'executive fiat' was one of the issues which erupted in the recriminations after defeat (Seyd, 1987: 122–3). Labour lost the election, securing only 37 per cent of the vote, its lowest level of support since 1931. The bold promise of 1974 to effect a fundamental shift in the balance of class power was a distant dream. Even the more modest aims adopted by Callaghan when he became Prime Minister in 1976 were unfulfilled. He had hoped for inflation below 5 per cent, unemployment below 3 per cent, a manageable balance of payments, devolution for Scotland and Wales, and resumption of the party's social aims (Callaghan, 1988: 398). Of these objectives only a reasonable balance of payments was achieved, and the unemployment level of 5.5 per cent (1.3 million) was a clear sign of the distress of the postwar social democratic strategy. The moderates in the party emphasised the severe economic and parliamentary constraints under which the Government had operated. Callaghan concluded that 'it was a miracle that we had governed as long and as effectively as we had and carried out as much of our programme' and asserted that the government 'had no reason to feel ashamed and much to be proud of' (Callaghan, 1988: 564). Those on the Left were furious at the abandonment of the radical programme and the imposition of cuts in public expenditure. It viewed the Government's performance as craven.

The battles which followed the election split the party and had a debilitating effect on its subsequent electoral performance. Callaghan resigned as Leader in 1980 and was succeeded by Michael Foot, a left–winger by repute who some thought capable of reconciling the opposing factions. However, he was unable to keep the party together, and in 1981 a number of prominent pro–EEC MPs defected to form the Social Democratic Party. Its alliance with the Liberals in the elections of 1983 and 1987 was never quite sufficient to gain a balance of power in parliament to force a change in the electoral system, but it took millions of votes from Labour. The Left won some important constitutional victories and some important policy commitments, including unilateral nuclear disarmament and withdrawal from the European Community. However, its power peaked in 1981 when Benn was beaten by Healey by the narrowest of margins in the election for Deputy Leader (Seyd, 1987: 128–36).

In 1983 compromises were manufactured which looked plainly contradictory. Healey as a potential Foreign Secretary on a platform preaching unilateral nuclear disarmament was not credible, and Labour's promise to restore full employment was not backed by policies which offered a realistic possibility of achieving this goal. Labour polled only 27.6 per cent of the vote, and the Conservatives, boosted by the military victory in the Falklands in 1982, gained a huge parliamentary majority, despite winning less than 43 per cent of the vote. Neil Kinnock was elected Leader in 1983 and adopted a strategy of winning back the centre voters by jettisoning left wing policies which were considered to be an electoral liability. Aided by the 'new realism' of union leaders whose powers had been severely restricted under the Thatcher Government, Kinnock gradually reduced the power of the Left within the party. He excluded politicians like Benn and Ken Livingstone from positions of influence, and presided over an offensive against sections of the Left at grassroots level by proscribing the Marxist groups Militant and Socialist Organiser (Shaw, 1988). The party also disowned activists in local government who resisted new legislation introduced by the Conservative Government. Labour increased its share of the vote in the 1987 general election, but only to 31 per cent.

By the late 1980s the party was able to stifle dissent within its ranks, but it was organisationally weak. Membership had declined steeply from the 1950s, from an estimated 1.2 million individual members in 1952 to 350,000 in 1980 (Whiteley, 1983: 7, ch.3). By the time of the 1992 election it was closer to 250,000, one of the lowest ratios of members to voters in the European socialist family. The youth wing of the party had been disbanded and by 1990 only 5 per cent of members were under the age of 26 (*Labour Party News*, September 1990: 20). The party was persistently short of funds, and in contrast to most of its counterpart parties in Europe it did not sponsor daily newspapers, research institutes, theoretical journals, or mass political educational programmes. Although there have been a number of active *ad hoc* groups, conferences and campaigns which drew in many trades unionists and socialist feminists, the combined resources of the British Left were scanty in comparison with those of its opponents. In particular it suffered from lack of support in the national press.

The failure of the Liberal–SDP Alliance to win the balance of power in 1987 led to a revival in Labour's fortunes. A hasty merger between the Liberals and the majority of the Social Democratic Party (eventually known as the Liberal–Democrats) split the centre, and the minority Social Democrats maintained a rival party under David Owen until it was dissolved in 1990. This provided the opportunity for Labour's centrist strategy to bear fruit, and it began to forge ahead in the opinion polls from late 1988. An overhaul of policies attempted to free the party from its 'tax, spend and nationalise' image (Smith & Spear, 1992). But despite a successful campaign in the 1989 elections to the European Parliament, at the general election in April 1992 Labour secured only 34.2 per cent of the vote and lost once again. The campaign was fought on the agenda set by the Conservatives in the 1980s, with an acceptance of privatisation and low personal taxation. Despite unprecedented postwar unemployment, homelessness and criminal violence at home, and a poverty–stricken and ecologically devastated world at large, the concepts of 'capitalism' and 'socialism' did not figure in the rhetoric of Labour leaders. The Left had been effectively silenced and the party was able to present itself as united, but this had been achieved at the cost of demobilising the membership and surrendering the vision of a povertyless, egalitarian society. Kinnock resigned the leadership soon after the election, along with his Deputy, Roy Hattersley, and the party elected John Smith as Leader and Margaret Becket as Deputy Leader.

CONCLUSION

Labour's 1974 Programme was one manifestation of a broader 'left turn' across Western Europe. In France the 1972 Common Programme between the Socialists and the Communists had made a similar commitment to expanding the state sector in order to gain public control over the economy. In Sweden, where the Social Democrats achieved over 50 per cent of the vote in 1968, there were moves by sections of the Left to go beyond the limitations of the welfare model, and in the early 1970s the demands for workers' share ownership were raised. Although the Social Democratic Government in Germany was the epitome of caution, over 100,000 people were involved in extra–parliamentary left–wing groups in the mid–1970s (Burns and Van der Will: 116–7). The German SPD secured its highest ever vote of almost 46 per cent in 1972, while the Austrian Socialists took over half the vote in three elections in the 1970s. In Italy, the Communist Party achieved its highest ever vote, over 34 per cent, in 1976, and it was pushing hard for a place in government. In Portugal, following the overthrow of the fascist dictatorship in 1974, it appeared at one stage that a communist dictatorship might be installed, but the Socialist Party emerged as the strongest electoral force and a left–wing constitution was adopted. The sense of confidence exuded by many left–wing socialists was buoyed by the defeat of the USA in the Vietnam War. The first signs of economic recession were greeted by the Left as an opportunity for radical change, although few suspected the depth of the forthcoming economic crisis.

The electoral statistics indicate that social democracy was at its most popular as the postwar boom drew to a close. But why were the parties of the Left attracting so much support? Was it an endorsement of 'revisionism', based on full employment and good social provision from mildly redistributive fiscal policies, or was it the expression of a desire to go much further down the path of socialisation? Of course the support for social democratic parties came both from moderates and radicals, but the swiftness and seriousness of the crisis exposed the incompatibility of the two approaches. In Britain the defection of a considerable number of voters from Labour to Liberal pointed to a cautious suspicion of the more left–wing alternative. The party became polarised in a way not seen since the defection of the leader, Ramsay MacDonald, in 1931. The Left wanted to 'take on' the system by either direct ownership or close regulation of the means of production, while the Right accepted the need to cooperate with private capital in an increasingly competitive world.

The deep–seated differences within the Labour Party were barely contained before 1979 and broke out into open warfare afterwards (Wainwright, 1987; Kogan & Kogan, 1983). There is nothing new in scraps between different wings of socialist parties, but the intensity of this infighting was a reflection of the seriousness of the problems which were unfolding. They were all the more damaging in that they tended to reinforce original positions and discourage self–criticism. The Left strategy was isolationist while the Right could hardly be said to have a strategy at all, merely the intention to manage the economy more humanely than the Conservatives. Many of the European socialist parties suffered from similar divisions. The German SPD was unable to agree on a new programme after losing power in 1982, the Swedish SAP was divided over the controversial issue of the wage earner funds in the 1970s and 1980s, while the French Socialists were in open disarray before the elections of 1993.

The dramatic loss of electoral support for Labour is part of a wider European phenomenon (see the conclusion to this book). Part of the explanation is the failure of Keynesian policies and the absence of alternatives which offer convincing solutions to the major problems of low growth and high unemployment. But the lower levels of support also reflect the shrinking of the industrial working class, the traditional constituency of socialism. The large Liberal vote of 1974 turned out not to be an exceptional reaction to a starkly confrontational political situation. The centre vote has consistently held up. In the 1989 European elections, when the centre was divided, the UK Greens scored an amazing 15 per cent despite their lack of resources (Rootes, 1991). The importance of this centre vote has caused Labour leaders to re–examine the role of the trade unions. The importance of the trade unions within the party (Minkin, 1991) was regarded by many social democrats from other European countries as a great strength, but many observers thought that the power of the unions in the 1970s alienated some of the centrist voters. The unions were not always bastions of democratic practice, and the wielding of the 'block vote' by union leaders at Conference created an unpopular image of manipulation in the eyes of many outside the party. The political importance of the unions led the Left to offer uncritical support for 'free collective bargaining', but this was advantageous to workers only in a favourable economic climate, and it was not conducive to planning the economy (Rowthorn, 1980: 146). The closeness of the union link, and also the big pay rises of the 1974–5 period, raised expectations which the Government failed to meet. In the 1979 election there was a 7 per cent swing to the Conservatives among trade unionists, much higher than the national average (Holmes, 1985: 161).

The irony of the appeal for 'free collective bargaining' in the 1970s was that the Conservatives under Thatcher had abandoned statutory approaches to pay. They were willing to let the market decide the price of labour, in the safe knowledge that the return of mass unemployment was a more effective way of combating union power. Unemployment and the consequent 'new poverty' created new divisions in society, and this has remained a major problem for European social democracy as a whole. The majority in work have witnessed increased living standards despite the reduced levels of growth, yet the poorest sections of society have become even poorer. Conservative calls for 'sound money' and low taxes have been attractive to many of those in work who felt that their jobs were secure. It has also made it difficult for Labour to devise redistributive policies based on higher taxation. To propose tax increases runs against the problem of perceived short–term self–interest as well as inviting the accusation that they will discourage wealth creation. The Conservative themes of individual liberty and 'rolling back the state' have also played on disaffection with excessive bureaucracy, associated with top–heavy hierarchical structures in the public sector.

The European context which faces Labour could hardly be more different than that of 1974. If Labour and the other social democratic parties in Europe are to recover some of their former electoral strength, they have to persuade voters that the social damage caused by neo–liberal policies is visible and unacceptable. Alliances with parties of the centre or 'new politics' parties such as the Greens are inevitable and will demand a greater willingness to tolerate differences than was evident in the 1974–79 period. But perhaps the most obvious conclusion to be drawn from the tribulations of the last Labour Government is that global economic power presents overwhelming constraints on political power in the nation state. Since 1979 the globalising tendencies of production and finance have accelerated, and the Single European Act and the Maastricht Treaty have advanced the emergence of a new European federation. Arguments have continued to flourish within the Labour Party about the pace and character of the development of European integration, but if egalitarian politics are ever to make an impact in any of the nation states, a European recovery programme is imperative.

3 The French Socialist Government

In 1981 the British Labour Party was pulling itself apart in the wake of its traumatic experience in government, but in France it was the parties of the Right which paid the price for being in government in hard times. When Francois Mitterand defeated the incumbent right–wing candidate, Giscard D'Estaing, in the Presidential election in May, he became the first socialist President of the French Fifth Republic. In the general election which followed, the Parti Socialiste (PS) won an absolute majority of seats in the National Assembly for the first time, and formed a coalition with the Parti Communiste Francaise (PCF). As the combined vote of the parties amounted to almost 54 per cent, it was a rare moment of majority strength for the Left in France. Both PS and PCF had strong left–wing programmes and proclaimed that they were in the business of making a break from capitalism, but despite the initial strength of their popular support, the Government quickly came across similar economic pressures to those which beset the 1974–9 Labour Governments in Britain. Both started with left–wing programmes based on rapid, state–led growth, and both abandoned their programmes in the face of a hostile international economic environment. Socialist aspirations evaporated as world market forces exerted their ruthless discipline. The experience of the French Socialists provides more evidence of the difficulty of resisting the short–term market logic of the world economy, and points to the need to develop effective international strategies if the socialist project is to remain relevant.

A closer inspection of the experience of the Left in France reveals considerable differences from the British situation, most strikingly in the existence of a large Communist Party. France had also undergone great socio–economic changes in the postwar period which differed from the British experience in three main respects. First, there was a considerable increase in population and a mass movement from country to town, whereas Britain had been a fully urbanised society for decades. Employment in agriculture declined from 29 per cent of the total workforce in 1949 to less than 8 per cent in 1981 (Hanley, Kerr & Waites, 1984: ch. 2; Hough, 1982: pp. 19–21; Kuisel, 1987: 19). During this period the percentage employed in industry rose slightly, to 36 per cent in 1979, and there was a large increase in the numbers of clerks, administrators and people in the professions (Holmes & Fawcett, 1983: 8–9, 174–5). The second distinctive feature concerned the place of France in the world economy. The annual growth rate of 5.2 per cent between 1950 and 1974 was far greater than that of Britain or the United States (Kuisel, 1987: 18–9), and since the 1950s France had moved away from a high level of self–subsistence to a far greater interdependence with the world economy (Hall, 1990: 173–5). The third feature was the widespread use and acceptance of central economic planning, and although this declined in importance in the mid–1970s, it was one of the reasons why there was a more widespread acceptance of the principle of state intervention in the economy than was the case in Britain (Hough, 1982: ch. 5). In common with most countries in continental Europe, the state in France had historically played a very active role in promoting economic development, initially to catch up with Britain. In summary, France's economy and population expanded rapidly in the post war period and the country became fully urbanised and integrated into the economic systems of Europe and the world.

It is not surprising that given the rapidity and extent of the changes outlined above, the socialist movements in France underwent something of a transformation in the years leading up to 1981. Ever since a majority of delegates at the Congress of the SFIO (Section Francaise de l'Internationale Ouvrière) at Tours in 1920 voted to form the Communist Party and affiliate to the Third International, there was a strong Communist presence in French politics (Mortimer, 1984; Kriegel, 1972). In the inter–war period the Socialists were electorally stronger than the PCF, which suffered from internal upheavals which reflected the power–struggles in the Soviet Union. This Socialist lead disappeared after the Second World War, for the PCF's exemplary role in the Resistance and the vital part played by the Soviet Union in the defeat of fascism enhanced the popularity of the communists. In the life of the Fourth Republic (1945–58) the PCF secured about a quarter of the total vote, whereas the Socialist share of the poll dropped to less than 16 per cent in the election of 1956. The fortunes of the Socialists continued to decline in the Fifth Republic, and they won less than 13 per cent of the vote at the election of 1962. The PCF consistently polled around 20 per cent of the vote between 1958 and 1978.

The readjustment of the French Left was given a significant impetus in 1965 when a loose federation of the socialist and radical groups outside the Communist Party was formed to support the Presidential candidature of

Mitterand, who came from a small independent radical group. Mitterand won 45 per cent of the vote in the second ballot, and although he was beaten by a wide margin by De Gaulle, the success in mobilising the 'broad Left' vote was an important step towards the development of a new party. The PCF continued to win more votes than the Socialists, but the gap closed in successive elections until 1978, when the Socialists polled a quarter of the total vote and surpassed the PCF. The communists did not embrace a strategy of 'peaceful transition' to socialism until 1964, and for many years they were ambivalent on the issue of political pluralism (Nugent & Lowe, 1982: ch. 4). The rhetorical freedom permitted to them by their isolation from government enabled them to adopt a consistently blistering critical stance, and the iron discipline within the party meant that it invariably spoke with one voice. But hierarchical discipline within parties tends to isolate the leadership, which can easily lose sensitivity to the mood and aspirations of its potential constituents. Dramatic signs that this was happening to the PCF occurred in the general strike of May–June 1968.

The events of 1968 had important implications for the subsequent development of left–wing politics in France. The word 'explosion' has been used in relation to the events to illustrate the startling and rebellious nature of the political crisis which erupted in nights of streetfighting between riot police and student protesters, and developed into a general strike which paralysed the Gaullist regime (Lefebvre, 1969: Singer, 1970). De Gaulle had founded the Fifth Republic in reponse to the threat of civil war which stemmed from the Algerian struggle for independence. The President took upon himself overall power for the direction of government, with scant regard for parliamentary opposition or pressure group mediation. Broadcasting was completely controlled by the state and the left–wing parties looked as though they would remain in the wilderness for many years to come. This was the context in which the student protests began in 1968, partly concerned with 'internal' University issues such as overcrowding, the imposition of petty rules, and the uncritical nature of the teaching, but also concerned with external matters such as the Vietnam War. The student strikes and sit–ins developed into an escalating series of demonstrations, barricades and baton charges. To the surprise of both Left and Right, a strike call to workers from the students soon resulted in a general strike involving ten million workers.

The strike paralysed the French Government, but it also took the parties of the Left by surprise. The initital reaction of the PCF, through its daily newspaper *L'Humanité*, was hostile to the students and their 'petit–bourgeois adventurism'. Only when the workers spontaneously came out on strike did the PCF redirect its ire against the state. The PCF leaders were alarmed that a general strike had broken out without their initiative and control, and all the party's efforts went in to channelling the strike action towards tangible economic demands and away from political appeals for industrial democracy which sought to give real power to workers outside the organisation of the CGT. The Grenelle agreements, signed by the Government, the employers and the CGT, raised the minimum wage by one third and secured increases in pay and pensions, but the rank–and–file were not impressed and the strike continued. Although Mitterand declared that the socialists were ready to assume power, they had a poor electoral base and were wary of embracing the communists in such a volatile situation. The strike collapsed in the days following De Gaulle's second broadcast appeal, which was followed by a huge pro–government demonstration. In the elections at the end of June, amid a torrent of red scare propaganda, the Right gained a sweeping victory. Once 'direct action' had failed to unseat De Gaulle, the Left became demoralised.

The leader of the PCF, Waldeck Rochet, later argued that the party had faced a stark choice between working for reforms or moving towards insurrection (Mandel, 1968: 17). While the risks involved in insurrection were real, it was also clear to many young left–wingers that the PCF was unwilling to countenance any strong reforms which might undermine its own institutional power within the working class. The PCF showed little interest in workers' democracy and vilified the student leaders. Dramatically, the party was revealed as a conservative force (Barjonet, 1968: ch. 6), much to the satisfaction of the various anarchist, Trotskyist and Maoist groups which wielded disproportionate influence during the tumult. The events of 1968 exposed the contradictory position of the PCF as a Leninist party which preached revolution but refused to contemplate the insurrectionary option. Waldeck Rochet used the experience to support his pursuit of a broad alliance of the Left aiming for parliamentary success. Four years later the PCF signed up to a 'Common Programme' with the Socialist Party. In the mid–1970s the PCF flirted with Eurocommunism, symbolised by the dropping of the commitment to the 'dictatorship of the proletariat' at the Congress of 1976. However, clearly worried that the party might lose its distinctive culture and be overtaken by the Socialists, the PCF in 1977 suddenly and decisively reverted to a more 'hardline' position, insisting on strict party discipline and support for the communism of the Soviet Union and Eastern Europe. In doing so it cleared the way for the Socialists to cultivate the 'New Left' support which enabled them to outpoll the PCF for the first time since the 1930s.

The only short–term successes for the Left in 1968 came with the popularity of the CFDT, the trade union federation formerly associated with the Catholic Church, and the small Party of Unified Socialism (PSU). The CFTD had reacted positively to the demand for workers' self–management. The PSU, led by Michel Rocard, enthusiastically embraced the cause of the students and the implied radical democratic thrust. Significantly, although the PCF and the Federation of the Left both lost support in the election, the PSU doubled its small vote. The resonances of 1968 were found in the demands for *autogestion* – the extension of accountability in all areas of social and economic life – the demands for more democratic control in local politics, the appeal for solidarity between intellectual and manual workers, and in support for left–wing forces in struggle in the 'third world'. These were the dominant themes which emerged when the Federation of the Left was transformed into the Parti Socialiste at the Congress of Epinay in 1971, and the new party quickly accommodated the Rocard wing of the PSU. The socialist movement in France had a long tradition of factions, and the new PS adopted a constitution whereby different factions were explicitly recognised, permitting organised disputation of programmes as a necessary part of the internal democratic process (Hanley, 1986: 1; Nugent & Lowe, 1982: 78). In keeping with the libertarian spirit of 1968, the PS stressed the importance of decentralising power in all areas and warmed to the politics of new social movements. The Socialists prospered because they 'read' the lessons of 1968 and developed a politics which chimed with the aspirations of the *'soixante huiters'*.

INTOXICATION

The constitution of the PS advocated the transition from socialism to capitalism. The preamble claimed that the party is revolutionary, in the sense that 'because Socialists are consistent democrats, they believe no genuine democracy can exist in a capitalist society' (Lavau, 1987: 117; Hayward, 1990: 21). The promise of a 'break with capitalism' was a feature of PS rhetoric in the period leading up to the elections of 1981. Mitterand did not have a clear run to obtain the Presidential nomination of the PS, and required the support of the left–wing CERES (Centre d'études, de récherches et d'éducation socialiste) faction in order to survive the challenge of Rocard, who had become more moderate since his days with the PSU. CERES was formed in 1966 and for the most part comprised of discussion groups of professional people, ably led by Jean–Pierre Chevènement. It attempted to translate the spirit of the 1968 rebellion into transformatory policies, and held a series of conferences on specific themes which helped it to clarify its ideas and exert a considerable intellectual influence on the Party. In the mid–1970s it commanded about a quarter of the voting strength at Party Congresses, and although this fell to 14.4 per cent at the Metz Congress in 1979 it provided most of the ideas for the 1980 programme, the Projet Socialiste, which provided the basis for Mitterand's 110 propositions on which he ran for the Presidency (Hanley, 1986: 129). In 1972 Mitterand had talked about the conditions necessary to 'combat and destroy capitalism', and he had inveighed against the 'power of money and the dictatorship of a class' in response to the overthrow of the democratically elected government of Salvador Allende in Chile in 1973 (Mitterand, 1982: 52, 78). In 1981 he had to win left–wing voters away from PCF candidate Georges Marchais, and he outscored his rival by over 10 per cent. He then went on to defeat Giscard D'Estaing by a majority of over a million votes.

At the ensuing general election the PS won an absolute majority of seats in the National Assembly and secured 37.5 per cent of the vote, far and away its best–ever performance. The PCF, with 16.2 per cent, its lowest return since 1936, was offered a place in government and accepted the ministries of Transport, Civil Service, Health, and Training (Nugent & Lowe, 1982: appendix 6). The new administration, led by Pierre Maurroy as Prime Minister, set out on a 'dash for growth', reflating the economy and extending public ownership. One of the reasons for the success of the Left in 1981 was the inability of the Right to deal with the economic problems which followed the first oil price rise of 1974 and deepened after the second one in 1979. Unemployment had risen to 7.3 per cent and inflation to 13 per cent. The reflation took a number of forms. The minimum wage was raised by over 10 per cent in real terms and there were substantial increases in housing subsidies, family allowances, and old age pensions. The overall effect of these measures was worth 2 per cent of the gross domestic product (Hall, 1987: 55; Singer, 1988: 107). In addition there was a major job creation scheme, providing 100,000 jobs in the public services in the first 18 months (Hanley, Kerr & Waites, 1984: 59). The other major recipients of public funds were the owners of the 50 firms nationalised by the PS–PCF government, for compensation payments were very high, due to the intervention of the Constitutional Council (Holton, 1986: 72).

The programme of nationalisation was one of the most spectacular ever undertaken by a democratically elected government. In the first two years 12 industries were nationalised, including seven of the largest firms in France, while 36 banks and two finance companies were also taken into public ownership. The list included renowned giants such as Thomson–Brandt (electronics and telecommunications), Saint–Gobain (paper, glass), Rhône–Poulenc (chemicals, pharmaceuticals), CGE (electrical construction, engineering, electronics), and Dassault (areoplanes). French–based subsidiaries of multinational corporations were also nationalised, such as Bull (from Honeywell) and CGCT (from ITT, which had played a leading role in the overthrow of Allende in Chile) (Stoffaes, 1985: 144–5). With a fifth of the workforce now employed in a public sector producing a third of all exports, the industrial policy challenged the basis of French capitalism. Despite suggestions from Rocard and Jacques Delors that the state should take only a bare majority stake in the newly nationalised industries, Mitterand insisted on full public ownership (Holton, 1886: 72). In some areas, particularly electronics, virtually all manufacturers came into public ownership, giving the state the sort of control that the Labour Left had hoped for in its 1973 programme. But the satisfaction that the Left felt at this 'capture' quickly gave way to anxiety about the macro economic effects of the first year of 'intoxication', as Mitterand later termed it (Nay, 1987: 340).

It was to be expected that the sudden injection of demand into the economy would cause prices to rise and imports to outstrip exports in the short term. Inflation rose to double figures at a time when France's chief competitors were reducing their inflation rates. The trade deficit was high before the Left came to power, and the situation grew much worse in 1981–2 (Radice & Radice, 1986: 59–64; Hall, 1990; McCormick, 1985). Although world trade fell by 3 per cent in 1982, German exports to France increased by 29 per cent in the first three months of that year (Fitoussi, 1985). Business investment declined in real terms as the employers considered the whole package to be a frontal attack on their prerogatives. In addition to the measures outlined above, a one–hour reduction in the working week and an extra week of paid holiday were introduced, while the Auroux Laws improved the rights of workers (Ross & Jenson, 1985). A wealth tax was also levied. A small devaluation took place in October 1991, but the first major retreat came in June 1982 with a prices and wages freeze and a further devaluation. The economic indicators failed to improve, and the outright rejection of the reflationary strategy was agreed in March 1983, accompanied by a third devaluation.

It is possible that the Government would have had a better chance of sustaining its strategy if it had negotiated an early and substantial devaluation of the franc (Hall, 1987: 62; Ross & Jenson, 1988: 40; MacShane, 1986; Bell & Criddle, 1988: 154). Be that as it may, there was still another option open to the Government in March 1983, as there had been in December 1976 for the British Labour Government. The 'alternative strategy' was to take France out of the exchange rate mechanism of the EC and impose import controls, in addition to devaluation. Although this policy would have been within the emergency provisions of both the Treaty of Rome, which set up the EEC, and GATT, it would have meant a weakening of the commitment to further European integration (Hall, 1990: 177). Mauroy and Finance Minister Jacques Delors led the pro–EC group, and Mitterand backed them (McCormick, 1985: 55). But if the rigueur of 1982 might have been regarded as a temporary retreat, the decision of March 1983 signified the adoption of a new course, carried through with great energy until the defeat in 1986. The nationalised industries were made competitive, which meant an end to job protection, and the private sector was encouraged by tax concessions and investment incentives. Inflation was beaten by controlling the money supply, and by 1986 it was down to 2.6 per cent from its high point of 14 per cent in 1981 (Singer, 1988: 259–60; MacShane, 1986: 4). The change of course was consolidated by the appointment of Laurent Fabius as Prime Minister in the summer of 1984 and the withdrawal of the PCF and its Ministers from the coalition. Mauroy had resigned in the wake of the Government's climbdown on the proposed withdrawal of state subsidies from clerical schools. Fabius had replaced Chevènement as Minister for Industry at the time of the crucial economic policy choice in March 1983, and he set about loosening controls over the nationalised industries and reducing corporate taxation (Bell & Criddle, 1988: 119–25). In 1984–5 the level of unemployment benefit was reduced by 10 per cent, and as many of the registered unemployed were not eligible for benefit a 'new poverty' began to emerge, particularly in the old industrialised areas. Mitterand had made the fight against unemployment a priority of his Presidential campaign, but it rose from 1.8 million in 1981 to 2.4 million in 1986 (over 10 per cent). Although the rate of increase was not as great as that experienced in West Germany or Britain, the acceptance of mass unemployment compromised the visionary zeal which had carried the Socialists to victory.

The unpopularity of 'rigueur' was shown in the 1983 municipal elections and the 1984 elections for the European parliament, for the combined vote of the Left parties fell below the 40 per cent mark on both occasions (Lancelot & Lancelot, 1987: 87). Strikes occurred in the health service and in road haulage, and the supporters of Catholic schools successfully resisted the securalisation of the school system suggested by Mauroy and his education minister Savary. The strength of opposition and the level of unpopularity did not break the surface unity of the PS, but there were many tensions in the movement. Nicole Questiaux, Minister with responsibility for 'national solidarity', resigned in 1982 when her spending plans in the social security field were halted. Informal rivalry to become the party's Presidential nominee for 1988 was fought out in political clubs such as Rocard's *Convergences*, Fabius's *Democratie 2000* and Chevènment's *Republique Moderne*, but the Party closed ranks when Mitterand's popularity revived in 1985 (Machin, 1990: 38). Resistance to austerity from organised labour was limited. France has always had a relatively low level of unionisation, and there was only limited cooperation between the major union federations (Wilson, 1985). Above all, however, here as elsewhere in Western Europe, unemployment was the principal factor in taming disaffected workers. Indeed the Government had some difficulty in generating support among workers for the implementation of the Auroux Laws when it launched a national campaign of mobilisation early in 1984 (Lewis & Sferza, 1987: 109; Gallie, 1985). Even when the PCF left the Government, the expected militancy from the CGT did not materialise.

This brings us to the role of the Communist Party, first as a part of the Government, and then as a Left opposition. The PCF entered the Government from a position of weakness in 1981, and its electoral decline continued, for it polled only 11.2 per cent at the European election in 1984, and just under 10 per cent at the general election of 1986. It had lost over three million voters in eight years (Courtois & Peschanski, 1988). The 'crisis' moment from which the party failed to recover was the termination of its Eurocommunist phase in 1977–8, a retrenchment which disheartened the many thousands of activists who had tried to make it work at grassroots level (Jenson & Ross, 1984). Under the leadership of Marchais it clung to its old structure and image, but the reversion to a pro–Moscow position after 1978 proved to be electorally disastrous (Bell & Criddle, 1989; Ross & Jenson, 1988). Soviet Marxism had taken a hammering from the humanist Marxist tradition (Sartre, Lefebvre, Garaudy) which was influential in both the PCF and the PS, and the image of communism deteriorated further with the declaration of martial law in Poland in 1981, and the Soviet imbroglio in Afghanistan. The horror of the Khmer Rouge atrocities in the former French colony of Kampuchea also raised the spectre of 'Left fanaticism'. Vociferous opposition to the official line was suppressed firmly at the Congress of 1985, forcing former Politburo member Pierre Juquin to leave the Party and attempt to rally the 'alternative' Left to his Presidential ticket in 1988. The PCF stuck to its intransigent and marginalised position, and its failure undoubtedly helped the PS to consolidate its place as the dominant party of the Left. However, the decline of the Communist Party was so steep that it was no longer imperative for the PS to deal with it, and this weakened the pressure on the PS to lend some substance to its claim to be socialist.

This drift from radicalism in the PS was nowhere more in evidence than in the field of foreign policy. Although France was not a member of the military command structure of NATO, Mitterand fully realised that its 'independent' deterrent counted for little in the nuclear stand–off between the Soviet Union and the United States. Alarmed by the deployment of Soviet SS–20 missiles in Eastern Europe, he urged the countries of Western Europe to accept the American Pershing–2 and Cruise missiles, even indicating to the German voters in 1983 that they should reject the anti–nuclear stance of the German SPD (Howarth, 1990: 208). The 'nationalist' card was played on a number of occasions, as, for example, in the colonialist–style intervention in Chad, but perhaps the most disturbing example of national chauvinism overcoming all principles was the Rainbow Warrior affair (Singer, 1988: 203–8). The Rainbow Warrior was a ship owned by Greenpeace, the international environmentalist group, which was attempting to halt French nuclear testing in the Pacific Ocean. It was blown up by two members of the French Secret Service while harbouring in Auckland, New Zealand, in 1985, resulting in the death of one of the crew. The French Minister of Defence, Charles Hernu, denied all knowledge until the evidence against the Ministry was irrefutable. He had plotted the action in conjunction with the President's personal military attaché and the Director of the Secret Service. Those responsible resigned, although Hernu received the personal gratitude of Mitterand and a shameful standing ovation from the Socialist Party Congress at Toulouse in 1985. The Secret Service agents were quickly released, after the 1986 election, as the French Government held out the threat of banning New Zealand's dairy produce from the European Community. In attempting to claim the centre ground necessary for success in a Presidential election,

Mitterand made it clear that he was prepared to rattle sabres in the 'national interest'.

It was no surprise when the PS lost the election in 1986 under the new system of proportional representation. The hardship caused by the austerity programme and the failure to fulfil promises on unemployment were important factors, while left–wing supporters were disappointed by the enthusiastic promotion of profit rather than the promised 'break' with capitalism. The leaders of the PS derived some satisfaction from the result, for the electoral damage was limited. The party won 31.6 per cent of the vote (a loss of 6 per cent), and was still the largest party by a considerable margin because the right–wing vote was split between the UDF, the RPR, and the neo–fascist National Front (FN), which won almost 10 per cent of the vote. The UDF and the RPR formed a coalition Government under Jacques Chirac, but Mitterand remained President. The coalition, inspired by the neo–liberal policies enacted in Britain, began a privatisation programme which aimed to sell off 66 public firms. However, this came to an abrupt close with the financial 'crash' of stock–markets throughout the capitalist world in October 1987, by which time only 14 firms had been privatised (Story & de Carmoy, 1993: 196). The stock market had played only a minor role in financing French industry compared with Britain, but it had achieved a more prominent place in French economic life as a result of reforms introduced by the PS Government (Hall, 1990: 178). When Mitterand defeated Chirac in the Presidential election in 1988 he called another election under the old 'second ballot' electoral system which the Chirac Government had reintroduced. The PS returned to power with 35.9 per cent, and Rocard was appointed Prime Minister. The PCF made a slight recovery, polling 11.3 per cent, but this time remained in opposition.

The recovery of the Left in 1988 cannot be explained entirely in terms of the divisions among the Right and the financial crash. The support for the combined Left, including small parties, reached almost 50 per cent, a marked contrast to the level of support for the Left in Britain, Germany, or Italy. One of the reasons for the success of the PS was the decisiveness which it showed in moving from its 'Left Keynesian' phase to the profit–orientated policies of the 1983–6 period. After the 1986 election *The Economist* declared that France was a 'better specimen of capitalism than before', with high unemployment discouraging strikes, low inflation, a flourishing stock exchange and profitable nationalised industries (*The Economist*, 8 March, 1986). This image of capitalist efficiency was projected by Fabius, who had started his career as a Minister in 1981 by introducing France's first wealth tax. As Prime Minister he claimed that he was a pragmatist, that his wish was 'to make things more efficient', and that the state 'can't stand in for business' (*Sunday Times* 22 July, 1984). As Gaffney has pointed out, the discourse of the Party switched from a 'millenarian' vision promising a brave new world to one of 'modernisation', in which the latter was used to justify the neccesity of deregulation while blaming the social consequences on the global failure of capitalism (Gaffney, 1989: 181–97). The PS Government responded to the economic crisis by demonstrating that it could manage capitalism efficiently. But if 'efficiency' means mass unemployment, is there anything left of socialism?

The attraction of the PS as an efficient manager of the capitalist system came under severe strain after 1988 when unemployment remained high and world competitiveness did not improve. However, the PS managed to hang on to some idea of socialism by its enthusiastic support for a united Europe with social democratic guarantees for workers' rights and social provision. Jacques Delors left the Government to assume the Presidency of the EEC Commission in July 1984, and he vigorously projected the goal of a single market by 1993 complemented by the adoption of a 'Social Charter':

> 'Social Europe' became a key priority in the French EC Presidency of late 1989, presented by Mitterand as an indispensable element of social cohesion along the path to European union (Story & de Carmoy, 1993: 199).

The Social Charter was adopted by the European Council in December 1989 and was built into the Maastricht Treaty of 1991. The idea of a United States of Europe led by social democrats opened up possibilities for the resolution of global economic and ecological problems. It offered a long–term vision to offset the short–term failure to provide either full employment or redistribution of wealth. However, the moves towards greater European integration also revealed the extent to which power was moving away from the nation state. In the early 1980s the German Bundesbank became Europe's acting central bank, but it remained tied to its historic role as the guardian of 'sound money' and the enemy of inflation (Story & de Cecco, 1993: 329–33). These priorities were reflected in the financial provisions of the Maastricht Treaty which place restrictions on borrowing which could be met only by deepening the problems of low growth and high inflation. Social democratic goals could be realised in Europe only if there was a much greater federal budget, but this is being actively resisted by key interests. The whole process of European integration was therefore seen by many on the Left to be a cause of social distress rather than a potential solution, and this persuaded the Communist Party and some sections of the PS led by Chevèvenment to campaign for a 'no' vote in the referendum on the Maastricht Treaty in September 1992. The Treaty was accepted by a wafer–thin majority.

The PS in power attempted to widen the social basis of its support by embracing the interests of the new social movements. When Mitterand won the Presidency it was the first time in France that a majority of women had voted for the Left. He appointed Yvette Roudy as Minister for the Rights of Women in 1981, and various programmes were conducted to combat sexism at work and in advertising. A number of women were given senior governmental posts, although there were still few PS women deputies in the National Assembly (Jenson, 1990: 146, 158). The Socialist Government extended recognition and financial support to the leading anti–racist group, SOS–racisme, founded in the autumn of 1984 in response to the rising wave of racism which accompanied the rise of the National Front. The SOS leader Harlem Désir supported Mitterand's candidacy in the 1988 Presidential election. The group had tremendous success in mobilising young people against racism, and its open hand symbol stating 'don't touch my mate' (Touche pas a mon pôte) became nationally known (Ossman–Dorent, 1988). However, anti–racists grew disillusioned with the Government's willingness to expel illegal immigrants, and there was a furore over the public expulsion by aeroplane in 1991 under Prime Minister Edith Cresson.

Ecologists also became disappointed with the Government. Shortly after the PS came to power in 1981 the nuclear power station at Plogoff in Brittany was cancelled, but the nuclear energy programme remained central to the French electricity supply. When Rocard was appointed Prime Minister in 1988 he announced that he would 'open up' Government to embrace all groups which were not hostile to the PS, a clear indication of a desire to listen to the demands made by ecologists, feminists and anti–racists (Machin, 1990: 49–50; Ladrech, 1989). Brice Lalonde, former President of the French branch of Friends of the Earth and head of Géneration Ecologie, became Minister of the Environment. However, he was replaced after the regional elections in March 1992 when Géneration Ecologie and Les Verts won 14 per cent of the vote between them, while the PS secured only 18.3 per cent. The decision of the two ecological groups to fight the 1993 election on a joint ticket in rivalry to the PS passed a negative judgement on socialist attempts to give political expression to the concerns of the new social movements. Many of the PS activists had been zealous supporters of justice for the third world, but here again the rhetoric tended to outweigh achievement. Mitterand campaigned for more sympathetic attitudes towards the debt problems of the third world countries, and used the existing 'Club of Paris' mechanisms to work out better terms of repayment. In this area, as in others, the limited powers of a medium–size state were abundantly clear.

One area in which the PS did succeed in effecting radical change was in the administration of France. The decentralising measures taken by the Government were an important aspect of their 'self–determination' strategy, and they were well received. The old Prefect system was abolished. The Prefects were appointed directly by the Paris government with executive powers at departement level. Now local government was to have more freedom in administrative and financial matters, and a new tier of regional government, with considerable financial power, was introduced (Kesselman, 1985; Mazey, 1990). The success of decentralisation contrasts with Labour's botched plans to devolve power to Scottish and Welsh Assemblies. The central state apparatus in France was markedly different from Britain's in several respects. Many high–ranking state officials were members of the PS, indeed Fabius was a graduate of the Ecole Normale d'Administration (ENA), the elite training ground for public officials set up in 1945. Most key positions in the higher civil service were awarded to people loyal to the PS in the first few months of the Government, and they were supplemented by ministerial 'private offices' containing over 500 political appointments under Mauroy and Fabius. This figure was raised to 600 when Rocard became Prime Minister in 1988 (Wright, 1990: 129). Although the introduction of partisans invariably annoyed the career administrators and caused a certain amount of confusion due to 'dual administration', it was an effective check on the sort of obstruction experienced by the Labour Government in Britain in 1974–9. It has been argued that while the PS in power did not have a profound effect on the internal functioning of the state, there was a trend towards relating socialism and administration in a technocratic 'subculture' in both the PS and the higher civil service (Birnbaum, 1985: 140; Stevens, 1985). The socialists were attempting to promote a social democratic administrative ethos, rather like Sweden, whose system was much admired by Fabius. When Rocard formed his Government in 1988 it contained nine graduates of ENA.

ILLUSIONS OF PROGRESS?

The failure of the 1981 strategy provides a strong example of the immense difficulties involved in implementing social democratic goals in isolation during a period of international deflation. The ambitious rhetoric of the 'break' with capitalism owed much to the period in which the socialists had been in opposition, and in particular to their desire to lure voters away from the Communist Party. In practice the PS was a mainstream social democratic party which achieved a more limited goal of being the largest party in the centre ground of French politics (Bell & Criddle, 1988). Not only did the PS retreat from its bold 'Left Keynesianism', but it elected for a strong pro–market posture which quickly resulted in increased unemployment. The inability to resolve this problem of chronic high unemployment has plagued the recent history of socialism in France, as it has in Spain. In both cases the socialists adopted a rhetoric of modernisation and achieved a degree of success in posing as the managers of a high technology, internationally efficient economy. However, such a profound disjunction between socialist aspirations and social reality cannot be successfully sustained for long. The voters were sufficiently loyal to reward the PS with a second chance in 1988, but failure to tackle unemployment weighed heavily against its prospects of holding on to its support.

The change of course taken in 1983 involved a decision against reverting to temporary protection from the European market, and therefore a commitment to the idea of a more closely integrated Europe. This was explicitly and energetically projected as a 'golden opportunity' for the creation of a social democratic federation by Delors as President of the European Commission (Delors, 1989: 44). However, this possibility appears to many potential socialist voters to be too remote to offer realistic alternatives to the present condition of chronic unemployment, low growth, and the rise of violent right–wing nationalism. In the run up to the election of March 1993 the PS attempted to put the reduction of the working week on the political agenda. But as long as a government is obliged to provide the best possible conditions for capital accummulation it is difficult to reduce hours. The effect would be to raise labour costs and hit the competitiveness of French industry. This is precisely why the PS Government backed down on its 1981 commitment to a 35 hour working week. Effective action would have to be taken across the European Community, but this is a remote possibility.

The closeness of the Maastricht referendum and the hostility to the proposed GATT agreements reflected a feeling that the progress towards greater integration had been 'administered' without proper consultation. Insofar as executives of social democratic parties or trade unions have identified the possibility of real advantages in a United States of Europe, they have failed to generate a concomitant movement from 'below' which might mobilise around specific demands in such areas as working time, environmental protection, housing, transport, and training. Ironically, this problem of political remoteness was highlighted by Prime Minister Rocard in 1990, when he bemoaned the arrogance of politicians who regarded it as a 'duty and an honour' to impose upon people the social changes 'which the people are not sufficiently clear–sighted to desire spontaneously' (Rocard, 1992: 46). At least Rocard recognised the problems of political communication, participation and mobilisation. His removal by Mitterand and his replacement by Edith Cresson was a serious political mistake. Her unpopularity was reflected in the poor results in the regional elections of 1992 and Mitterand called on an old colleague, Pierre Bérégovoy, to take the party into the next general election. His determination to keep the franc at its level of parity with the German mark made it impossible to reflate the economy and offer some hope to the voters.

The PS and its allies scored only 20 per cent of the votes in 1993 and were swept from office by centre–right RPR/UDF alliance, which polled 39.5 per cent. The Communist Party achieved 9 per cent and the Ecologists were disappointed to poll only 7.6 per cent. During the election campaign Rocard made a speech calling for the complete renewal of the Socialist Party to create the sort of broad alliance which he had been advocating for some years. He succeeded to the party leadership after the election, but the 'big bang' which he touted will be difficult to achieve in the wake of the widespread demoralisation brought on by crushing defeat.

4 Corporatist Paths to Socialism?

For most of the 1980s social democratic governments in Sweden and Austria defied the neo-liberal litany of high unemployment, privatisation, and deregulation. Both these small countries (eight million inhabitants) are neutral and outside the European Community, and both maintained low unemployment and low inflation with growth figures comparable to their EC neighbours. Both countries operated 'corporatist' arrangements in which the state brought together private business interests and organised labour in order to plan production, set wage levels, and decide on infrastructural improvement, regional policy, and training programmes. However, these corporatist practices came under increasing strain as the decade proceeded.

This chapter will concentrate on the recent experience of the Swedish Social Democrats, although it will touch on the Austrian model and on some of the other examples of corporatist practices promoted by social democratic governments. Besides its international renown, one of the interesting theoretical products of the Swedish experience was the argument that its model of welfare capitalism provided a sound basis for the transition to fully-fledged socialism. The policy initiative which excited this possibility was the wage earner funds scheme, which promised the gradual transfer of the ownership of the means of production to employees. Perhaps the most influential transition theorist was Walter Korpi, whose *The Working Class Under Welfare Capitalism* (1978) and *The Democratic Class Struggle* (1983) contained detailed empirical research on the organisation and attitudes of the Swedish working class to support the argument that Sweden was ripe for socialist development. A number of large-scale empirical studies were also cited to support this hypothesis in *Beyond Welfare Capitalism* (1981) by Ulf Himmelstrand, Goran Ahrne, Leif Lundberg and Lars Lundberg. The transitional potential of Sweden was also enthusiastically espoused in *The Transition From Capitalism to Socialism* (1979) by the American socialist John Stephens. In the years which have elapsed since these works were published, the assumptions of postwar social democracy have been demolished in the intensified competitiveness of a global economy struggling to climb out of a prolonged economic crisis. To raise the issue of the transition from capitalism to socialism now appears fanciful, and in many respects the Swedish story exemplifies the riches to rags development of modern European socialism. However, it is instructive to ask why the potential for radical change identified by the transition theorists did not develop. What is revealed is a common trait in socialist theorists of this period, the overestimation of the strength of the labour movement as a whole combined with the underestimation of the power of capital, particularly in its international dimension.

THE SWEDISH MODEL

In the 1980s Sweden was the envy of many social democrats in other European countries, for the Social Democratic Labour Party (SAP) had been in government for more than half a century. It presided over a superb welfare system and boasted one of the highest living standards in the world. The SAP first entered government in 1932 after winning over 40 per cent of the vote. The advent of corporatist consensus was signalled by the 1938 Saltsjöbaden agreement between the Swedish Trade Union Federation, the LO, and the Swedish Employers' Association, the SAF. It was agreed that regular negotiations would take place in a Labour Market Council on matters such as redundancies, disputes and pay settlement. In return for this concession by the employers, the LO agreed to cooperate in raising productivity (Hamilton, 1989: 177). The strength of popular support, the high level of unionisation and party membership, and the fragmentation of the right–wing parties helped to mould a society committed to the welfare of all its citizens and the prosperity of its industries, seeing the goals of efficiency and equality as complementary rather than contradictory (Milner, 1989: 16, 60–1). The Swedish 'way' was theoretically based on ideas which in some respects were a development of the revisionism developed by Eduard Bernstein in Germany in the 1890s (Tilton, 1990). Unlike Germany, Sweden enjoyed the social peace to enact a consensual reformism. The major concession from the Social Democrats to secure the cooperation of the employers was the dropping of their proposed nationalisation programme after the Second World War, but successive governments raised high levels of taxation to finance excellent provision of welfare, public transport and education.

The economic strategy on which the success story of the 1960s and 1970s was based was advocated by two labour economists, Gösta Rehn and Rudolf Meidner. In order to ensure full employment, the state would foster an 'active labour–market policy', including retraining programmes and other attempts to increase mobilility of labour, regional investment, and direct provision of jobs through infrastructural work (Dahlberg & Tuijman, 1991). Inflation was to be averted by high indirect taxes, dampening down demand and financing a high level of social provision. 'Solidaristic bargaining' would ensure that all workers in an industry received commensurate increases (Olsson, 1990). This involved wage restraint for workers in large and successful firms, but it overcame the problem of low pay; Sweden had very low pay differentials. Small or relatively inefficient firms were squeezed, resulting in a concentration of ownership. As the Swedish giants prospered, so did all sections of society. The success of the model was greatly aided by the long postwar boom and the relatively low level of defence expenditure which flowed from its neutrality. This 'Left corporatist' model was strong enough to cushion Sweden from the worst effects of the international economic crisis which set in after 1974. The strength of the consensus was confirmed by the continuation of corporatist processes when the SAP was forced out of power by a 'bourgeois' coalition during 1976–82. Indeed that government reaffirmed the state's responsibility for employment protection by nationalising more industries than all of its SAP predecessors (Pontusson, 1984: 84).

By the mid–1960s some Swedish socialists began to contemplate more radical developments. Two related issues were confronted, both concerning the distribution of power in the productive process. The first was the LO's perception of 'excessive' profits among the richest companies caused by the self–limiting wage increases accepted as part of the solidaristic bargaining system. The second was the lack of power exercised by the workers in decision–making at enterprise level. The 1967 industrial policy of the SAP extended state intervention in investment and regional and sectoral planning, and introduced state representatives on the boards of large corporations. In 1971 it was decided that there would be two worker representatives on the boards of medium–size and large companies. In 1974 the employers' absolute right to hire and fire labour without consultation was ended, something which they took to be an infringement of their prerogatives. In 1976 a Co–Determination Act required management to initiate negotiations with unions on any proposed changes in work practices (Elder, 1988: 157–8; Hamilton, 1989: ch. 10).

The great issue which provoked political polarisation surrounded the 'wage earner funds' proposals, first put forward by Rudolf Meidner within the manual workers' federation, the LO, in 1975, and adopted as official LO policy the following year (Himmelstrand et al, 1981: ch. 19). When the proposal was finally put before the SAP for adoption in 1978 it declared that firms with more than 500 employees would be obliged to issue shares every year to wage earner funds, the shares representing 20 per cent of their profits. The funds were to appoint shareholders representatives, mainly from the unions, to the boards of enterprises. It was estimated that with average profits of 15 per cent it would take 25 years for labour to achieve a voting majority in a company (Himmelstrand et al, 1981: 266). The response from business and the bourgeois parties was predictably hostile, for this measure posed a direct threat to the existing relations of production. However, many within the SAP were afraid that the proposal would break the consensus which had hitherto been beneficial to the working class, and they blamed this new radicalism for the election defeat of 1976. The opposition was galvanised by the funds issue and assisted by the vociferous support of the majority of the press. In opposition the SAP decided to adopt a weaker version of the funds proposal in 1981.

THE TRANSITION THEORISTS

Let us consider more closely the argument that the Swedish model could act as a stepping stone to the achievement of socialism. Korpi reasoned that the immense strength of the organised working class in Sweden had tilted the balance between capital and labour decisively in favour of the latter. In adopting solidaristic wage bargaining the Swedish labour movement focused power at the centre (the LO and also the TCO – the white collar workers' federation) rather than with individual unions (Korpi, 1978: 231). The strong links with the Social–Democrats, and the willingness of members to vote for the party and join it in large numbers had produced a situation in which labour was well positioned to win the 'democratic class struggle'. The wage–earner funds debate was a major battle in the broader struggle. The demands were founded on the labour view that excess profits were being made largely as a result of the solidaristic bargaining process. The funds proposals maintained the principle of solidarity, extended real powers to the collective worker, and implied a foreseeable qualitative change in the ownership of the means of production (Korpi, 1978: ch. 12; Korpi, 1983: 231–6). Korpi was aware that this would put the unions in a dual role as representatives of the wage earners and owners of the firms, and he recognised that the unions' own democratic structures would quite rightly come under careful scrutiny. He advocated universal and equal suffrage in the elections to the boards administering the funds, thereby giving a voice to the unwaged (Korpi, 1983: 234–5). At the time Korpi wrote his two books it was not clear which way the SAP would move on the funds. He recognised that the SAP faced a choice of historical significance, and he called on its leaders to formulate a 'provisional utopia' and demonstrate a way of moving towards its attainment (Korpi, 1983: 232). In reasserting a form of gradualist Marxism, Korpi explicitly rejected both Leninist and corporatist interpretations of the political role of organised labour. Leninism rejected parliamentarianism as an effective means of change, while corporatism minimised the significance of political competition, emphasising agreements between the 'big' actors in all major decision–making (Korpi, 1978: 4). In Korpi's view, decisive struggles were fought out politically, but a 'key part' of these struggles was generated by 'conflicts of interest in the sphere of production' (Korpi, 1983: 208). In view of the significance given to the political struggle, it is not surprising that both Korpi and Himmelstrand analysed the reasons for the 1976 defeat of the SAP. Supported by an abundance of survey findings, they concluded that a more left–wing stance would have found a receptive audience, and that the party's support of nuclear energy had been unpopular.

Himmelstrand also rejected the idea that social democracy had forged a permanent integration of the working class into capitalism, and he argued that the Swedish working class had engaged in a number of stages of development which had opened up the possibility of a transition to socialism (Himmelstrand et al, 1981: 23–4, chs. 21, 22). The situation in the late 1970s and early 1980s posed critical problems for the SAP, for the end of the post–war boom exposed the contradiction between the increasingly social character of productive forces and the private character of the relations of production, and this was bound to limit the possibility of compromise between class interests. Himmelstrand pointed out that the strategy to push for economic democracy as the 'next stage' of the historical struggle for democracy was closer to Marx's thinking than the Leninist model (Himmelstrand et al, 1981: 309), and in many respects it was a renewal of the gradualist Marxism advocated by Karl Kautsky earlier in the century. Although the wage earner funds promised a transfer of ownership along with a boost to investment, there was a danger that the scheme, along with other measures of participation, would place excessive power in the hands of union technocrats, so Himmelstrand recommended the widespread democratisation of all elements of society in order to counteract such a possibility (Himmelstrand et al, 1981: 207, 312–5).

Stephens was also impressed with the level and strength of organised labour in Sweden and the potential for the transition to socialism. He distinguished between the welfare statism which was common to most advanced capitalist countries after the Second World War, and 'production politics', which relocated the question of the ownership and control of the means of production to the centre of political debate, as it did in Sweden in the late 1970s. He described three conditions for the development of production politics; first, ruling without petty bourgeois coalitions, second, a high level of white–collar unionisation, and third, a long period of government by the socialists (Stephens, 1979: 197–8). In his view, Sweden was the only country in which all three conditions prevailed. The wage earner funds provided a more subtle and effective method of transition than nationalisation. The policy promised to socialise the economy without compensation, and also offered new sources of capital formation, which, as Stephens pointed out, was 'likely to be a serious problem in all capitalist countries when and if the current recession is over'. He considered that the brilliance of the funds lay in the fact that even in terms of capitalist efficiency they provided 'a practical solution to an immediate problem' (Stephens, 1979: 205). The wage earner funds did indeed promise a beneficial effect on investment and competitiveness, but naturally the employers were not impressed by a proposal which posed such a threat to their ownership and control. Although SAP Leader Olof Palme asserted in 1979 that the funds were 'inevitable', some leading figures in the SAP were concerned that such radical proposals ran counter to the political culture of compromise and involved serious risks. This was the tense situation which faced the SAP when it won the election of 1982 with 45.6 per cent of the vote, securing a parliamentary majority with the support of the communists.

THE EDIFICE CRUMBLES

Palme faced strong opposition to the funds, grouped around the October 4 Movement, and the bourgeois opposition organised protest marches in 1983. The 1983 Law set up five regional employee investment funds, financed by a payroll tax and a profits tax on larger firms (Milner, 1989: 135). Each fund was authorised to own no more than 8 per cent of a firm's shares, but as five funds were created it was possible for the collective workers to obtain an important stake in some enterprises. However, the funds ceased to receive profit shares from 1990, relieving the long-term threat to the ownership of Swedish capital. The enactment of the legislation in 1984 triggered the suspension of centralised bargaining, for the employers federation, the SAF, refused to cooperate with the government, despite the attempts by Palme to persuade them that the workers required some incentive to secure the moderation of wage demands (Walters, 1987: 70). The weakening of centralised bargaining, hitherto dominated by the LO and the SAF, had in fact already begun with the decision of the employers in metal (cars and engineering) to insist on separate bargaining in 1983 (Lash, 1985: 218–24; Mahon, 1991). However, a return to more flexible central bargaining system occurred in 1985, and the elements of corporatism were still in place by the end of the decade. Another fund which gave real power to the unions was introduced in 1985. 'Renewal funds' were financed by a 10 per cent tax on a firm's profits exceeding a certain level, to be used for training and research and development. However, the funds remained in the Central Bank without earning interest until unions and management agreed on how to use them. This provided the unions with their most meaningful participation in decision-making and it also overcame the 'free loader' problem, whereby some firms neglected training while recruiting staff trained by other employers (Rehn & Viklund, 1991).

The hostility of the Swedish employers to the wage earner funds was expressed by former Volvo President and the 1991 Chaiman of the SAF, Gunnar Johansson, who described them as 'an attempt to introduce a socialistic economy by the back door' (letter, 3 October 1991). He also complained that the funds would result in 'one actor dominating the whole stockmarket', although in fact there had always been a high degree of concentration of ownership in the Swedish economy. In seeking to move away from corporatist arrangements and to reduce the level of taxation (and with it social expenditure), the greatest threat posed by the employers was to move their business out of the country. The head of Volvo, Pehr Gyllenhammar, argued for decentralised wage bargaining throughout the 1980s, and he represented an enormously powerful interest. In 1988 Volvo accounted for 12 per cent of Sweden's exports and employed 6 per cent of the country's manufacturing workforce (Milner, 1989: 145), while Saab, the 'other' motor manufacturer, was bought out by the American–based multinational General Motors. Rehn and Viklund have argued that the big exporters in Sweden such as Volvo, Electrolux, Ericson, and SKF, have been able to 'almost blackmail' the Government at central and local level, and also operate more independently from the SAF (Rehn & Viklund, 1990: 321). One of the ways in which they circumvented national agreements was by introducing profit–sharing schemes and allocating personal bonuses (Mahon, 1991: 305–6). In 1990 the employers disbanded their central negotiating secretariat. Under business pressure to retain competitiveness in the world system, the SAP Government was forced to preside over a significant decrease in public expenditure as a percentage of gross national product, from 67 per cent in 1982 to approximately 50 per cent in 1991 (*The Guardian*, 7 August, 1991). This pressure also led the SAP to depart from long–standing commitments to steeply progressive taxation and cheap public services (Sainsbury, 1991).

Although the SAP retained power in the elections of 1985 under Palme and 1988 under his successor Ingvar Carlsson, its support dropped slightly on each occasion (44.7 per cent in 1985 and 43.7 per cent in 1988). After the 1988 election the SAP needed the support of the Left Party Communists and the Greens. Industrial unrest grew in the late 1980s and inflation climbed to 7 per cent by 1990, abnormally high by Swedish standards. Unemployment grew from 1.4 per cent in 1989 to 3.1 per cent in the summer of 1991, a remarkably low figure in comparison with other developed economies, but a disturbing rise in a country which had not experienced this problem. Growth remained at less than 2 per cent per annum throughout the 1980s, slightly lower than the average for Western Europe. Austerity measures were introduced in January and October 1990, involving cuts in welfare provision and public sector employment, as well as the privatisation of electricity and telecommunications. These policy changes were presented as part of a programme 'renewal', but, as Sainsbury has pointed out, this was perceived as a 'reorientation to the right' (Sainsbury, 1993: 59). Sweden's share of the world market declined slightly, and here again the compelling logic of the world market imposed its shadow on events. Her competitors had been able to discipline their workforces by the use of unemployment, and provide incentives through tax cuts and privatisations. Sweden remained tied to high levels of public expenditure, and 40 per cent of the work force were employed in the public sector in 1990 compared with less than a quarter in the countries of the European Community (*The Guardian*, 16 February, 1990). Acknowledging the need to be on the inside of the world's largest free trading bloc, the SAP Government formally applied for Swedish membership of the European Community in July 1991.

The Social Democrats lost the election of September 1991, polling 37.6 per cent of the vote, its lowest proportion since 1928. The new centre–right coalition led by the Conservative Party leader Carl Bildt came to power pledged to 'break the pattern of economic stagnation and to re–establish Sweden as a nation of growth and enterprise with a strong and expanding economy' (Brodin, 1992: 20) Armed with an array of conventional free market policies, including privatisation of industry and insurance, marketisation of health care and child care, the sale of council houses, the introduction of education vouchers, and the abolition of wage earner funds, the dismantling of the Swedish model commenced. The consequences of this diet were felt suddenly and dramatically. Mass unemployment returned for the first time since the 1930s, the level rising from 3 per cent to double figures within eighteen months. The economy experienced negative growth and swingeing cuts in welfare expenditure were announced in September 1992 and January 1993.

WHAT WENT WRONG?

The Swedish 'transition' theorists have been criticised on a number of counts. We can identify three major interrelated elements which enable us to understand why the hopes of the theorists in question have been stilled – the international economic context, class power and class consciousness, and the role of the state. Pontusson has pointed out that the writers in question made little estimation of the likely effects on the class struggle of changes in the accumulation process in response to the downturn in growth experienced since 1974 (Pontusson, 1984: 85, 95). The Swedish economy is one of the most 'open' of the advanced industrial nations. An index of openness (the ratio of exports to GNP multiplied by 100) indicates that Sweden's openness increased from 22 in 1965 to 35 in 1985, compared with average world figures of 24.9 in 1965 to 29.1 in 1985. In other words Sweden changed from being less open than average to being considerably more open than average. Sweden in 1985 was relatively more 'international' in its economic activity than West Germany (33), the United Kingdom (29), France (25), Japan (15), and the USA (7) (Husted & Melvin, 1990: 7). As the significance of exports has increased, so has the power of the exporters. However much state intervention can maintain investment with schemes such as the wage earner funds and the renewal funds, the ultimate power to invest rests with management. The possibility of shifting operations to countries with lower taxation and more flexible bargaining arrangement placed an enormous constraint on the SAP government. Two major firms, Tetra Pak and IKEA, moved their headquarters out of the country. With the advantage of hindsight we can say that the lack of a global political–economy perspective was the greatest weakness in the analyses of the transition theorists.

The second element turns on the perception of class power. The writers used high levels of unionisation and party membership as an indication that the workers were actively class conscious, and Korpi and Himmelstrand provided survey findings to support this. As Pierson has pointed out, they tended to underestimate the tendencies in the modern accumulation process which weaken class homogeneity (Pierson, 1986: 122–3). From the outset the idea of the wage earner funds was associated with the the major manual workers' federation, the LO, and was premised on the strength of labour and the SAP. In the 1980s the strength of the LO fell in comparison with the white collar unions, and certain sectors of the LO became very hostile to public sector workers who were regarded as living off the productive workers and holding back their just rewards (Svenson, 1991). Gosta Rehn and Birger Viklund commented that the strong LO unions, particularly the Metalworkers', changed from being the leaders of social reform to being 'self–centred and "red–necked"'. They expressed no support for equal opportunities, accepted higher differentials, and joined the liberal criticism of the public sector, 'using a rather tough language against their fellow workers' (Rehn & Viklund, 1990: 324). The unions have found it difficult to respond positively to the demands of feminists and environmentalists, as one might expect from entrenched bureaucratic organisations facing new challenges in a harsh climate (Micheletti, 1991: Taylor, 1993: 144). A good example of the difficulty which the SAP faced in responding to conflicting pressures was the decision in September 1990 to postpone progress on decommissioning nuclear power stations. Although this saved money and satisfied the power workers, it dismayed green opinion (Sainsbury, 1991: 51; Therborn, 1991: 117–8).

The divisions of interest between different elements of the broad working class may have been difficult to anticipate in the late 1970s, but it was not hard to see that support for the SAP had levelled out at about 43 per cent, following its high point of 50 per cent in 1968. Since 1970 the vote for the Communists held steady at 4 or 5 per cent, indicating the relatively small support for a radical reworking of the Swedish model. In order for an important initiative like the wage earner funds proposals to command popular support it was essential to link them to a wider democratic movement, particularly in the areas of the environment and the position of women in society. The entry of the Greens into parliament with over 5 per cent of the vote in 1988 indicated some support for the new social movements, but since the 1960s the overall vote for the Left hovered around the 50 per cent mark. The campaign of the bourgeois parties in 1991 was essentially a libertarian one, feeding on suspicions of the bureaucratic Social Democratic state and the power of the union bureaucracies, and associating them with the defunct communist systems of Eastern Europe. The surprising success of the right–wing populist New Democracy Party and the 'new right' Christian Democrats (both approximately 7 per cent) indicated that there was some attraction to the association of liberty with 'rolling back' the state. Both Korpi and Himmelstrand recognised the danger of placing too much power in the hands of the labour bureaucracy, but they did not anticipate the extent to which such 'labour power' was vulnerable to the ideological onslaught of free market ideology.

Finally, there is the question of the role of the state. Pontusson has argued that the state was limited in its capacity to nationalise private property by the terms of the Swedish model (Pontusson, 1984: 87). In that sense the historical compromise stemming from 1938 contained an important obstacle to effecting a transition to socialism. In Sweden the state apparatus was thoroughly permeated by supporters of the SAP, but it was also firmly tied to a corporatist model which many considered to be under threat from the wage earner fund proposals. Faced with an intense international competition for profitability, the Swedish state came under great pressure to provide the most favourable conditions for capital accumulation. Even when the state apparatus is not obviously sympathetic to conservative forces, it is obliged to act in the interests of those who control the levers of economic power; as Offe has commented, this is the 'institutional self–interest of the state' (Offe, 1984: 120; also Poulantzas, 1978: 225). Nor was the state apparatus exempt from the same sort of processes at work in the private sector. Leading civil servants were lured out of state service by high salaries in the top companies.

AUSTRIA

The Austrian Socialists (SPO) managed to develop and preserve the corporatist institutions of the 'social partnership' throughout the 1970s and 1980s. The SPO polled more than 50 per cent of the votes in three successive elections in the 1970s under the leadership of Bruno Kreisky, which constitutes the strongest sustained performance of any social democratic party (Sully, 1988). Since then it has polled 48 per cent in 1983 and 43 per cent in 1986 and 1990. The party also claims one of the highest membership rates of any of the affiliates to the Socialist International. As in many of the European countries, some of the lost support has gone to the Greens, who polled just under 5 per cent in 1986 and 1990. Unlike Sweden, Austria has a large nationalised sector of the economy, and the state industries were used in a counter–cyclical way after 1974 to maintain investment and employment (Radice & Radice, ch. 8). This, combined with self–discipline in the corporatist processes which permeate every level of Austrian life, produced low unemployment, low inflation, and growth comparable with its neighbours (Fitzmaurice, 1991: ch. 5). Voluntary control of wage settlements succeeded in limiting the rate of inflation even after the second oil price rise of 1979. The first wage–price pacts had been struck in 1947 by the highly centralised Austrian Trade Unions Federation and the Federal Chamber of the Economy (März, 1988). Ten years later incomes policy was placed in the hands of a 'parity commission' comprising representatives of unions, employers and government. Under Kreisky the social partnership idea was extended to encompass a wide range of actors rather than the handful of key figures which is normally associated with corporatism. Chambers developed in all industries, with obligatory membership for all relevant interest groups, and over 200 advisory councils were formed to participate in decision making and administration (Gerlich et al, 1988).

In recent years there has been a tendency to limit corporatist practices to the major decision–making areas, in keeping with the trend towards de–regulation and flexibility which has swept the advanced industrial world (Gerlich, 1992). There has also been political opposition to the idea of social partnership from the far–right Freedom Party, which polled over 16 per cent in the election of October 1990. Opposition to corporatism has also come from 'new politics' groups, on specific issues such as the building of nuclear power stations and a hydroelectric dam (Sully, 1981: 168–72; Parkin, 1989: 32, 319–22). They were met by intolerant reactions from the authorities, who presented a solid tripartite bloc behind their industrial 'consensus'. Peace activists protesting Austria's high profile in arms trading have also felt the heavy hand of state coercion. This raises an ever present danger of corporatism, the possibility of dominant interests operating in an insensitive way to intense minorities which challenge the parameters of assumed consensus. If new social movements are estranged from politics by this 'freezing out', the 'old' socialist movements run the risk of failing to renew their ideas. It has also had implications for the most identifiable 'outsiders' of all, the guestworkers. Although the interventionist policies of the Austrian state have helped to keep down unemployment, curbs on the numbers of guestworkers have also played an important part. The 'Aliens Act', which came into force from January 1993 was the third major measure in a year controlling the entry of foreigners (*Socialist Affairs* 1, 1993). These measures, of course, make life very uncomfortable for the legal guestworkers.

SOUTHERN EUROPE

In Spain and Greece the socialist movements used their positions in government in the 1980s to adapt or develop corporatist structures. Both socialist movements were propelled into power after spectacular surges shortly after the overthrow of the right–wing dictatorships. The Spanish Socialist Workers Party (PSOE) polled under 30 per cent in the 1977 elections but swept to power with over 48 per cent of the vote in 1982. It retained power in 1986 and 1989 despite diminishing electoral support (44 per cent and 40 per cent). In Greece the Panhellenic Socialist Movement (PASOK) received less than 14 per cent of the vote in the election of 1974, but swept to victory with 48 per cent of the vote in 1981. It retained power in 1985 with 46 per cent of the vote, but was defeated in the two elections of 1989, winning 39 per cent in June and 41 per cent in November, elections dominated by the accusations of corruption levelled against veteran PASOK leader Andreas Papandreou, which were later disproved.

PSOE established itself as by far the strongest political party in Spain in the 1980s. Under Franco there existed 'state corporatist' structures for planning economic development, but of course the absence of democratic processes meant that no free negotiations between genuine representatives took place. Nevertheless there was an attempt to create negotiated agreements in the new democracy, and the 1977 Moncloa Pact was a notable early example (Martinez–Alia & Roca, 1988: 138–40). Shortly after coming to power the PSOE Government made its commitment to 'pactismo' clear, and the product was the 1982 inter–confederation accord between government, the employers federation (CEDE), and the two main trades union confederations, the Workers Commissions and the General Union of Workers (UGT). This was succeeded in 1984 by the 'social and economic accord', athough this time without the support of the Workers Commissions, the federation in which the communists play a leading role (Share, 1989: 75). In the late 1980s it became more difficult to secure the cooperation of the labour organisations, largely due to the level of unemployment, which was over 15 per cent for most of the 1980s and early 1990s. The dreadful record on unemployment was presented as the unfortunate price to pay for modernising the economy. Inflation had to be controlled in order to produce high growth rates, a balance–of–payments surplus, and membership of the European Community. Although more resources were devoted to welfare and education, Spain still lagged behind most other leading industrial nations (Gillespie, 1989: 76).

PSOE acted as a centre party, tightly controlled by the leadership of Prime Minister Felipe Gonzales and, in the 1980s, by Alfonso Guerra (Gillespie & Gallagher, 1989). The government recommendation to the electorate to vote in favour of Spain's entry into NATO in 1986 angered many left–wing activists and helped to regenerate the fragmented forces of the Marxist Left. They came together as Izquierdo Unida under the popular leader Julio Anguitta, attracting over 9 per cent of the vote in the 1989 elections and retaining that level of support in 1993. Because the old state apparatus was tinged by the fascist past, PSOE implanted its own members into leading administrative posts, but this created the danger of clientalism – favours for tasks rendered – rather than democratising the structure of the state (Pridham, 1989). The party has not been renowned for its internal democracy, but it engaged in a widespread consultative exercise in order to produce a long–term strategic manifesto, the Programma 2000, which was approved in 1990 (Gillespie, 1993). Largely developed by Manuel Castells and Manuel Escudero after canvassing more than half a million citizens, the programme calls for a regulated market economy and a higher level of social welfare, as well as a renewal of socialism on a European scale. The corporatist tendencies exhibited by PSOE have to be seen in the context of Spain's history and its rapidly changing place in the world. It has left behind the isolation and authoritarianism of the Franco years to become part of the European Community (1986), and rapid growth and an influx of multinational investment have accelerated the secularisation and urbanisation of the country. In contrast to the dictatorial corporatist state of the Franco era, the PSOE Government was willing to grant regional devolution, and lessen the power of the army, the police and the church (Story, 1993). Although there appears to be little substance to PSOE's socialism, it was able to claim more support for its efforts than the Socialists could retain in France. The Socialist victory in the election of 1993, despite its record on unemployment, revealed the widespread fear of a return to the Right.

The rhetoric of Papandraeou and his PASOK colleagues was at times closer to Marxism than the social democratic tradition (Macridis, 1984: 64; Lyrintzis, 1989: 35–6). However, despite the anti–American blasts PASOK kept Greece in NATO and allowed the Americans to retain their military bases. Membership of the European Community in 1986 appeared to have a moderating influence on the PASOK leadership. A 'left Keynesian' approach to economic and social policy in the early 1980s gave way to austerity policies, producing unemployment of 10 per cent by the end of the decade, much of it concentrated among the young (Spourdalakis, 1988: 225–32; Lyrintzis, 1989: 40–3). Although some measures of socialisation were carried through, there were many restrictions on the freedom of workers to strike and the PASOK Government maintained the existing corporatist labour practices of the Greek state, which were heavily bureaucratic. PASOK's internal structures were undemocratic, and it helped to fashion an authoritarian state in which the military, the diplomatic service and the judicial system were exempted from democratic control. The power of patronage was even more extensively operated than in Spain, with most leading civil service posts being occupied by party appointees

(Spourdalakis, 1988: 242–54; Gillespie & Gallagher, 1989). The predictable danger materialised with the widespread accusations of corruption which culminated in the downfall of the Government and legal action taken against Papandreou and some of his closest supporters. More than half the Greek electorate voted for the two parties of the Left, PASOK and the Progressive Left Alliance, in both the 1989 elections, but because the Progressive Left played an active part in prosecuting the PASOK leaders for corruption, there was no possibility of a Left coalition. Instead the right–wing New Democracy Party led by Constantine Mitsotakis formed a government, and embarked on a privatisation drive to dismantle the large public sector.

CONCLUSION

The fall from power of the Swedish Social Democrats and the subsequent attack on the welfare state consensus provide more evidence of the difficulty of defending egalitarian policies in the world economy. As Sweden, Austria, and possibly Norway prepare to enter the European Community, their capacity to preserve or restore the old social democratic practices will be greatly diminished. However, to what extent is it possible for some of the practices of 'left corporatism' to find a place in the Community? While *laissez–faire* deregulation may have helped corporations in one country to gain a short–term competitive edge over corporations from another, the broader socio–economic effects have been baleful. Europe as a whole continues to suffer from the low growth and mass unemployment which started after 1974, while environmental and infrastructural problems increase in scope as the public funds necessary to tackle them are diminished. The experience of Sweden since 1991 offers more evidence against the panacea of neo–liberal economics.

The examples of Sweden and Austria show that interventionist policies can produce low unemployment and low inflation at the same time, with broadly competitive growth. Austria had the added advantage of a strong public industrial sector to secure cooperation, while Sweden was more vulnerable to the power of its highly concentrated multinational private sector. The Swedish wage earner funds and renewal funds were imaginative schemes for transferring real power to working people while at the same time helping industries to improve their competitiveness through investment and training. The solidaristic wage bargaining system was unusually egalitarian and effective in maintaining high levels of employment. However, countries can no longer claim the kind of relative autonomy within the world economy which might enable such 'expensive' solutions to flourish. Theoretically, a United States of Europe might offer such an arena, but there is a long way to go before a federal state is created. As it stands, restrictions on borrowing and budget deficits in the

Maastricht Treaty legally inhibit conventional Keynesian counter–cyclical measures.

Finally, one aspect of corporatism which has discredited social democratic politics must be mentioned, the question of corruption. In the states where a large public sector has been part of the corporatist package, there have been spectacular cases of corruption involving socialist politicians. Austrian, Spanish and Greek socialists have been implicated. In Italy the large public sector has been created and controlled largely by the Christian Democrats, but the Socialists shared power with them throughout the 1980s and the majority of the party's parliamentary representatives have been implicated in accepting bribes for awarding contracts. It is doubtful that the party will survive such a disgrace. The serious implication for socialism is that it provides an argument for dismantling the public sector, even though swindling and corruption is a regular feature of private capital. The greatest safeguard against corruption is always openness and democratic accountability, which socialist parties have always gestured towards but have not always promoted.

5 Germany

Before the unification of Germany in 1990, the Federal Republic (BDR) in the West was the largest and richest economy in the European Community and the Democratic Republic (DDR) in the East was, with Czechoslovakia, the leading economy in the Soviet zone. The combined strength of the new Germany is statistically impressive. Its population of approximately 80 million is second only to Russia, while its gross national product, almost one third that of the European Community, makes it the third largest producer in the world. With low inflation and a consistent foreign trade surplus, Germany has the strongest currency in the Community, and its central bank effectively operates as the European central bank (Marsh, 1992). What happens to socialist politics in Germany will have a profound effect on the future of European socialism. This chapter will look at the recent history of socialism and communism in both the BDR and the DDR in order to establish the character of the German Left. We will also look at the effect on institutional socialism of the politics of new social movements, represented in Germany by the Greens (*Die Grünen*).

Germany was the first country to develop a united socialist party, in 1875, and in the early part of the twentieth century the Social Democratic Party was the largest socialist party in the world. However, doctrinal divisions were never far from the surface, and Germany has witnessed most of the great doctrinal struggles in European socialist history. In the 1860s and 1870s the Marxists opposed the Lassalleans in the formation of the new party, and in the 1980s the great revisionist debate between Kautsky and Bernstein rocked the party. In the years preceding the First World War the left opposition led by Luxemburg and Liebknecht bitterly opposed the party leadership, and this split surfaced bloodily in the German Revolution of 1918–19. It is often forgotten that the German party split before the Russian Revolution, with the formation of the Independent

Social Democratic Party (USPD) in 1916. The division was redefined by the formation of the Communist Party (KPD) in December 1918, and the 'reform versus revolution' polarity divided the enormous support for the Left in the Weimar Republic and contributed greatly to the triumph of the Nazis in 1933. When the nation divided into two states in 1949, the doctrinal and organisational split between communism and social democracy was translated into a territorial division. The SPD was not permitted an independent existence in the East, and the Communist Party was soon banned in the West. The German experience therefore catalogues the catastrophic consequences of the rancorous rupture of the international socialist movement.

When the people of Berlin breached the wall which divided their city on 9 November, 1989, it was the beginning of the end of the postwar settlement. It signalled the demise of communist power in the German Democratic Republic, and in the first and last free election held there, in March 1990, the formerly omnipotent communists, reconstituted as the Party of Democratic Socialism (PDS), polled only 16 per cent. The Social Democrats (SPD) achieved only 22 per cent of the votes, and the conservative alliance dominated by the Christian Democrats claimed an overwhelming victory. This gave a green light to the rapid reunification of Germany. In Moscow in September 1990 a treaty restoring full sovereignty to a united German state was signed by representatives of the two German Governments and the Second World War allies, the USSR, the USA, France and Great Britain. The agreement took force on 3 October, and in the first free all–German elections for 58 years, held in December 1990, the Christian Democratic Union/Christian Social Union (CDU/CSU) gained 44 per cent of the votes and formed a coalition government with the Free Democratic Party (FDP – 11 per cent). The SPD won only 33.5 per cent, the PDS 2.4 per cent, and Alliance 90, a group of East German Greens and independent socialists, gained 1.2 per cent. Germany has a mixture of constituency (first vote) and party list (second vote) representatives to ensure proportional representation for parties which pass a 5 per cent threshold, but because special arrangements had been made for the representation of parties from the East, the PDS and Alliance 90 won seats in the *Bundestag*. The Greens in West Germany gained only 3.9 per cent of the votes and lost their entire parliamentary group, which had totalled 42 before the election. The result was a ringing endorsement of the 'fast track' approach to unity taken by Chancellor Helmut Kohl and in particular his decision to exchange defunct East German Marks for *Deutschmarks* at the rate of one–to–one (Poguntke, 1992b: Padgett & Paterson, 1991). It was also a considerable blow to the Social Democrats, who had considered that the former DDR was fertile ground for democratic socialism.

THE SOCIAL DEMOCRATS IN WEST GERMANY

Kurt Schumacher and the other SPD leaders were shocked by the party's narrow defeat in the 1949 election, in which it mustered less than 30 per cent of the vote (Edinger, 1965: ch. 5). But more than a decade of official anti–Marxist propaganda, as well as the association of socialism with the Soviet 'enemy', conspired against Schumacher's ambitions. Germany was the front line of the cold war, and the politics of the Federal Republic were dominated by perceptions of the communist threat. The SPD remained in opposition until 1966, when it joined a 'grand coalition' with the CDU/CSU, with the SPD's Willy Brandt as Vice–Chancellor and Minister of Foreign Affairs. This lasted until 1969, when for the first time the SPD vote exceeded 40 per cent (42.7) and it formed a government with the liberal FDP. The SPD remained in office with the FDP until 1982, since when its electoral fortunes have declined.

To a great extent the SPD's behaviour in government was shaped by its development in the years in opposition. The recovery of Germany in the 1950s has often been referred to as the economic miracle, orchestrated by the Finance Minister Ludwig Erhard. It was premised on the need of the Americans for a strong economic power to act as a bulwark against the threat of Communism from the East. American businessmen with pre–War German connections successfully urged the United States government to dismiss the idea of deindustrialising Germany (van der Pijl, 1984: 145), and West Germany joined the Organisation for European Economic Cooperation in 1948. Marshall Aid began to flow in 1949. The strategy adopted within the Federal Republic was given the name 'social market economy', although the 'social' side of this was restricted to some measure of workers' participation in industry until the extension of the welfare state in the mid–1950s. The early period was marked by a low level of consumption and high unemployment (Armstrong, Glyn & Harrison, 1984: 140-9), providing the basis for the rapid growth of the economy, which, at 7.1 per cent per annum between 1955 and 1959, was the highest in the world and compared favourably with that of the United States (3.3 per cent) and the United Kingdom (2.2 per cent) (März, 1988: 34). One of the reasons for German economic success was the consistent undervaluation of the mark, which helped German exports, mainly to other European countries. The central bank, the *Bundesbank*, was given wide autonomous powers to prevent a recurrence of the sort of economic disasters which had undermined the Weimar Republic. Investment was encouraged by the 'long loan' policy of the banks, while good industrial relations were aided by the organisation of industry–wide unions and their inclusion on the supervisory boards of firms.

Viewed historically, there should be little surprise at the success of the German economy. Following unification in 1870, Germany quickly caught up with the industrial production of Britain. Losing two world wars slowed its economic advance, but the termination of military aggrandizement in 1945 released its economic potential. A large, skilled workforce and a developed infrastructure survived the damage of the war, and the absence of a large defence expenditure provided the country with an enormous advantage over Britain and France, who were both paying heavy defence bills as a result of their colonial past and the cold war. For example, until recently half of Britain's expenditure in research and development was devoted to military purposes, compared with with less than 10 per cent in Germany (Kennedy, 1988: 622).

The military situation had other effects on West Germany. It was integrated into the West European Union and the North Atlantic Treaty Organisation (NATO) in 1954–5, while in retaliation the Warsaw Pact was formed with East Germany as a founder member. The rapid economic recovery of the West contrasted with the poverty of the East, which had suffered in economic terms for its dependence on the Soviet Union. Almost three million citizens out of a population of 18 million fled from East Germany between 1949 and 1961, when the SED regime under Ulbricht erected the Berlin Wall to stem the outflow. In the Federal Republic anti-communism was shrill and authoritarian. The Government applied to the Constitutional Court for a ban on the German Communist Party (KPD) in 1951, and this was granted in 1956. There were waves of arrests, interrogations, dismissals, and black lists of those who had been members of the KPD or even associated with organisations in which the KPD operated (Cobler, 1978; Graf, 1976: 108; Hülsberg, 1988: 19–21). In developing the new 'enemy within' the leaders of West German society could conveniently set aside the question of the Nazi past, and many former Nazis achieved leading positions in business and public administration (Childs, 1966: ch. 4). The East German regime's denial of basic civil liberties to its citizens, and its willingness to shoot them if they tried to escape to the West, intensified the anti-communism.

In the polarised economic and political climate the SPD found itself under severe pressure to move away from its Marxist heritage. The process became possible after the death of Schumacher in 1952 and crowned by the adoption of a new programme at the 1959 Conference at Bad Godesberg. All vestiges of Marxism were shed in favour of the new commitment to 'as much market as possible, as much planning as necessary' (Dyson, 1989: 151; Graf, 1976: ch. 7; Carr, 1987: 196–7). In a *Bundestag* debate in 1960 Herbert Wehner, on behalf of the SPD, announced the party's full support for NATO in the face of the communist threat (Paterson, 1977: 185). Wehner, a former KPD member, was one of the leading figures behind the transformation of the SPD. Another leading moderate, Willy Brandt, achieved international prominence as the mayor of West Berlin at the time that the wall was built, and the visit to Berlin of US President Kennedy appeared to endorse the 'reliability' of the SPD in the fight against communism. In 1957 Kennedy had written an article in *Foreign Affairs* in which he argued that the fidelity of the SPD to the West was unquestionable and that it was foolish for the Americans to rely entirely on the Christian Democrats (van der Pijl, 1984: 217). After Bad Godesberg the SPD's electoral support began to rise, and part of this increased popularity was due to Brandt's favourable image as candidate for Chancellor.

The SPD entered a grand coalition with the CDU/CSU in 1966, after the FDP Ministers withdrew from the right–wing coalition headed by Ludwig Erhard. With the advantage of hindsight the concerns expressed at the time about a 'profound economic and social crisis' (Freund, 1972: 48–9) appear to be greatly exaggerated, for the falterings in economy proved to be temporary, as did the flickering support for the neo–Nazi National Democratic Party. However, the Nazi past cast a long shadow, and there was a great fear of economic instability and a surge of extremist politics. In political terms the coalition provided the SPD with the opportunity of exercising ministerial responsibility and enhancing the status of its leaders, particularly Brandt, who was Deputy Chancellor and Minister of Foreign Affairs, and Wehner, who was Minister for All German Affairs. However, the absence of a large left–wing opposition created a vacuum which encouraged the development of an extra–parliamentary opposition, and the late 1960s in Germany (as elsewhere) saw a proliferation of street confrontations between police and demonstrators (Burns & van der Will, 1988: ch.3). When the SPD formed a government with the FDP after the 1969 election, however, the hostility of the CDU/CSU opposition had the effect of reducing the tension between the SPD leadership and the left wingers of its youth organisation, the Jusos. In the late 1960s and early 1970s large numbers of young people came into the party, but in 1971 the party executive gained the power to form and dissolve party organisations and to control their finances, and in 1975 the executive gained the power to sanction all publications (Braunthal, 1983: 23–6).

The distinctive contribution which the SPD leaders brought to government was not in the area of social reform but in improving the relationship between the two German states. Brandt and Wehner immediately began work on a policy which was soon to become known as *Ostpolitik*, whereby the two Germanies would recognise each other and the Federal Republic would legally accept the border between Poland and East Germany. Although it did not appear to non–Germans to amount to much more than an acceptance of the status quo, it eased East–West tension and contributed to the development of closer economic and social relations between the two states, and for that matter between the Soviet bloc and the countries of the NATO alliance. The preliminary work undertaken by Brandt and Wehner in the grand coalition bore fruit after 1969, and was symbolised by the meeting between Brandt and the East German Premier Stoph at Erfurt in 1974 and sealed by a series of treaties in which the two states recognised each other as well as the border between Germany and

Poland and other post–war changes.

In 1969 Brandt declared that he would be the Chancellor of domestic reforms (Prittie 1974: 231), yet in this area the record of the SPD was modest. There were minor reforms which introduced flexible retirement age, improved training, better safety–at–work regulations, and measures to rehabilitate the handicapped. In the field of education the SPD encouraged the introduction of comprehensive schools, but the difficulty here lay in the fact that education is the responsibility of the State governments in the federal system (Braunthal, 1983: 253–6). There are a number of possible reasons for the SPD's lack of radicalism in office. We have noted that its dramatic rise in support was achieved after Bad Godesberg. Schumacher's gradualist Marxism did not project a popular image to a society bent on rapid material recovery in an atmosphere of rabid anti–communism. The failure of the SPD under Schumacher made it difficult for the Left to make an impact in the party. In addition, the SPD needed the support of its coalition partner, the FDP, which was ideologically opposed to state intervention in the economy.

The oil price rise of 1973–4 provoked a deflationary response from the major economic powers, and while this provided a further constraint on the SPD's policy options, it was committed to public expenditure cuts even before the price rise. The chief advocate of this economic caution was Helmut Schmidt, the Finance Minister, who succeeded Brandt as Chancellor in 1974. Brandt resigned when one of his advisors was unmasked as a spy for East Germany. Schmidt saw fighting inflation as his priority, even at the cost of rising unemployment and cuts in public expenditure. Left–wing critics justifiably argued that some reforms could have been carried through without great expense, such as reform of the University system, the development of co–determination, and improvements in the labour process. As with the British Labour Governments, the focus on management of the economy appeared to exclude consideration of any sort of reform. It was considered that provided that certain economic indicators were strong, the electorate would respond favourably, but there was an electoral price to pay for the rejection of radical reform. The Government's financial conservatism was also encouraged by the independent power of the Federal Bank to set interest rates. The strong competitive position of the economy was shown in increased export–led output, which helped to arrest the growth of unemployment. However, not even the competitive power of the economy enabled the Germans to withstand the onset of the full world economic crisis in 1979–80. In both 1981 and 1982 there was a fall in the rate of growth, and unemployment rose from 3.2 per cent in 1979 to 7.5 per cent (over two million people) in 1982 (Radice & Radice, 1986: 49). These difficulties, together with the split within the SPD on the proposed stationing of Cruise and Pershing II nuclear missiles, persuaded the FDP to withdraw their support in 1982.

In industrial policy, the corporatist idea of 'concerted action' was introduced by the SPD Minister of Economics Karl Schiller in 1967. This was designed to bring together government, unions and employers to formulate industrial policy. Although the employers were initially reluctant, they were the chief beneficiaries in the late 1960s (Berghahn, 1988: 119). In 1976, after eight years of negotiations between the government, the trade union federation (the DGB) and the employers' federation (the BDI), it was agreed to extend the system of workers' participation on supervisory boards so that instead of the workers having one third of the representatives they would have half in large enterprises, although one of those representatives would be from senior staff and the Chair of the Board would retain the deciding vote (Braunthal, 1983: 115–8). The employers challenged the new Codetermination Law in the Constitutional Court in 1977 and effectively ended the 'strong' version of concerted action, but informal trilateral contacts were sustained throughout the 1980s, despite the fact that for many years real wages failed to rise (Dyson, 1989: 155–6). The most notable strike action taken during the SPD's period in office was the attempt by the metal workers to win a 35 hour week in 1979. Not only was this their first official strike for 50 years, but the focus on hours rather than cash reflected a developing consciousness of the desirability and social justice of a shorter working life. Although unsuccessful, attempts to internationalise the action showed signs that organised labour was beginning to recognise the need to match the internationalisation of capital.

Although the Brandt Government pledged itself to give more democracy to the people, it actually increased the authoritarian tendencies within the German state, following the decree of January 1972 which prohibited 'extremists' from entering or staying in the public service. The decree was used almost exclusively against the Left, and quickly became known as the *Berufsverbot* (ban on admission to the professions). It has been estimated that it produced over a thousand rejections of applicants on political grounds, hundreds of dismissals from the service, and over 2,000 disciplinary proceedings against public servants (Braunthal, 1989: 248–9). To protect people from the over–zealous application of the ban, new guidelines were issued in 1976 which stipulated that disloyalty had to be 'proved'. However, the following year SPD leaders criticised the Young Socialists for supporting the Russell Tribunal, an international body set up to investigate the problem. In 1976 Brandt admitted that he had made an error in signing the decree, but it was not until 1979 that routine investigations were scrapped. The practice of *Berufsverbot* extended to private firms and even trade unions, working on blacklists derived from official information (Cobler, 1976: 33–4). It also led to the massive expansion of the intelligence service reponsible for the 'defence of the constitution'. The experience for individuals vicitimised under the system was frightening, and the whole intimidatory process was a lamentable episode in the history of German Social Democracy.

One of the justifications for the *Berufsverbot* was the growth of terrorism in the 1970s. Between 1970 and 1978 over 200 people were convicted of terrorism, 28 people were assassinated, and 93 were injured (Braunthal, 1989: 317). The chief perpetrators were the Red Army Faction, led by Andreas Baader and Ulrike Meinhoff. Meinhoff was found hanged in her cell in 1976, while Baader, along with Gudrun Ennslin and Jan–Carl Raspe, died 'in mysterious circumstances' while awaiting trial in Stuttgart–Stammheim gaol in 1977. Terroristic attacks developed in the late 1960s after the murder by the police of a student at a demonstration and the attempted murder of the student leader Rudi Dutschke (Burns & van der Will, 1988: 94–5; Baumann, 1977). The complacency of West German society in relation to its Nazi past was seen in the number of former Nazis in positions of power, and these were the targets of the RAF. The moderation of the SPD created a vacuum in Left politics and a sense of powerlessness among many young people in the face of an increasingly authoritarian state. Although there were probably no more than 200 active terrorists, there were thousands more prepared to shield them. The arrest of their leaders and the offer of reduced sentences effectively brought terrorism to an end by 1980.

The move towards a non–ideological, technocratic image under Schmidt's leadership made it difficult for the SPD to agree on a long–range party programme in the 1970s. The international political situation played an important part in the divisions within the Party, and re–emphasised the extent to which German politics was dominated by enmity between the USA and the Soviet Union. The 1983 election was dominated by the debate over whether to permit the deployment of US Cruise and Pershing nuclear missiles in West Germany. The initiative had come from Schmidt himself in 1977, but the majority of the party opposed an action which effectively brought on a second phase of the cold war (Paterson, 1989: 194–6). The divided SPD lost almost 5 per cent of its support in the 1983 election, after which the party voted overwhelmingly to oppose the nuclear weapons programme. The differences within the party made it difficult to develop a new programme. It proved difficult to reconcile 'new politics' concerns with the environment, abortion on demand, minimum income guarantee schemes, guest workers' rights, and the abolition of nuclear energy, with traditional labour concerns for full employment and high wages, and the business demand for high profits (Merkl, 1988; Padgett, 1987). After many years of debate a new programme was adopted at the Berlin Congress of December 1989, reaffirming the liberal principles of Bad Godesberg but giving a central place to environmental protection (Padgett, 1993).

The selection of Oskar Lafontaine as Chancellor candidate in 1990 signalled a move to the Left, for he had been a clear advocate of coalition with the Greens (Lafontaine, 1992), and had called for a general strike against the deployment of nuclear missiles in 1983. In economic policy Lafontaine advocated a new 'economic realism', attempting to combine capitalist efficiency and social justice. This constituted an attempt to convince the voters that social democratic measures could be more efficient than those of the Right, as well as being more compassionate. These measures included tax incentives for reinvested profits and increased investment in ecologically friendly technologies. And it also included a form of solidaristic labour market policy which would involve some sacrifices from 'core' workers to aid part–timers, the unemployed, and many women workers (Dyson, 1989: 159–60). The development of a new ethical market reformism was curtailed by circumstances which could hardly have been foreseen. From the time of the collapse of the Berlin Wall German politics became overwhelmingly concerned with the issue of German reunification and the problems of integrating the former DDR. Lafontaine warned that Kohl had seriously misjudged the immense social and economic difficulties of integrating the East German economy in an unplanned way, but this failed to match the mood of the times. Following the poor performance of the SPD at the polls, Lafontaine was replaced as leader by Bjorn Engholm.

Within months of the election the economic and social plight of the East vindicated Lafontaine's fears. The early state elections in Hesse and the Rhineland Palatinate produced good results for the SPD, giving the party a majority in the Upper House, the Bundesrat, which meant that to some extent they were placed in the position of sharing responsibility for the problems stemming from unification. The severity of these problems was not confined to economic hardship, for it included neo–Nazi attacks against guestworkers. The need to take concerted action against this resulted in a 'solidarity pact' between the government and the SPD in March 1993. This raised the possibility of a renewal of the old 'grand alliance' of the late 1960s. Election results at state level in 1992 went against both of the major parties, while support grew for the Greens and the extreme right–wing Republican Party. The SPD struggled with the dilemma of supporting a sense of national solidarity while at the same time preserving an oppositional distance from which it could present a coherent alternative. Its difficulties were compounded by the resignation of Engholm in April 1993.

THE SOCIALIST UNITY PARTY IN THE GERMAN DEMOCRATIC REPUBLIC

It is possible to distinguish four phases in the history of the DDR. First, the grim years of the establishment of a state fashioned after the Soviet model which was highly provisional in character, and still subject to the economic burden of reparations to the Soviet Union. After the death of Stalin in March 1953 and before the the June rebellion by disaffected workers in East Germany there was a real possibility of negotiating reunification, a 'unique opportunity' as Brandt later described it (Brandt, 1978: 29). However, the leaders of the two new states were anxious to preserve their rather precarious positions, and Adenauer played an important role in ensuring American rejection of Soviet overtures on reunification (McCauley, 1986: 59–63). After the 1953 rising more attention was paid to increasing living standards, but the state was threatened by its failure to satisfy consumer needs. The revival of the economy was hindered by the emigration of millions of people to the West, a problem grimly 'resolved' with the building of the Berlin Wall in 1961.

The sealing of the frontiers ushered in a third phase which both consolidated the grip of the SED on state and society and which saw significant increases in living standards in the 1960s and early 1970s. When Erich Honecker took over power from Walter Ulbricht in 1971 the economy appeared to be in good shape and the relationship with the Federal Republic was being stabilised. The high point of his leadership was the ninth Party Congress in 1976, for by this time the GDR was the richest country in COMECON, the communist economic bloc, and was the tenth leading manufacturer in the world. However, closer relations with the West enabled East German dissidents to talk to their fellow citizens via West German television and newspapers (Woods, 1986: ch. 2). The quandary of German communism became clear; material success could not bring the increased tolerance for which so many yearned because the regime lacked legitimacy. The end of the third phase was symbolised by the crackdown on dissident intellectuals such as singer–poet Wolf Biermann, political theorist Rudolf Bahro, author of the influential *The Alternative in Eastern Europe* (Bahro, 1984), and the distinguished scientist Robert Havemann (Woods, 1986: ch. 4).

The final phase in the history of the DDR began shortly after the great oil price rise of 1974, as the economic expansion stuttered in the wake of the downswing in the world economy. Increasing global pressure to raise the productivity of labour passed its ruthless verdict on the weakest firms. Unemployment rose and was used as a discipline to hold down labour costs and drive up productivity. These processes were accelerated after the second oil price rise in 1979. In the short term the centrally planned economies could boast the retention of full employment and enjoy cheap energy supplies from the Soviet Union, but in terms of their competitive position in the world market the problems were mounting and became visible once the western economies began a partial recovery in the mid–1980s. East Germany did not have the debt problems which beset Poland, Hungary, and Yugoslavia, but it was closely linked to the world economy by its special trading status with the European Community (Palmer, 1988: 78–9). The economies of Eastern Europe played an increasingly intermediary role in the world economy during the 1970s, exporting manufactures to the third world while importing better quality manufactures from the United States, Japan, and Western Europe. When inflation raised the price of those imports the countries of Eastern Europe had difficulty in purchasing the capital and consumer goods it had ordered from the west, while it found its own goods more difficult to export. Often the simple way out was to extend credits, which exacerbated the problems, and the planned economies lacked the internal mechanisms to deal with these problems as ruthlessly as the advanced capitalist countries. The crisis was bad enough for advanced capitalism, but even worse for the communist states (Frank, 1980: ch. 4).

The most noticeable material damage to the country under SED rule was the dreadfully high level of pollution and the failure to deliver the quality of consumer goods taken for granted in West Germany. Like the other states of the Soviet bloc, the decisive political factor in the collapse of the dictatorships was the accession to power in the Soviet Union of Mikhail Gorbachev in 1985. The Soviet Union had exerted an effective veto on all the countries in the Warsaw Pact, and the GDR had followed the Soviet Union very closely for most of its life. For example, when Malenkov declared a 'new course' of producing more consumer goods in the Soviet Union in 1953, the GDR followed suit. When Malenkov fell, the GDR abandoned its new course. When Krushchev introduced a highly unsuccesful plan to decentralise the economic planning mechanism, the GDR followed suit, and duly abandoned the experiment when Khrushchev was ousted in 1964 (McCauley, 1986: chs. 3, 4; Childs, 1982, chs. 1–3). It is true that East Germany formally had a multi–party system, but the Liberals (LDPD), Christian Democrats (CDU), Farmers (DBD) and National Democrats (NDPD) were completely subordinate to the ruling SED and acted as nothing more than state–controlled transmission belts for interest articulation and mobilisation. East German elections were a charade.

The major internal opposition to the regime came from ecologists, peace activists, and democratic socialists, and the churches provided a space for this opposition to develop (Ball, 1988: 34–5). In January 1988 a small group of demonstrators produced their own banners following the official rally to commemorate the murder in 1919 of the founders of the German Communist Party, Rosa Luxemburg and Karl Liebknecht. The authorities arrested the demonstrators, many of whom had previously applied for exit visas, not in order to emigrate from East Germany, but merely to protest at the continued ban on travel to the West, symbolised by the wall. The authorities rushed through their visa applications with the aim of permanent exclusion, but pressure from within the GDR and abroad helped their lawyers to negotiate the right to re–entry. This drew more attention to the issue of freedom to travel and broadened the oppositional current. New Forum was founded as an oppositional alliance founded in September 1989 (Reich, 1990: 71–4), prior to the visit of Gorbachev to East Germany, an occasion on which he expressed his disapproval of the authoritarianism of the regime run by Honeker and Erich Mielke, the Security Minister (Minnerup, 1989: 5). The old guard was soon to pay for its intransigence.

Early in 1989 the Hungarian Communist Government became the first to announce that there would soon be free elections, and in the summer it opened its border with Austria. East German citizens on holiday took the opportunity to emigrate to West Germany via Czechoslovakia, Hungary, and Austria, thereby reopening the vital issue of freedom to travel. In order to stem the tide the East German government banned all visa–free travel, but this sparked mass demonstrations, in Leipzig and other cities. In October Honecker was forced to resign at a meeting of the SED Politburo, to be replaced by Egon Krenz, and on 9 November thousands streamed through the Berlin Wall in the absence of any authority to stop them. This heralded the complete collapse of SED power. Within a month the SED Central Committee and Politburo had resigned, and the new Prime Minister, Hans Modrow, was left as a caretaker Prime Minister until the elections in March (Sword, 1990; Hawkes, 1990).

THE ALTERNATIVE LEFT

In many European countries the 'alternative left' has been largely peripheral to the political process, but in Germany it has had a significant impact. In the 1960s the radical opposition was focused on the Socialist League of German Students, the SDS, under the guidance of its leading theoreticians, Rudi Dutschke and Hans–Jurgen Krahl (Burns & van der Will, 1988: 102–18). Dutschke urged a strategy of countering ideological control and authoritarianism by a combination of militant action on the streets and a 'long march through the institutions' such as the state administrations and the universities. There was also an emphasis on the emancipatory potential of third world revolutions, such as Vietnam, and this provided the major thrust of the huge demonstrations which occurred between 1967 and 1969. After the passing of the Emergency Laws in May 1968, which introduced the ban on radicals in state service, the organisational focus of protest was the Extra–Parliamentary Opposition (APO), and it was stung into intensive action by the attempt on the life of Dutschke in April 1968.

By the early 1970s the APO was more or less defunct and the opposition fragmented, a small minority engaging in terrorism and many thousands joining a number of 'K' (*Kommunist*) groups espousing Trotskyist or Maoist positions. In a less radical way many more became involved in pressure group protest through 'Citizens Initiatives' (*Burgerinitiative*), grassroots organisations mainly concerned with single issues such as pollution or the building of nuclear plants. Hundreds of thousands were involved in such groups, which were loosely linked together by a Federal body (Burns & van der Will, 1988: ch. 5) Another major element of radical protest developed after the decision by NATO in 1979 to deploy Pershing and Cruise nuclear missiles in Germany. This provoked an amazing mobilisation of a peace movement across non-communist Europe, and some of the largest demonstrations were in West Germany. The women's movement played a decisive role in the organisation of alternative politics which led to the formation of the Greens. Although there was a major socialist-feminist organisation founded in 1976, the Democratic Women's Initiative, for the most part the activities were local and autonomous, although the movement as a whole could still mobilise on national issues such as abortion (Haug, 1986). The demand for women's rights became an integral aspect of the programmatic and organisational life of the Greens.

The Greens came together as a party of a new sort early in 1980, with a programme which immediately located them to the left of the SPD, a position they have since maintained (Padgett & Paterson, 1991a; 65–6; Hülsberg, 1988: ch. 5). They achieved a startling breakthrough in the Federal election of 1983 by polling 5.6 per cent of the vote and attracting a disproportionate support from young voters (Kolinsky, 1986: 42). Much publicity was generated by the sight of casually attired young representatives articulating radical policies in the sombre world of middle aged dark-suited men. In 1985 all five leaders of the Greens' *Bundestag* group of representatives were women (Hülsberg, 1988: 54–63). In 1987 the Greens increased their vote to 8.3 per cent, despite the repeated assertions from political commentators that their internal divisions would lead to their demise (Ambos, 1988). The Greens have demanded environmental protection, abandonment of nuclear energy, reduction of the working week, democratic control of the economy, full and equal rights for women, and a reordering of the world economy in order to end the exploitation of the third world. In addition the Greens advocated German neutrality (Hülsberg, 1988: ch. 10).

The demand for the radical democratisation of society was matched by the adoption of radical democratic procedures within the party (Hülsberg, 1988: 120; Poguntke, 1993). Rotation of offices meant that representatives could hold office for no more than six years and could be re-elected only once. Following the 1983 election all but two Green representatives stepped down halfway through their term in the *Bundestag*. Members were not permitted to hold more than one office, and full-time functionaries were not allowed to become political representatives. All representatives were made accountable, and all party meetings were thrown open to all members. Financial rewards for representatives were limited, with payments over a certain amount going back to the party. In addition, there was strict equality of representation of the sexes, based on a quota system. These measures reflected the conviction of Green members that the structures of all the established parties helped to sustain a system of domination. Hence the Greens often referred to themselves as a 'non-party'. However, this raises two problems, the danger of assimilation into the system they oppose, and the problem of sustaining high rates of participation. The assimilation problem brings us back to Michels' 'iron law of oligarchy' mentioned in chapter one. Coalitions with all three major parties have been attempted, and compromises have therefore been made. But in general the Greens have stayed faithful to collective leadership and the rotation of party positions. The participation problem turns on the fact that the bulk of Green support is not attracted to joining a political party and it is therefore a grassroots party without a stable membership base (Poguntke, 1992b).

The problem of assimilation and compromise led to open opposition between two tendencies which have been broadly distinguished as 'realos' and 'fundis' (Hülsberg, 1988: ch. 8). The 'realos' aimed to seek coalition with the SPD if agreement could be reached on specific issues. This has led to Red–Green coalition Governments in Hesse (on two occasions) and in West Berlin (at the time the Wall came down). A coalition between the SDP, FDP and the Greens was formed in Bremen in 1991, and in Hamburg the SPD Government was supported by the Greens. The 'fundis' consistently opposed such compromises and continue to argue for the idea of a deindustrialised society. The 'realos' regularly won the decisive votes at Party Congresses following raucous debates, but the differences could no longer be contained following the electoral setback in 1990. Their opposition to unification and their refusal to campaign actively undoubtedly damaged them. Many fundamentalists left the party in May 1991, following the 'realo' decision to streamline decision–making processes and create a more effective campaigning organisation (Poguntke, 1992a: 25–6). The Greens polled well in state election results in 1991 and 1992, and their union with the East German group Alliance 90 (*Bündnis 90*) at the Congress in Leipzig in May 1993 gave them a fully national profile.

CONCLUSION

German reunification has elicited conflicting opinions on the place of Germany in the world (Markovits & Reich, 1991, 49–52). Some have feared that the old dream of German domination of the continent is being realised, and that the historical strength of militarism and nationalism is not easily discounted. However, there is a more widespread view that Germany's present strength derives from its adherence to liberal democracy, a united Europe, and an aversion to militarism. There can be little doubt that Germany is the powerhouse economy of Europe, with a quarter of all Community market shares and a key geographical position for the opening up of the former communist states (Markovits & Reich, 1991). However, there is little evidence that this means domination. Germany has played a leading role in hastening European integration (Paterson, 1993), and most German politicians are happy that the creation of a European central bank and monetary union will lead to a share of economic reponsibility which has fallen on Germany. Because the German economy is the strongest in Europe, the interest rates set by the *Bundesbank* act as a limit on those of other countries, as speculators can sell other currencies to buy marks if interest rates were reduced elsewhere. As the legal imperative of the Bundesbank is price stability, a deflationary policy has consisently been pursued, and Germany, instead of becoming the 'locomotive' of European recovery, has been accused of being responsible for 'Eurosclerosis', i.e. low growth and high unemployment (Solow, 1991). Although the German economy began to expand rapidly again in the late 1980s, the integration of the five eastern states led to a big increase in unemployment, higher taxes and lower growth. 'Recovery' leapt to the top of the political agenda, not only in Germany but in Europe as a whole.

The priority of price stability and monetary control was written into the Maastricht Treaty and, if implemented, would prolong Eurosclerosis. Clearly this is not in German interests, but it is not clear what sort of a European recovery programme the various parties might favour. Naturally the German trade unions and SPD favour a strong social charter, but this is also approved by German business, for without it investment would move to those Community countries offering lower labour costs than Germany's. Other priorities for the Left are a reduction in the working week or life, improving the environment, and securing effective equal opportunities. In the course of the 1980s the SPD adopted an anti–nuclear stance, an economic policy emphasising environmentally–friendly growth, and committed itself to quotas to ensure equal gender representation on all party bodies. It has embraced the goal of a socialist Europe, and in that respect has advanced a long way from Schumacher's 'nation state' focus in the postwar years (Telo, 1991: 133–7). There is a measure of agreement between the Greens and the SPD on a number of issues, particularly the campaign for a shorter working week, which was a focal point of Red–Green politics before the 1987 election (Hülsberg, 1988: 188). Peter Glotz, a leading SPD theoretician, hailed the idea as a 'concrete utopia' which could inspire a European–wide movement (in Gorz, 1989: 190). Both the Greens and the SPD are committed to the development of international strategies on such issues as environmental protection, working hours, democratic accountability, the conversion of arms industries, and minimum social provision (Engholm, 1991: 7–9; Parkin, 1989: ch. 15). In the long term, Red–Green cooperation offers the hope that the SPD can recover its sense of 'vision', while giving the Greens the opportunity to come in from the margins of German and European politics.

6 Communism in Western Europe

The Communist Party of Italy (PCI) gained 34.4 per cent of the vote in the general election of 1976, the highest level of support for a communist party in Europe since the Czechoslovak election of 1946. In the elections of 1973 and 1978 the French Communist Party (PCF) won over 20 per cent of the vote. In Portugal in 1979 the Communist Party achieved just under 20 per cent of the poll (Waller & Fennema, 1988: 262–3). Elsewhere in Western Europe the communist parties had limited electoral appeal, although they wielded a disproportionate influence in trade union activities. By the early 1990s the French communist vote had slipped into single figures and the Italian party had dissolved and reconstituted itself as a democratic socialist party. Communism throughout the continent was reduced to a marginal political force. This chapter will examine the difficulties faced by communists in attempting to promote anti–capitalist politics in modern liberal democracies, paying particular attention to Italy and Spain.

Communists were proud to be associated with the 'party of Lenin', yet the historical link with the Russian Revolution presented certain problems. The boldness of the Bolshevik endeavour to change the world and deal a death blow to capitalism gave to communists a model of uncompromising achievement through strict discipline which made the social democrats look pusillanimous in comparison. But communists were working in liberal democracies in which political rights had been won after centuries of popular struggle, and the alternative presented by the Soviet Union and its satellites had limited appeal. However much Marx may have intended the 'dictatorship of the proletariat' to be more democratic than existing liberal societies (Balibar, 1977), the examples on offer were hard to defend, especially after the military suppression of the Czechoslovak experiment in 'socialism with a human face' in 1968. Communism had initially defined itself by its willingness to take the revolutionary road to socialism, but it was clearly in no position to do so in Western Europe. As Wallerstein has argued, the *de facto* renunciation of insurrectionary tactics came about because 'neither the Soviet nor the west European communist leadership ever really thought the situation permitted it' (Wallerstein, 1984: 118). These ambiguities on key issues appeared to consign even the most powerful communist parties to a purely negative role in their national politics, awaiting an opening which might come about as a result of shifts in the global struggle between the two military superpowers, the United States and the Soviet Union.

The cold war period sharpened the differences between the social democratic parties and the communists, leaving the latter frozen out of political power at central state level, although some successes were achieved in municipal politics. The long postwar economic boom produced greatly increased living standards and full employment, and insurrectionary options finally appeared to be redundant. At the same time the global position of communism was bolstered by revolutionary successes, first in Cuba and then in the mid–1970s in Vietnam, Laos, Cambodia, Ethiopia, Mozambique, Angola, and Guinea Bissau. The apparent weakening of American global power encouraged communists to explore the possibilities of broad alliances which might free Western Europe from American hegemony. The détente between NATO and the Warsaw Pact eased the way for such alliances by diminishing the ideological power of the 'red menace' (Block, 1980: 260–2). The politically favourable global situation induced communist leaderships to break out of their isolation and play a more constructive role in their national politics. This was the background to the phenomenon which came to be known as 'Eurocommunism'.

The Eurocommunist strategy asserted the independence of national communist parties from the organisational and ideological leadership of the Communist Party of the Soviet Union. The Soviet model was no longer deemed to be the prototype for communism in the West. It pledged respect for the liberal principles of political pluralism, alternation of power, and civil liberties. Indeed the Eurocommunists sought to extend democratic rights in the social and economic sphere, and declared their willingness to make alliances with other 'progressive' parties and movements. Eurocommunism was an attempt to dispel suspicions that communists had no respect for democratic institutions. The major public declarations of Eurocommunism took place in the years immediately following the oil price rise of 1973–4. In retrospect we can see this event as a trigger for an extended international depression, but at the time it was a shock which many viewed as temporary. It did not become evident that it was a cyclical long–term downturn until the second oil price rise of 1979 quickly produced mass unemployment on the scale of the 1930s. Eurocommunists were quick to seize on the onset of the crisis to boost their claims for emergency coalitions and interventionist measures, but it would be wrong to see the

Eurocommunist strategy as a response to the crisis. By this time many communists in Western Europe had accepted the analysis expounded by the theorists of 'state monopoly capitalism' in the 1960s which propounded a notion of the 'general crisis of capitalism' because it assumed that deep cyclical crises were a thing of the past (Kindersley, 1981: 189; Jessop, 1982; ch. 2). Eurocommunism was developed against a background of the perceived success of welfare capitalism rather than its crisis. As Kindersley argued in 1981, 'Eurocommunism is not a product of the crisis, but has rather been lent credibility by it' (Kindersley, 1981: 205).

Eurocommunism, then, sought a place in national political life for a 'strong' reformism which retained a vision of a future socialist society, something which had all but vanished from the thinking of social democracy. In the lengthy evolution of the new strategy we can identify two political moments of vital importance, 1956 and 1968. At the twentieth Congress of the CPSU in 1956, First Secretary Nikita Khrushchev exposed the crimes of Stalin before the Central Committee (Lane, 1982: 87–97). The effect on the communist world was enormous, for the myth of Stalin's leadership held the international communist movement together with a quasi–religious bond. If Stalin could be denounced as a tyrant, what sort of system permitted such degeneration, and which aspects of Stalinism were still present? The Italian leader, Palmiro Togliatti, immediately took advantage of the situation to call for 'polycentrism' in the international communist movement and to argue that the crimes committed under Stalin could not be entirely attributed to his personality but required a critical review of how the system arose and how it operated (in Daniels, 1985: 228–30). Togliatti led the PCI to accept constitutional legality in the programme adopted at the eighth Congress in December 1956 (in Lange & Vannicelli, 1981: 33–8; Amyot, 1981: 49–51). In the same year Soviet tanks invaded Hungary to suppress the attempt by the Nagy Government to break out of the Soviet sphere of influence. Communists throughout Europe were shocked into resigning; approximately 250,000 in Italy and 50,000 elsewhere (Claudin, 1978: 38). The spell of Moscow omnipotence had been broken. Within a few years China and Albania openly broke fraternal relations with the USSR.

In the spring of 1968 two events shook Europe, the general strike in France and the victory and defeat of the reform movement in Czechoslovakia. Manuel Azcarate, one of the leading spokesmen of Eurocommunism, declared that these events were decisive in the formation of Eurocommunism (Azcarate, 1981: 28–9). The gulf between revolutionary rhetoric and pragmatic politics was shown up dramatically in the reaction of the French Communist Party (PCF) to the dramatic upheavals of May and June, as we saw in chapter three. The party was already attempting to forge a common programme with socialists, and its initial reaction to the student demonstrations was one of outright hostility to such 'adventurism'. They became more sympathetic only when the workers spontaneously escalated the protests by going on general strike, and then they tried to channel the strike movement into purely economic demands. The leader, Waldeck Rochet, was obliged to renounce the possibility of insurrection because of the obvious dangers involved, yet the party could not even produce an effective radical reformist line because of the rigidity of its Marxist–Leninist dogma. The future leaders of Eurocommunism drew two lessons from the events. First, communist parties had to renounce the option of taking power illegally, and second, they needed to convince people that they wanted to extend democracy, not extinguish it. This involved not simply a change of message but also a searching self–criticism by communists and a renovation of party life in order to appeal to the new radicalism.

The Prague Spring resulted in invasion by troops of the Warsaw Pact and the forcible suppression of the liberalising reforms undertaken by the Dubček government. The communist parties in the West could not possibly condone this invasion, for to do so would wreck their democratic credentials. A major breach opened between these parties and the CPSU, and the Italian party in particular was severely critical of the invasion and openly hospitable to refugees from the Czechoslovak reform leadership (Narkiewicz, 1990: 72). The West European communists had to go further than merely expressing the view that the Soviet system was 'inappropriate' for the West; they had to condemn this specific act and be prepared to condemn others. Nevertheless the CPSU was still able to convoke two international conferences of communist parties, one in Moscow in 1969 and a 'pan–European' one in Berlin in 1976. While the West European parties were able to assert their independent lines, their presence acknowledged a commonality of some sorts, and at the very least an acknowledgement of the binding mythical power of the Russian Revolution. In many ways they were still part of the same family despite their disagreements. Fraternal visits to congresses and conferences continued, and there were international journals and movements on specific international issues. Perhaps most significantly, the parties in the West were slow to reform their own organisations, retaining the principle of democratic centralism as a disciplinary weapon. In 1969 the Manifesto group was expelled from the Italian party for breaking the rules of democratic centralism, and in 1970 the humanist Marxist Roger Garaudy was expelled from the French party (Claudin, 1978: 45–6). By 1975 the Eurocommunist strategy was sufficiently coherent to enable the major parties to issue joint declarations, first by the Italians and the Spanish at Leghorn in July and then by the Italians and the French in Rome in November. All three parties signed a Joint Declaration in Madrid in March 1977, three months before the first free elections in Spain, following the demise of the Franco dictatorship (Lange & Vannicelli, 1981: 357–61). All three declarations pointed out the failings of capitalism as evidenced by the 'crisis' brought on by the oil–price rise. They committed the parties to uphold and extend democratic processes and all civil liberties, and they hailed the new opportunities for the peaceful development of socialism in Western Europe offered by détente. Interestingly, the Leghorn declaration emphasised that the commitment to constitutionalism was not a tactical device, clearly revealing the sensitivity of the party leaders to criticisms that the communists simply could not be trusted. Social democrats such as former British Labour Party leader Harold Wilson and Foreign Secretary David Owen took this line, although others like Kreisky, Brandt, Soares and Palme, were more conciliatory.

There was a major risk in the new strategy. If communists became too conciliatory, what was to distinguish them from social democratics, and why should people prefer them? If they continued to extol Leninism, how could they avoid comparison with the Soviet Union and its unhappy satellites? In France the new line attracted a massive increase in membership from under 400,000 in 1972 to over half a million in 1978 (Courtois & Peschanski, 1988: 51–2). However, the new Socialist Party was more successful in broadening its electoral appeal, and the Marchais leadership reverted to a tightly disciplined pro–Soviet stance. In Italy the PCI was much larger in membership and electoral support than the Socialist Party, which was one of the weakest European parties in the Socialist International. The PCI was therefore in a stronger position to make a success of the new strategy, particularly as it could claim that it had always pursued an independent line. In Spain there was no arena for political competition until after Franco's death in 1975, but the Communist Party of Spain (PCE) expected to be the major left–wing force, and was anxious that it should develop its politics in a democratic context. Despite the central role played by Carrillo in the development of Eurocommunism, it quickly became clear that PSOE would become the leading party on the Left. It seemed, in short, that there was a cost in adopting a strategy more amenable to compromise, for part of the attraction of the old communism was precisely its uncompromising nature.

ITALY

The experience of fascism had an important influence on the development of the Italian Communist Party, which was founded at the Congress of Livorno in 1921. The Fascists seized power in 1922, and for five years the PCI led a semi–legal existence before being formally banned. It was unable to emerge into the open until the Partisan War against the Fascists and the Germans in 1944. In its early years the PCI was in a minority in the socialist movement as a whole, and its natural constituency, the manual workers, formed a relatively small portion of the total workforce by West European standards. Insurrectionary tactics were therefore of little relevance to the Italian situation. They might have been pursued in the wake of the defeat of the German army, but only at the cost of Anglo–American military intervention. The Italian Communist Party after the Second World War was a mass party rather than a tightly knit band of revolutionaries, and it had over two million members by 1947 (Barkan, 1980: 51–3). It organised successfully among farmworkers, poor peasants and intellectuals as well as industrial workers.

Togliatti used the intellectual reputation of his predecessor as leader of the PCI, Antonio Gramsci, to support the development of a distinctively Italian road to socialism (Mancini, 1980; Gray, 1980). Togliatti had been a comrade with Gramsci in the Factory Council movement in Turin in 1919, co–authoring articles on workers' democracy. Gramsci spent twelve years in a fascist prison, from where he wrote a number of notebooks (the *Quaderni*) which contained some of the richest insights of twentieth century socialist thought. The notebooks were published in Turin in six volumes between 1948 and 1951, and in a new edition in 1975. A key concept was 'hegemony', the consolidation of power by 'intellectual and moral leadership' rather than by force. Developed in his 'Notes on Italian History' in relation to the moderates of the Action Party during and after Italian reunification in the nineteenth century, there were clear messages for socialists of the twentieth century. Gramsci argued that 'there can, and indeed must, be hegemonic activity even before the rise to power, and... one should not count only on the material force which power gives in order to exercise an effective leadership' (Gramsci, 1971: 59). The necessity of achieving consent for a group's ideas while still in opposition suggested an educative politics within the existing framework of power, and Gramsci placed special emphasis on the importance of winning the battle for ideas on the cultural level, in the 'ethical state' or 'civil society' (Gramsci, 1971, 258 ff).

This perspective was considerably more sophisticated and sensitive than the approach of the Comintern, which was based on the success of the Bolsheviks in 1917 and dictated by the requirements of Soviet foreign policy. Gramsci pointed out that the conditions which had faced the Bolsheviks differed greatly from those which faced Western socialists. He wrote that 'in Russia the state was everything, civil society was primordial and gelatinous; in the West, there was a proper relation between state and civil society, and when the state trembled a sturdy structure of civil society was at once revealed' (Gramsci, 1971: 238) The methodological differences between Gramsci and the Marxism of the Comintern leaders was also made clear in his writings on what he termed the 'philosophy of praxis', or historical materialism. Here he rejected 'mechanistic' interpretations of Marx's thought which saw political events as simple reflections of changes in the economic structure, ignoring the contradictory and developmental nature of the structure as well as the specific ideological and sociological factors at play (Gramsci, 1971: 381–418).

Gramsci's advice on the sort of party which might succeed in introducing socialism to Italy was contained in his work 'The Modern Prince'. Machiavelli's *Prince* was written over 400 years earlier, but Gramsci saw the relevance of the concern for achieving national unity by winning the support of key classes in Italian society. The Communist Party had to become the modern prince, and in a country in which the industrial workers were still in a minority it would have to reach out to other classes and relate to their concerns. He reminded readers of Marx's dictum that popular beliefs were also a material force (Gramsci, 1971: 165). Gramsci spoke of the importance of a phase in the class struggle which he termed 'the war of position', as distinct from the 'frontal attack' of a revolution or the 'war of movement' epitomised by mass strikes and demonstrations (Gramsci, 1971: part 2, ch. 2). According to Gramsci, the 'war of position, once won, is decisive definitively', indicating that long struggle in all aspects of national life during periods of relative stability would pay dividends (Gramsci, 1971: 239). It followed from this emphasis on ideological and cultural struggles that Gramsci viewed the party's educational role as vital, and here he called for the emergence of 'organic intellectuals' who could disseminate radical interpretations of social reality to working people (Gramsci, 1971: part 1, chs. 1, 2). It is clear from the Prison Notebooks that Gramsci's Marxism had little in common with that of the Third International. However, disputes have raged as to whether the Eurocommunist repackaging of Gramsci was an accurate reflection of his intentions. After all, he praised Lenin, did not explicitly reject democratic centralism (Gramsci, 1971: 189–90), and did not disavow the possibility of revolution. Nevertheless, there was enough in the Notebooks for the PCI to use Gramsci not only to justify a strategy of broad alliances but also to encourage the promotion of 'oppositional' cultural forms through festivals, journals, books and films (Femia, 1981). The depth and breadth of Marxism in Italian intellectual life has been impressive.

Gramsci's ideas were of tremendous importance for the PCI, but his works did not specify what sort of alliances could be formed in order to promote the struggle for socialist hegemony. Berlinguer chose to go for the 'historic compromise', or alliance with the Christian Democrats (DC), the governing party of the Right (Sassoon, 1981). Berlinguer announced the initiative in the autumn of 1973, in a series of articles in which he argued that the violent overthrow of Salvador Allende's democratically elected socialist Government in Chile earlier in the year indicated that it was not possible to transform society with the support of only one half of those who voted (Amyot, 1981: 202–5; Pasquino, 1980: 96–7). The pursuit of such a grand alliance was linked to the strong desire by the PCI to be accepted as a responsible political actor in the mainstream of Italian life, prepared to take tough decisions in the national interest. They could demonstrate to the Italian people that they were more efficient and less corrupt managers than the power–holders who had dominated the post–war period, and at the same time retain a vision of an egalitarian democratic socialist society. A grand alliance would also act as a bulwark against the extreme right, represented in Italy by the MSI, which had increased its share of the vote alarmingly from 5.8 per cent in 1968 to 10.7 per cent in 1970. Fascist terrorism had claimed sixteen lives in a bombing in Milan in December 1969, and this fuelled the sense of social crisis. Nevertheless, many on the Left considered that it was unacceptable to make common cause with the pillars of Italian conservatism (Abse, 1985).

An alternative alliance might have been forged with the Socialists (PSI), and possibly also the Radicals, but this would still have fallen short of winning a parliamentary majority. Even if such an alliance had managed to form a government, it would have been faced with a $20 billion international debt, vociferous demands from its own voters, and the sort of 'capitalist counteroffensive' which the Labour Government faced in Britain at that time (Block, 1980: 277). The PSI declared itself in favour of a left alliance in 1976 (Pasquino, 1980: 98; Sassoon, 1989: 241), but in view of the party's consistent anti–communism there was more than a suspicion of opportunism. In that year the PCI's pursuit of the grand alliance appeared to be vindicated by the spectacular result in the general election, which saw them record 34.4 per cent of the vote, over 7 per cent higher than in 1972. Bettino Craxi became leader of the PSI in 1976 and was able to take advantage of the historic compromise by stressing the independent, modernising and secular approach of his party (Di Scala, 1988). From then on the PCI share of the vote dropped in successive elections (30.4 per cent in 1979, 29.9 per cent in 1983, and 26.6 per cent in 1987), while the PSI increased (9.8 per cent in 1979, 11.4 per cent in 1983, and 14.3 per cent in 1987. The PCI ceased its support of the Christian Democratic government by the end of 1978, and officially dropped its commitment to the historic compromise in 1980 (Sassoon, 1989: 238). The Socialists courted the Christian Democrats so effectively that Craxi headed a coalition as Prime Minister from 1983 to 1987.

Did the PCI gain anything from the historic compromise? Ostensibly very little, for although the Government of 1976–9 was often called the Andreotti–Berlinguer government, it was not a coalition government but simply relied on the parliamentary support of the Communists. The politician most likely to have engineered a genuine coalition, Aldo Moro, a centrist Christian Democrat, was murdered by Red Brigade terrorists in 1978. The strategy involved some startling compromises from a party claiming to be more than just social–democratic. The party declared in 1975 that it no longer called for unilitaral withdrawal of Italy from NATO, opening the possibility of communist ministers sharing responsibility for the strategy of an anti–communist military bloc. The pressing problem of inflation produced a call for 'creative austerity' from Berlinguer in 1977, acknowledging the need for sacrifices but calling for them to be weighted against the rich. While this was common coin from social democratic parties, communist leaders in the past would have routinely served up blanket condemnations of the ruling parties for managing a decaying capitalism. In terms of reforms, the major achievement which was promoted by the compromise was the creation of the national health service, which came into operation in 1980 (Amyot, 1981: ch. 13). It also helped to promote reform in family law in 1975, a law against sexual discrimination in 1977, and the legalisation of abortion in 1978.

The PCI offended many secular thinkers and radical women with its unwillingness to make the issues of divorce and abortion a campaigning priority (Sassoon, 1989: 109). The PCI was anxious not to offend Catholic sensibilities and did not wish to make these issues too 'political'. The issues were decided by referenda, the 1974 one achieving 59 per cent support for divorce and the 1981 referendum securing 68 per cent support for the relatively liberal abortion law which was being challenged by conservatives. The procrastination of the PCI on abortion led its women's organisation, the UDI, to abandon its links with the Party (Abse, 1985: section 7; Buttafuocco, 1980). Finally, many on the Left were angry at the PCI's zeal in supporting repressive legislation (e.g. detention without arrest, detention without trial), in response to terrorism throughout the 1970s. The PCI did not achieve the governmental power it sought, and was unable to halt the creation of a relatively stable coalition led by the Christian Democrats and the Socialists. An important indicator in this shift to the right was the reversal, by the 1985 referendum, of the indexation of wages to prevent erosion by inflation, a notable victory won by the trade unions in 1975 with the support of the PCI (Pasquino, 1988: 30–2). The strategy of courting the Christian Democrats meant that the party had missed an opportunity to harness the concerns of the young, particularly the new social movements emerging around feminism and ecology. Like the SPD in Germany it expanded its membership greatly in the early 1970s (from 1.5 million in 1969 to 1.8 million in 1976) and then disappointed them when the promise of power through compromise was not fulfilled. However, the party had some success in winning participation from sections previously outside its orbit, such as Catholics and former state officials, and in the 1980s about 20 'independent leftists' were elected as Deputies on the PCI ticket. In the late 1980s it moved towards achieving a quota of 50 per cent for women representatives at all levels of the Party, and the womens' parliamentary group have operated with considerable independence (Pasquino, 1988: 28–9).

'Renewal' was a long process which was not settled by the time of Berlinguer's death in 1984, or during the following four years under the leadership of Alessandro Natta. It fell to Achille Occhetto to complete the process in a most decisive way, by breaking with the communist tradition once and for all. The most important policy switch which occurred in the late 1980s was the renewed commitment to being a 'left alternative' to the centre–right coalition of Christian Democrats, Republicans, and Socialists. However, the international policy remained ambiguous. The PCI was very close to Gorbachev, who still considered himself a communist, but as long as this alliance was in place it was difficult to imagine the party achieving its other goal of entering the Socialist International. This ambiguity was resolved only when the CPSU was suspended in 1991. Organisationally, the final vestiges of democratic centralism were discarded (Bull, 1991: 107–8). Occhetto promised a new sort of party for a new era:

> We need to find a new form for a Party so it is capable of drawing into action and struggle the subjects of today's contradictions, those of the year 2000 and not of the 19th Century. For instance, our traditional idea of the social alliance of workers and peasants is meaningless today, even of it is still represented by the emblem of the hammer and sickle. Today the decisive problem is the relation between the world of work as a whole and cross–class contradictions such as those of ecology, women's liberation etc. (*The Guardian*, 25 January, 1990).

In 1989, five days after the breaching of the Berlin Wall, Occhetto proposed the disbandment of the PCI and the formation of a new party. For a full year the party went through a soul–searching discussion about its past and its future. The PCI changed its name to the Democratic Party of the Left (PDS) at a special Congress in Rimini in February 1991, with the support of about 70 per cent of the delegates (Pasquino, 1993). A sizeable left–wing minority led by by Armando Cossuta left to form a new party, *Rifondazione Communista* (PCR), with elements from non–party organisations such as Proletarian Democracy. At its founding Congress in January 1992 it claimed 120,000 members (Casini, 1992: 49).

The PDS, like the PCI before them, adopted a strong pro–European position. Its rejection of 'communism' led to its acceptance by the Socialist International in September 1992, despite the fact that there were two other Italian affiliates, the Socialists (PSI) and the Social Democrats (PSDI). At the same time the formation of the Party of European Socialists, a development that Occhetto had supported, likening the existing situation to the period in the last century when parties were first formed in nation states. As a new 'European nation' was being founded he considered it imperative that socialists should move 'away from their ancient history' and work together on issues such as the reduction of working hours (*The Guardian*, 25 January, 1990). However, the desire of the PDS to play a significant role in the development of a trans–European politics was hampered by the political crisis which enveloped the country after the elections in April 1992. In the elections the PDS polled only 16.1 per cent of the vote, despite the fact that *Rifondazione Communista* polled only 5.6 per cent and that the vote of the PSI fell to 13.6 per cent. The total 'left' vote fell by approximately 6 per cent. Before the elections both the PDS and the PSI were implicated in financial scandals in Milan involving contracts for the large public sector. After the election the allegations spread to include most of the leading echelons of the PSI, and then later to leading individuals in the former Communist Party. The resignation of the respected leader of the left opposition within the PDS, Pietro Ingrao, in May 1993, was a severe blow to the party. Nevertheless, it is likely to remain as the leading force on the Italian Left. As a communist party it was fixed as the 'enemy' by its political opponents, who were able to enjoy undisturbed political power with corrupt complacency. Now that the 'red scare' has been ended by the collapse of communism, and the established parties have been badly hurt by the corruption scandals, the successors of the PCI may at last succeed where Berlinguer failed.

SPAIN

The Spanish Communist Party was the first Communist Party in Western Europe to participate in Government, but the experience was brief and brought to a bloody end with the victory of Franco's fascists in 1939. Before the Civil War broke out the PCE was a small party with approximately 5,000 members, much smaller than the Socialists and the Anarchists (CNT), and smaller even than the independent Marxists of the POUM. The decisive factor in its dramatic expansion during the Civil War was the dependence of the Republican government on aid from the Soviet Union. Historically this ensured the dependence of the PCE on the CPSU, and most of the exiled PCE leadership lived in the Soviet Union until they were free to return to Spain in 1977, following Franco's death in November 1975. The party sought a broad alliance against Franco, but this was difficult to achieve because of the party's record in the Civil War, when it persecuted members of rival left–wing groups. However, the PCE was the chief oppositional force during the Franco years, despite ruthless persecution, and this earned it great respect.

    When Khrushchev launched his destalinisation campaign in 1956 it was broadly welcomed by PCE leaders (Preston, 1981), and the 'liberalisation' was marked by the elevation of Santiago Carrillo to the leadership in 1959, succeeding Dolores Ibarruri. However, the PCE still showed no signs of acting independently of the wishes of the CPSU, and an indication of the limits of its tolerance was the expulsion of Fernando Claudin and Jorge Semprun in 1965 for proposing an interpretation of developments in Spain which anticipated many of the Eurocommunist positions which were adopted in the early 1970s (Story, 1979: 158). The invasion of Czechoslovakia was the decisive event which impelled Carrillo to engage in a radical strategic rethink. Carrillo returned to

Spain in February 1976 but had to remain underground. It is then that he wrote his book, *Eurocommunism and the State*, which appeared the following year. At the Conference of Communist Parties in Berlin in 1976 Carrillo caused a furore among the CPSU and East European delegates by rejecting any notion of international discipline between the Communist Parties, and pledging his own party to to a pluralist view of socialism (Preston, 1981: 36–7). Carrillo's work emphasised the acceptance of a multi–party system, the complete independence of the PCE from the Soviet Union, and a widening of its class appeal, not just to workers and peasants but the 'immense majority' of the population in an anti–monopolist alliance of 'the forces of labour and culture' (Carillo, 1977: 40). At that time there was a worry about what role the army would play in the post–Franco settlement, and here the experience of Allende in Chile reinforced the PCE view of supporting a broad alliance in cementing the transition to parliamentary democracy. The attempted military coup in 1981 substantiated this fear of a return to right–wing authoritarianism.

The PCE accepted the restoration of the monarchy and concluded a constitutional agreement with the Socialists (PSOE) and the conservative UCD, which led to free elections in the summer of 1977. The PCE polled only 9.4 per cent of the vote compared with the 29.3 per cent share of PSOE. In 1979 the PCE increased its share to 10.7 per cent. The congress which followed the 1977 election rejected Leninism and adopted more self–critical and sensitive positions towards the problems and aspirations of the young and women (Rodriguez–Ibanez, 1980: 90–3). About this time a major debate developed concerning the internal democracy of the PCE and the authoritarian tendencies of Carrillo himself. The debate was started by Jorge Semprun, who had been expelled with Claudin in 1965. His autobiography appeared in 1977 and achieved immense publicity, mainly because he accused Carrillo of consistently using Stalinist methods (Semprun, 1979). A group developed within the PCE to renovate the party's structures, but many of its members were expelled in 1981. In the elections of 1982 it slid disastrously to 4.1 per cent and PSOE won a tremendous victory with 48.4 per cent of the vote. After the election Carrillo was replaced by Gerardo Iglesias as leader and many of the reformers were brought back into the party, causing Carrillo to found his own 'Platform', which in 1987 became a party, the PTE–UC. Carillo's small group eventually went into PSOE in 1991 (Gillespie, 1993). In 1982 another split occurred when a pro–Soviet faction under Ignacio Gallego broke away to form the PCPE in protest against the party's lack of militancy. By the mid–1980s there were three communist parties in Spain (Botella, 1988: 80–1), and many leading communists left the PCE to join PSOE (Camiller, 1984). Nevertheless, in the late 1980s there was a successful attempt to form an electoral alliance of communist groups known as Left Unity (IU), and in 1989 under the leadership of Julio Anguita it polled 9.1 per cent of the vote. It retained this level of support in 1993. The main strength of the PCE is its pre–eminence in the largest trade union federation, the Workers' Commissions. In 1985 there was a successful call for a general strike against the PSOE government's harsh economic policies, although the PCE did not have the political strength to force major changes in government policy (Botella, 1988: 81–3). In the late 1980s and early 1990s Left Unity shared power at municipal level in Barcelona and Seville, and this presence served as a reminder to PSOE not to take its left–wing support for granted.

CONCLUSION

It would be wrong to ascribe the electoral decline of the communist parties to the adoption of Eurocommunism. The French vote held up reasonably well when the PCF followed a Eurocommunist line, and then diminished sharply when it reverted to a more hardline approach. The Italian Party increased its vote dramatically in the 1970s under Berlinguer, after which it declined. The explicit break with the communist tradition cost it some support in the 1992 election, but the PDS is still the best supported left–wing party. The disintegration of the PCE in the early 1980s as a result of factional disputes demonstrated how difficult it was for the communists to democratise their own structures after a lifetime of disciplined adherence to democratic centralism. When Left Unity openly acknowledged the pluralism within in its own structures, it made a noteworthy electoral recovery. Apart from Italy, the communist parties and their successors may be able to secure between 5 and 10 per cent support and act as a 'brake' on social democratic parties moving to the centre. This is possible in France, Spain, Portugal, Greece, and Sweden. In other countries the alternative Left vote is more likely to go to Green parties or 'Red–Green' parties such as the Danish Peoples Socialist Party and the Dutch Green Left, which the former Communist Party of the Netherlands helped to create. In some cases there may be two 'alternative' parties claiming radical support in sufficient strength to gain parliamentary representation. This trend towards diversity in political representation requires a form of political pluralism which has not been a notable feature of either social democratic or communist politics in most parts of the continent.

When Stalin invented Marxism–Leninism it was part of a process in which the communist party became exalted to an almost sacred presence, a structure which subjugated all groups and individuals to the will of the leadership, and presented members with the truth which had to be followed uncritically. This was the fetishism of the monolith. It offered certainty and the power of disciplined and decisive action. The party was the party of Lenin, the heir of the Russian Revolution, the vanguard of the international historical struggle against capitalism. But its organisational strength was its greatest weakness, for 'top down' organisations inevitably lose touch with their members and react dogmatically to events. The Western communists never quite escaped from the historical grip of the Soviet experience. The association was present in the name, and it raised questions about the democratic trustworthiness of the parties. When capitalism experienced its last great depression, in the 1930s, communists were able to point out that the Soviet economy could expand at an amazing rate and provide full employment. From the late 1970s it became clear that the communist regimes in the East were unable to deal with the crisis in the world system. This failure cast doubts on the 'efficiency' claims of communists in the West and left them vulnerable to the claims that communism had no place for innovation and individual flair.

7 Socialism and New Social Movements

So far the discussion of socialism has concentrated on mass political parties which identify themselves as a part of a socialist 'family' and compete for political power at national level. This does not account for all the activity which falls within our broad definition of socialism as the historic protest against the effects of the capitalist system. Campaigns on specific issues have proliferated, some concerned to support socialist–led liberation struggles in Africa or Latin America, others concerned with domestic issues such as racist attacks or punitive taxes. Smaller socialist and anarchist groups have been particularly active in these areas. While there is nothing new in that, there is another phenomenon which is more recent and which some would claim is vital for the future development of socialism, namely, the rise of the new social movements. While social democratic and communist parties in Western Europe have suffered from declining membership and falling electoral support, a range of radical demands has been forced onto the agenda of European politics by new social movements. These demands have focused on the oppression of women, the ecological degradation of the planet, the threat of nuclear war, the resurgence of racism and the exploitation of the third world.

This chapter will explore the nature and origins of the new social movements and the attempts which have been made in socialist theory to identify and endorse their anti–systemic potential. Theorists such as Herbert Marcuse regarded these new forms of social protest as fulfilling a revolutionary role which had been relinquished by socialist and communist movements, but this is clearly far from the consciousness of the majority of the new activists. More recently, Immanuel Wallerstein has pointed to the necessity of a realignment of old and new 'antisystemic movements' to confront the power of the capitalist world system. The politics of new social movements have had some impact on socialist politics, although the relationship has been limited, uneven, and fraught with mutual suspicion. Are there indications that a new cooperation between the old and the new anti–systemic movements is likely, or possible?

THE NATURE AND ORIGIN OF NEW SOCIAL MOVEMENTS

There is now a burgeoning literature which attempts to account for the origins and organisational development of new social movements (Dalton & Kuechler, 1990; Scott, 1990; Melucci, 1989: ch. 2). The emphasis has fallen variously on 'either new grievances caused by economic and political rationalisation or rising expectations and changing value preferences in affluent societies' (Kitschler, 1990: 182). There has been a relative neglect of the international dimension of the phenomenon. The causes seized on by young radicals in the late 1960s were predominantly international in character, and this internationalism has accompanied the rise of the new social movements. It reflects the growing incapacity of nationally orientated political action to tackle a variety of problems which do not respect territorial boundaries. The focus on issues which transcend the framework of national politics is one factor which has distinguished new social movements from 'old' political parties or interest groups. A second factor is their articulation of a range of demands which are difficult or impossible to realise within prevailing economic and social relations. A third factor is their challenge to the established organisational structures of the state–orientated parties and pressure groups. It is possible for such movements to find expression in political parties and pressure groups, but the movement is always broader than any single organisational form and the membership is permanently vigilant concerning the dangers of integration into 'old' politics. New social movements place emphasis on extra–parliamentary activity, adopting a suspicious stance towards the hierarchical and bureaucratic structures of the states and the old political parties. Often the internal structures and processes of these movements will be radically democratic, involving rotation of offices, open meetings, positive discrimination and limitation of rewards. The 'new' politics is concerned to review its own practices and discourse with the intention of maximising participation and minimising the discrimination which operates implicitly in meetings. A variety of groups with different organisational forms may coexist within a broad movement. These groups are often quite small, facilitating more direct and flexible participation than is possible in mass parties, and their different styles and specific concerns make it easier for participants to find a group with which they are comfortable (Melucci, 1989: ch. 3).

It has often been said that there is nothing new about these social movements, but in terms of mass mobilisation and impact we have witnessed a qualitatively different level of activity in the past quarter of a century. Sociological approaches to the origins of new social movements have emphasised the effect of changes in the social structure during the postwar boom. As Inglehart has pointed out, advances in education and consumption (e.g. television, motor cars, private housing) undermined traditional socio–political affiliations and values. This produced a shift in values, from concern with economic and physical security to concern for the 'quality of life', or from material to post–material values (Inglehart, 1977; Inglehart, 1990). Membership of new social movements tends to come from relatively highly educated people in non–manual occupations, sometimes labelled the 'new middle class' (Carter, 1985). Since the late 1960s this social group has been expanding vis–a–vis the manual working class, as a result of changes in the mode of production, prompting writers such as Touraine and Bell to speak of a post–industrial society (Touraine, 1974; Bell, 1973).

The use of the prefix 'post' involves a risk of exaggeration. Developments in the forces of production and alterations in the specific forms of production relations do not constitute a departure from the logic of the capitalist accumulation process. And while the values of more affluent and formally educated people may be discernibly different from those of the 'old' working class, they are surely just as material (Wilde, 1990: 66). There is a danger that in linguistically denoting the end of an era, developed forms of social protest are dismissed as being historically redundant or at best residual. Just as in the past many socialist theorists assumed erroneously that the manual working class would automatically adopt a socialist consciousness, some theorists are now prone to assume that manual workers will never achieve such a consciousness precisely because of their position in society. A gulf is imputed between the limited horizons of the 'integrated' manual workers and the idealistic concerns of the new social groups (Kitching, 1983, Gorz, 1982). If this argument is accepted then it is difficult to conceive of movements developing with sufficient strength to challenge the existing power structures. 'Socialism' would fade into history. However, there is perhaps more in common between the 'new' and the 'old' in the struggle against oppression than the post–industrialist theorists have sugggested.

The radicalism of new social movements was in part a response to the 'ordering' of the agenda by the old 'antisystemic' movements which had helped to establish a highly bureaucratic welfare/warfare state apparatus. The establishment of the welfare state and the consolidation of the American alliance through NATO set the parameters of the political agenda of social democracy. This 'ordered' consensus seemed to permit no questioning of the cold war, the efficacy of nuclear energy, the desirability of high growth irrespective of its ecological consequences, the oppression of women, ethnic minorities, and the development of economic imperialism. The welfare state compromise raised expectations which it could not fulfil, and groups discovered that they could place issues on the agenda by having recourse to direct action (Arrighi, Hopkins, & Wallerstein, 1989: 38). The Civil Rights issue and the Vietnam war acted as a catalyst for these anti–establishment tendencies, not simply in the USA but also in Europe. The United States engaged in a protracted struggle against a weaker enemy it could not defeat. The domestic opposition to the war was unprecedented, and the assured confidence of the power elite was shattered. There were massive anti–war demonstrations throughout Europe, often met with considerable state violence. Large sections of European youth protested against the subservience of their states and their social–democratic parties to the US government, emboldened by the refutation of its economic and military might. At the same time the invasion of Czechoslovakia by the forces of the Warsaw Pact buried the remaining illusions in communism as a force for human emancipation.

It was evident that the old organised labour movements were held in contempt by many of the new protesters, as for example during the May events in France in 1968. Here the protests were directed not simply against the remoteness of state power and the arrogance and complacency of old capitalist elites, but also against the remote and authoritarian labour movement elites (Arrighi, Hopkins, & Wallerstein, 1989: ch. 5). The revolutionary aspirations of the 'new Left' of that period were confounded, but the new social movements emerged from that anti–establishment protest movement. They have shown the power to mobilise and to challenge, transcending national boundaries in the process, but their ability to affect outcomes has remained in doubt. This is partially due to their conscious renunciation of hierarchical and bureaucratic organisational forms, and partially due to the focus on 'single issues' taken by many participants, which discourages alliances with more established interests. This is reminiscent of the old dilemma faced by anarchists in the nineteenth century; failure to compromise will lead to marginalisation, while compromise will lead to assimilation and deradicalisation. Can the new social movements be effective without losing their radical edge? Can they help to restore the emancipatory imagination of socialism?

CONTAINMENT AND LIBERATION

The work of Herbert Marcuse (1898–1979) in analysing modern forms of social containment and in identifying the radical potential of new forms of opposition remains unsurpassed. He sought to use both Marx's theory of alienation and Freud's theory of the unconscious in order to gain a better understanding of the conditioning and containment of social consciousness and the possiblities for transcending that containment (Kellner, 1984; Geoghegan, 1981). In *One Dimensional Man* (1964) he argued that the technical organisation of contemporary industrial society had virtually silenced critical thought. This had been done not in a coercive way, but rather by inculcating acquisitive and competitive values through the techniques of mass advertising, information, and entertainment, and by the very abundance of such attainable and desirable products (Marcuse, 1974: 24). In so far as criticism occurred, it was confined to the operation of specific parts of the social process and did not stray beyond the limits of the 'contained' society. 'Big' questions about the nature and goals of society were excluded from the prevailing discourse, yet the illusion of free choice and open criticism was preserved:

> Advanced industrial society is indeed a system of countervailing powers. But these forces cancel each other out in a higher unification – in the common interest to defend and extend the established position, to combat the historical alternatives, to contain qualitative change...The reality of pluralism becomes ideological, deceptive (Marcuse, 1974: 53).

This process of containment and deception was underpinned by the lavish choice of goods being made available for the first time to a mass of consumers. The modern industrial society manipulated its citizens through the creation and partial satisfaction of false needs, but the hollowness of this atomised society was encapsulated by Marcuse in concepts such as 'repressive liberty', 'democratic unfreedom', 'new totalitarianism' and 'enforced tolerance' (Marcuse, 1974: 31, 16–7, 60, 177).

On the final page of *One Dimensional Man* Marcuse pointed to the fact that the assimilating power of modern society had not reached a sub–stratum of 'the outcasts and outsiders, the exploited and the persecuted of other races and other colours, the unemployed and the unemployable', and their resistance to the establishment was deemed to be revolutionary 'even if their consciousness is not' (Marcuse, 1974: 199–200). This was a major shift from the traditional socialist emphasis on the manual working class as the privileged agents for the transition to socialism, and it was not warmly received by most Marxists. It appeared to be closer to the third world liberation theory of Frantz Fanon, who emphasised the oppositional nature of the lumpenproletariat (Fanon, 1985: 103). When Marcuse went on to enthuse over the emancipatory potential of the rebellious students of 1968 he seemed to echo the idea of the 'intellectual proletariat' propounded by Marx's old anarchist protagonist, Mikhail Bakunin (Bakunin, 1971: 183).

Marcuse did not discount the transformative potential of the working class. In *An Essay On Liberation* (1969) he maintained that the working class was 'still the historical agent of revolution' because of its numerical weight and the weight of its exploitation. However, it shared the stabilising needs of the system and had become a 'conservative, even counter–revolutionary force'. He concluded that 'objectively, in itself, labour still is the potentially revolutionary class: subjectively, for itself, it is not' (Marcuse, 1969: 16). He argued that the American working class was already 'integrated into the system' but that the same could not 'yet' be said of the European working class (Marcuse, 1970a: 85). The radicalisation of the working class depended on the work of 'catalysts outside its ranks', but it was only possible if economic stability and social cohesion began to weaken. However, he made it clear that he was not seeking a new revolutionary agent to replace the working class. He argued that it was 'nonsense' to say that middle–class opposition was replacing the proletariat as the revolutionary class, or that the lumpenproletariat was becoming a radical political force. But he saw the emergence of 'relatively small and weakly organised (often disorganised) groups' functioning as 'potential catalysts of rebellion within the majorities to which, by their class origin, they belong' (Marcuse, 1969: 54).

He was uncertain about the potential of socialist or communist parties to regain their emancipatory thrust. He spoke of the obsolescence of parliamentary parties, which would inevitably 'fall victim to the general and totalitarian political corruption which characterises the political universe'. He rejected revolutionary centralism and 'underground' activity because of its vulnerability to the 'streamlined apparatus of repression' (Marcuse, 1970b: 472). He claimed that the Marxist–Leninist parties had been integrated into the 'bourgois–democratic process' (Marcuse, 1969: 54), and he saw little point in developing 'radical work within the party' (Marcuse, 1970a: 103). However, he did not shut the door entirely on the potential of orthodox political parties, writing in 1972 that the communist parties and the unions were still a 'potentially revolutionary force' (Marcuse, 1972: 41). He reiterated this view in 1977, stating that the working class was still a 'potentially revolutionary subject', but he stressed that this was an expanded working class which could not be conflated with the industrial working class. He recognised that a turn to the Right had occurred and expressed some sympathy with the Eurocommunist movement in its attempt to win over a large anti–capitalist – 'but not yet socialist' – opposition which was not part of the manual working class. He argued that capitalist ideology was 'wearing thin' in the face of environmental poisoning, nuclear threat, and the return of mass unemployment (Marcuse, 1989: 288–91).

Although he was vague about the forces which might challenge containment, he was convinced that nothing short of a 'biological revolution' in the instincts of people was required (Marcuse, 1969: 16–7). He pointed to a variety of protests for a better life which might combine into a movement for qualitative radical change, including protests about pollution, noise, and urban decay, and he emphasised the 'linguistic revolt' through which protesters disclosed the manipulative motivations of the economic and political power–holders (Marcuse,

1969: ch. 2; Marcuse, 1972: 16–7). In the 1970s he highlighted the significance of the women's liberation movement in challenging the oppressive social basis of modern life. He hoped that the various oppositional movements would install 'new moral and aesthetic needs' which would drive towards 'new relationships between the sexes, between the generations, between men and women and nature', and he claimed that freedom was 'rooted in the fulfillment of these needs which are sensuous, ethical, and rational in one' (Marcuse, 1972, 16–7).

Clearly it would take a radical democratic restructuring of society if the control and containment identified by Marcuse were to be broken. The idea of such restructuring has been developed in recent years in notable contributions from Carol Gould (1988), John Keane (1988), Carole Pateman (1989) and Anne Phillips (1991), and in the new utopianism of André Gorz (1985). Not surprisingly, these writers are rather vague when it comes to discussing how these ideals can be advanced in inauspicious times. The next section will briefly review how particular new social movements have challenged existing power structures, and how they have related to the old anti–systemic movements.

FEMINISM

The struggle for the emancipation of women is not new. Mary Wollstonecraft's *Vindication of the Rights of Woman* was first published in 1792 (Wollstonecraft, 1992), and women conducted a long struggle for the right to vote (DuBois, 1991). Nevertheless, feminism as a mass movement emerged across Western Europe and North America in the late 1960s and early 1970s. The radical protests of the 1960s had been directed not simply against policies in the defined public sphere of politics, but against the exercise of power in the practices of everyday life. In this respect the slogan of 'the personal is political' became particularly important for women in struggle against the systematic limitation of opportunities embodied in a wide range of social practices and often backed by discriminatory laws. The disparity between the numbers of men and women in employment has gradually narrowed, challenging the imputed domestic role of women as housewives, and challenging the formal and informal discriminations practiced against women in employment. The spread of effective contraception in the 1960s gave women increased control of fertility and further widened their life choices, as did the general improvement in educational provision. One of the first books to highlight the issue of the subordination of women in late capitalist society was Kate Millett's *Sexual Politics*, which identified patriarchy, the domination of men over women, as the most significant and sustained feature in the evolution of society (Millett, 1971). This concept of patriarchy was developed influentially by Shulamith Firestone in *The Dialectic of Sex*, (Firestone, 1971), and it clearly contradicted the conventional socialist focus on the centrality of class struggle.

There have been numerous attempts within the women's movement to reconcile socialist and feminist perspectives (Barrett, 1980; Rowbotham, 1972; Rowbotham, Segal & Wainwright, 1979; Hamilton & Barrett, 1985; Haug, 1992). The concept of patriarchy stresses the historical enormity of the oppression of women, pointing to its existence before capitalism and its persistence in the communist dictatorships. Michèle Barrett, from a socialist feminist perspective, has argued that patriarchy is of limited use as a concept for helping to understand the historical changes in the oppression of women, but Marxist accounts which reduce the oppression of women to the requirements of capitalist accumulation are also inadequate. Women's place in society could not be accounted for simply in terms of the reproduction and availability of labour power. Clearly there is a crucially important ideological dimension to the oppression of women which was continuous from pre–capitalist to capitalist systems, and was also manifest in countries calling themselves socialist. Barrett asks whether feminist demands for quality could be met within capitalism, and concludes that the sexual division of labour and the ideology of gender are too entrenched to be transformed without a complete transformation of the relations of production (Barrett, 1980: 148–59). Hartmann accepts a more positive role for patriarchy, but she also uses it explicitly as a descriptive term rather than an analytic one:

> Capitalist development creates the places for a hierarchy of workers, but traditional marxist categories cannot tell us who fills which places. Gender and racial hierarchies determine who fills the empty places. Patriarchy is not simply hierarchical organisation, but hierarchy in which particular people fill particular places. It is in studying patriarchy that we learn why it is women who are dominated and how (Hartmann, 1979: 13).

This combination of mode of production as an analytic concept and patriarchy as a 'struggle concept' has also been adopted by Maria Mies in her interpretation of the position of women in the international division of labour (Mies, 1987: 37–8).

Autonomous action to combat women's oppression has been particularly important, because the old socialist parties and trade unions have been guilty of excluding women in a variety of ways. The form of this autonomous action has naturally differed from country to country, but Pasquinelli's description of the trajectory of the Italian women's movement moving from 'the political' in the 1970s to 'the social' in the 1980s applies to most of the countries of Western Europe (Pasquinelli, 1984: 131). In the 1970s there were attempts to form national women's organisations and journals, and legal struggles for abortion and contraception rights and anti–discrimination legislation drew in women in large numbers. In the 1980s these attempts at national organisation were largely abandoned, but there developed a range of local initiatives, normally working around specific issues such as rape and domestic violence. In France the Movement for the Liberation of Women (MLF) gave an institutional focus to feminism in the 1970s but was much weakened by the 1980s (Jenson, 1990: 131–7). In Britain, the last attempt at a national conference of feminists ended in disarray in 1979 (Weir & Wilson, 1984). In Sweden, the most influential women's groups of the 1970s declined in membership and activity in the 1980s, but ad hoc groups have emerged around numerous centres and engaged in protests and strikes (Eduards, 1991). In Germany, the early focus of the modern feminist movement was the campaign for abortion on demand. The Democratic Women's Initiative tried to provide a common platform for issues of particular relevance to women following its foundation in 1976, but no single group established a leading position (Haug, 1992).

The pattern of national mobilisation in the 1970s followed by local initiatives in the 1980s does not apply to Spain, Greece, and Portugal, where right–wing dictatorships were in place until the mid–1970s. The immediate focus of radical political activity was the consolidation of basic political rights, but women's movements succeeded first in getting equality written into their new constitutions and then in gaining legal reforms through the socialist governments which were in power in the 1980s (Threlfall, 1989; Stamiris, 1986). Ireland was also late in gaining legal rights for women, and the strong Catholic lobby succeeded in winning a referendum which authorised a Constitutional ban on abortion in 1983 (Mahon, 1987; Girvin, 1986). In the communist countries, women were fully integrated into the workforce, but few reached positions of administrative power and they were obliged to carry the full burden of the domestic tasks (Molyneux, 1990). Autonomous Women's Groups have emerged since the revolutions of 1989. In Poland a small Polish Feminist Association was formed during the first phase of Solidarity's legal existence in 1980. Following the fall of the Communist regime it faced the task of resisting the Catholic Church's social programme, which aimed at illegalising abortion, despite the evidence of opinion polls which showed big majorities in favour of maintaining existing rights (Wilde, 1991; Malone, 1992; Corrin, 1992).

How has 'second wave' feminism related to socialist parties and trades unions? It was clear to many feminists that the labour organisations had often reproduced the subordination of women in their own policies and practices. Radical feminists have been unconvinced of the need to work within the old socialist or labour movements. Others have exerted pressure on such organisations by effectively mobilising outside their ranks, as for example in the German Greens or the Women's Party in Iceland, which won 5 per cent of the vote in the 1983 general election. Some socialist feminists have worked within the old organisations to force them to give a higher priority to the oppression of women, and there is some evidence that women have done better in countries with a strong social democratic tradition, such as Denmark, Sweden, and Norway. Segal has argued that in the advanced industrial countries the position of women has measurably deteriorated only in the United States, where there is no socialist party (Segal, 1991: 90). The French Socialist Party's creation of a Ministry for Women under Yvette Roudy in 1981 led to programmes for labour force equality and campaigns against sexism in the media, generally promoting a consciousness of the problems specific to women (Jenson, 1990: 146). The British Labour Party and the German Social Democrats also committed themselves to similar action if they were returned to power.

Socialist parties have taken on board some of the social demands made by feminists, such as improved nursery provision, and have also attempted to do something about the obvious inequalities in the representation of women and men in their own organisations. The Norwegian Labour Party was the first of the major social–democratic parties to adopt quotas, requiring 40 per cent of all party posts to be filled by women in 1983. The German SPD is committed to a similar quota by 1998 (Brooks, Eagle & Short, 1990: 12). In both cases the quotas can be seen as a response to the adoption of quotas by their 'Left libertarian' rivals (Kitschelt, 1990), the Norwegian Socialist Peoples Party and the German Greens. The British Labour Party has had reserved seats on its national executive committee for women for many years, but they are elected by the whole Conference rather than by women alone (Wainwright, 1987: ch. 4). Reserved places for women in the shadow cabinet of the Labour Party were introduced in 1989, and quotas have been under consideration. The representation of women in various European parliaments remains below 20 per cent in the largest countries of Western Europe, but exceeds 30 per cent in the Scandinavian countries. In general, the parties affiliated to the Socialist International field more than the average number of women parliamentary candidates and have more than the average number of women representatives, and in recent years these parties appear to have attracted a higher proportion of women members (*Socialist Affairs* 1991, 1, 49–51). However, numbers are not necessarily a reliable indicator of increased power, either in political parties or in society in general. Hege Skjeie has pointed to the possibility that women are being integrated into 'shrinking institutions', gaining positions which are no longer as powerful as before, while men continue to dominate in positions of real power (Skjeie, 1991). However, greater representation should at least expose this 'real power'.

Many active feminists have been disappointed by the slow pace of change in combating sexism, and have opted for autonomous group activity as a space in which to find relief from its pervasive power. However, in two decades many of the legal discriminations against women have been removed and most aspects of the oppression of women have forced their way on to the agenda of public debate. The focus on power in the structures of everyday life has added a feminist dimension to the previously flagging debate about the nature of power in modern society. This fundamental questioning of the nature of power in society will cause great discomfort to power–holders in capitalist institutions which have prospered most from existing inequalities, both in terms of maximising the exploitation of the workforce and in the ideological sense of 'divide and rule' social control. Nor can these issues be restricted to Europe or the advanced industrial world, for feminists have been active in forging solidarity with the struggles of women in the third world. The Women's International Democratic Federation developed a worldwide network of affiliates (*The Guardian*, 19 October, 1991), and other successful international coordination organisations are Forum 85, the International Women's Tribune Centre and ISIS, the Women's International Information and Communication Service (Dankelman & Davidson, 1988: ch. 10). In confronting issues about the roles of women in the third world, the overlap of 'new movement' concerns becomes clear; women's lives cannot be separated from questions about the global economic order and the environment (Mies, 1987).

ECOLOGY

Historically, environmentalist movements have sometimes expressed romantic or even reactionary ideas of protecting not only nature but the old social order, irrespective of the inequalities and oppressions which came with it (Bramwell, 1989: ch. 8). But the ecology movement which emerged in the early 1970s has been infused with a radical idealism, appealing for international action to avert what is perceived as the crisis of sustainable life. New parties representing 'green' concerns have begun to make an impact. Between 1980 and 1991 Green parties won seats in ten national parliaments within Europe, and most of the continent's Green Parties came together to form the European Greens in 1983, since when congresses have met regularly (Parkin, 1989: ch. 15). Following the elections for the European Parliament in 1989 Green MEP's from France, Belgium, Germany, Portugal, the Netherlands and Italy formed a parliamentary group.

The essence of the Green critique of socialism is that the latter's historical commitment to production as a means of furthering human progress leads to an instrumental and destructive view of non–human nature (Porrit, 1984: 44; Dobson, 1990: ch. 5). Social democratic and communist parties have consistently advocated high growth rates with little concern for environmental damage. Both movements have been drawn into the logic of capitalist competitiveness, with its tendency to perpetuate accumulation at all costs. In addition, both movements have appealed primarily to a constituency created by that logic, and workers have naturally tended to prioritise their own economic security. On the other hand, socialists have consistently attacked the human degradation involved in the process of production under capitalism and have pointed to the need for society to gain control of production rather than being driven by the logic of endless accumulation. So in the sense that socialists and ecologists recognise the urgent need to increase social control of production, there is a strongly shared concern (Ryle, 1988; Wolf, 1986; Williams, n.d.). Many socialists remain sceptical about the more catastrophic visions of ecological disaster adopted by some Greens, while the latter are justifiably wary of the historical association of socialism with the 'domination' of nature, and the linking of industrial production with social progress.

The ecological concerns expressed in the past two decades have questioned the entire nature of capitalist industrial and agricultural development. Perhaps the most influential early text was E. F. Schumacher's *Small is Beautiful* (1973) in which he criticised the 'inability to recognise that the modern industrial system, with all its intellectual sophistication, consumed the very basis on which it has been erected' (Schumacher, 1973: 17). The themes included the danger of the exhaustion of raw materials, the spread of pollution, the inherent danger of nuclear power, and the plight of the third world. Although cautious in suggesting political remedies, Schumacher was clear that when it came to furthering an ecologically sound world, without a 'transformation of ownership...everything remains make−believe' (Schumacher, 1973: 261). Another influential book in Europe was the attempt by Gorz to switch the focus of socialist thought towards the dangers of ecological breakdown and to alternative 'utopian' thinking. A collection of articles written between 1971 and 1974 appeared as *Ecology as Politics* in 1975. The ecologists' cause was aided by the collapse of confidence in exponential growth in the mid−1970s. Above all it has been the magnitude of ecological problems which has become visible in the last two decades and which has ensured that the issues have not been marginalised or easily incorporated in the discourse of conventional party politics.

The melt−down of the nuclear reactor at Chernobyl in the Ukraine in April 1986 was perhaps the most frightening signal of the destructive potential of modern technology. Apart from the immediate and subsequent deaths caused by the accident, the radioactive fall−out spread across the whole of the continent, rendering pastures as far West as Britain too dangerous to sustain animals for human consumption for years to come. Nor could the accident be attributed merely to Soviet technological incompetence, for a similar accident had almost occurred at Seven Mile Island in the United States in 1979. The effect of Chernobyl on nuclear energy programmes was startling, with cancellations for reactor orders coming in from all over the world, and socialist and communist parties in Europe finally began to be persuaded by their anti−nuclear members (Spence, 1987; Medvedev, 1990). Another horrendous accident was the poisonous gas leak at Bhopal in India in 1984, which killed 3,000 people and which exposed criminal disregard for safety standards in the super–exploited third world. European forests have withered due to the effects of acid rain. The pollution of rivers was graphically illustrated in 1986 when the River Rhine turned red following the Sandoz chemical warehouse leak. Alarm has been voiced about global warming, a phenomenon caused by the massive increase of gaseous emissions which could lead to catastrophic flooding and changes in the distribution of rainfall. The clearing of the rain forests, largely by multinational corporations, contributes to this warming effect, and there has been much publicity about its destructive cultural and climatic effects.

The international dimension of Green politics has succeeded in developing awareness of the inter–relatedness of factors which respect no national boundaries. In addressing the enormous danger of corporate capitalism's desperate struggle for profit, it has effectively enlarged the focus of debates about the nature of economic and political power. The appeal of this form of action can be seen by the popularity in Britain of two pressure groups founded in 1971, Greenpeace and Friends of the Earth, which have over 400,000 members between them. European socialist and communist parties have responded by 'greening' their economic programmes and pledging the abandonment of nuclear energy. In Germany, the SPD has given environmentalism a central place in its latest party programme (Padgett, 1993: 33), and Red–Green coalitions have been formed at state level. Increasingly, trade unions are becoming involved with Green issues, particularly those concerned with health and safety at work, but also with wider issues concerning the environment in which workers live, as well as their safety as consumers.

OTHER MOVEMENTS

Although feminist and environmentalist groups claim the largest sustained mobilisation of activists, other movements have made a considerable impact. The peace movement exploded in size following the decision in 1979 by NATO chiefs to deploy Cruise and Pershing II nuclear missiles throughout Western Europe. The ensuing demonstrations were the biggest ever seen in Europe (Magri, 1982). The end of the cold war and the dissolution of the Warsaw Pact has naturally led to demobilisation, despite the Gulf War and the war in Yugoslavia. Peace campaigners are now organised across Europe in the Helsinki Citizens Assembly and European Dialogue as vehicles for campaigning for peace, disarmament, and openness.

'One world' groups have sprung up across Europe in an attempt to force some concrete action on the questions of third world debt and sustainable development. In this area socialist writers and politicians have been very active in pointing out that it is the people of the third world who have been forced to bear the brunt of the world economic crisis (George, 1988; Amin, 1990; Kinnock, Lestor & Ruddock, 1988). Willy Brandt, as President of the Socialist International, helped to place North–South relations at the head of the International's agenda. Brandt headed an Independent Commission on International Development Issues, which produced two reports, in 1979 and 1983, known as the Brandt Commission reports, analysing the deteriorating condition of the third world in the world economy and suggesting practical measures to avert a potential catastrophe (Brandt, 1980; Brandt, 1983). These reports inspired the growth of local committees to highlight the issues. The Socialist International produced its own report with recommendations for improving North–South cooperation in 1975 (Socialist International, 1985). The link between third world poverty and environmental degradation was made in the report of the World Commission on Environment and Development, chaired by the Norwegian socialist leader Gro Harlem Bruntland (World Commission, 1987). Unless the debt problems of the third world countries are resolved they will be condemned to chronic poverty (MacEwan, 1990; Jackson, 1990: ch. 5). Many of the participants in 'one world' groups have considered themselves not to be socialists, but have nevertheless reached an awareness that the drive for profit is at the heart of the problems of the third world. The debt crisis, disadvantageous terms of trade, and insensitive International Monetary Fund and World Bank programmes, impress themselves on activists motivated by a sense of compassion rather than a theory of capitalist exploitation. As the dangers of a 'Fortress Europe' develop, the 'one world' groups will have their work cut out to make their case, but the socialist parties will be reminded of their international duties by their sister parties in the Socialist International.

Anti–racist groups have developed in response to the rise in support for racist political parties and the savage attacks against the safety and rights of ethnic minorities throughout Europe (Harris, 1990; Cheles, Ferguson & Vaughan, 1991). In the elections to the European Parliament in June 1989 over seven million people voted for parties of the extreme Right. There has been some success in mobilising opposition to racism, particularly the French SOS Racisme, founded in 1984 and led by Harlem Désir. It has acted as a coordinating and mobilising body, accepting people from many other groups provided that they accept the emphasis on solidarity (Ossman–Dorent, 1988). It has been notable for the energy and imagination of its protests, and its ability to reach a wide audience, particularly among the young. Thousands of young people from across Europe travelled to the huge anti–racism demonstration in Paris in January 1993. In Germany the anti–fascist movement has been able to mobilise widespread demonstrations against the surge of violence against immigrants which has developed since reunification. The European Community has 15 million people whose ethnic origins are outside Europe, and draconian measures to hunt out illegal immigrants will lead to harrassment of them all. It is clear that decisive anti–racist action is required at all levels.

CONCLUSION

New social movements developed during a period of retreat and defeat for the 'old' anti–systemic movements. Without necessarily associating themselves with socialism, the activists have exposed and challenged the exercise of formal and informal power, from the personal level to the global economic level. However, the concerns of the new social movements have rarely been prioritised by socialist parties. For example, socialist movements have often treated sexism and racism as secondary issues which cannot be resolved until capitalism is abolished, thereby effectively marginalising the struggles which are most important in the lives of women's groups and ethnic minorities. Wallerstein has persuasively linked the phenomena of sexism and racism to the development of capitalism. He accepts that the subordination of women and xenophobia existed before capitalism, but he argues that capitalism has exacerbated and systematised these problems. Sexism is viewed as 'the relegation of women to the realm of non–productive labour, producing the 'double humiliation' of an increased intensity of work with a loss of status. Racism is seen as 'the stratification of the work–force inside the historical system', which produced a justification for low rewards for productive labour. He has added 'ageism' to this list, for capitalism has systematically developed the non–waged work of the young and the old (Wallerstein, 1983: 24–6, 76–80, 102–4; Wallerstein, 1991, ch. 2). These oppressions are products of a divisive accumulation process, and the struggles against them indirectly challenge that system.

On the plight of the less developed countries, the relevance of socialist theories of imperialism and dependency is clear. 'One world' groups have been active in attempting to coordinate 'fair trade' schemes and subsistence alternatives to the IMF 'growth' packages, but the enormity of the problems requires urgent and sweeping inter–governmental action by all major international actors. For those in the developed part of the world to recognise the need to legislate against the super–exploitation of the poorer countries, an alliance between 'third worldists' and socialists is fundamental. At the moment the possiblity of such concerted action is hampered by the fact that the strength of socialists and 'new' politics groups in the European Parliament does not translate into effective political power. Europe is not yet a state, and without it there is no one major actor with the will or power to lead effective action for the world's poorest people. Ecologists too are finding that the sympathies of politicians quickly amount to little when economic sacrifices have to be made. The inadequate agreements reached at the Earth Summit in Rio de Janeiro in

June 1992 revealed to many ingenuous ecologists that the interests of capital accumulation constitute a powerful barrier to remedial action.

To some extent the new social movements have succeeded in shifting the priorities of the old movements. For example, labour movements have begun to pay serious attention to equal opportunities, sexual and racial harrassment, environmental protection of workers and their neighbourhoods, and the demand for a shorter working life and flexible hours. For socialists schooled in conceiving class struggle in terms of industrial action and the nationalisation of the means of production, the issues of the new movements may seem distant and diversionary. However, the broad working class, comprising those dependent on the sale of their labour power (Meiksins, 1986), has been subjected to new cleavages produced by changes in the accumulation process. Solidarity expressed through old labour movements and communities can no longer be assumed, nor do the old parties appear capable of winning majority support. It is therefore imperative that different priorities and concerns be recognised and pulled together through pluralist negotiation. Fragmentation renders the old and new social movements impotent against the interests of international capital. The historical strength of socialist theory has been its ability to show how the power of private property effectively disempowers those without it. Whatever the failures of strategy and tactics displayed by the variety of socialist movements, the argument that the power of capital is the crucial factor in conditioning social relations on a world-scale retains its force. Without concerted attempts to articulate the old and new 'antisystemic' movements, the system will continue to assert its power and reproduce the oppressions touched on in this chapter.

8 The Rise and Fall of Soviet Communism

No social order is ever destroyed before all the productive forces for which it is sufficient have been developed, and new superior relations of production never replace older ones before the material conditions for their existence have matured within the framework of the old society (Marx, 1969: 21)

In the long struggle between two irreconcilably hostile social systems – capitalism and socialism – the outcome will be determined, in the last analysis, by the relative productivity of labour under each system (Trotsky, 1973: 40)

Since 1917 the fate of European socialism has been inextricably linked with the Russian Revolution and its aftermath. The seizure of power by the Bolsheviks and its preservation against all odds led to a new and unforeseen form of political rule which inspired a formal split in the world socialist movement. The development of the communist movement has coloured all aspects of socialist experience in Europe, and the collapse of communist power in its homeland provides a timely moment for appraisal. A number of questions arise in trying to understand the development of Soviet communism. How and why did the Bolsheviks impose a dictatorship, and how was it consolidated? What effects did this have on the international socialist community? What were the decisive factors in the collapse of the system? Could the system have been reformed from within? In order to answer these questions, this chapter will emphasise the significance of four 'moments' in the history of the Soviet Union at which crucial decisions were taken when alternative courses were possible. The years 1921–2 mark the first moment. The others were the 'second revolution' of

1928-9, led by Stalin, the development of de-Stalinisation under Khrushchev from 1956 to 1964, and the attempt at radical reform led by Gorbachev after 1985.

BOLSHEVISM

The Russian Social-Democratic Party was founded in 1898 in difficult circumstances. The Russian Empire was ruled by an autocratic Tsarist regime which persecuted all political opposition. In addition Russia was a huge rural country of 125 million people with a level of industrialisation less than a quarter that of neighbouring Germany (Bairoch, 1982: 281). Serfdom had been abolished only in 1861, and Russia had one of the lowest literacy rates in Europe; at the outbreak of the First World War fewer than a third of the population were able to read and write (Pethybridge, 1974: 140). On the face of it, Russia looked an unlikely place for the first successful workers' revolution.

Although the working class was small, it was highly concentrated in large factories in a few major cities. There were about three million workers in big factories, producing two thirds of industrial output, and about five million in small-scale industry (Nove, 1972: 17). There were good opportunities for socialists to recruit workers to their cause, but to do so they had to escape the attentions of the Tsarist secret police. The problem of operating successfully in dangerous circumstances was confronted by Lenin, who demanded a highly centralised and totally disciplined party of professional revolutionaries whose lives would be 'directed' by a small central committee. As the party's operations would necessarily be secret, open democracy could not be practiced, and indeed Lenin described broad party democracy in such circumstances as a 'useless and harmful toy' (Lenin, 1988: 199-200). Determined to form a 'vanguard' party, he engineered a split in the Social Democratic Party at its 1903 congress. Lenin's group became known as the Bolsheviks, but most of the membership belonged to the Mensheviks, led by Martov. The Mensheviks wanted to develop a mass party, on the lines of the other members of the Second International. The revolutionary strategies of the two groups were similar. Both expected the forthcoming Russian Revolution to be a 'bourgeois' revolution which would introduce parliamentary democracy. But as the Russian bourgeoisie was very weak and closely associated with the old Tsarist order, the socialists would be in a powerful position to take advantage of the constitutional settlement (Harding, 1977: 100-8; Lane, 1982: 36-43).

It is often stated that Marx had expected the proletarian revolution to succeed first in one of the advanced industrial nations. In fact he had an open mind on the subject, and stated that it was quite possible that a workers' revolution in one of the less developed countries could ignite similar revolutions in more advanced states (Marx, 1976: 74-5). This view was adapted to Russian conditions by

Leon Trotsky in his theory of 'permanent revolution'. Like Lenin, he saw Russia as the weakest link in the capitalist world–system, but he was convinced that the workers could not and would not carry out a revolution on behalf of the bourgeoisie, but instead would be compelled by the situation to seize state power and spark sympathetic revolutions in Western Europe (Trotsky, 1975; Mandel, 1979: ch. 1). The weakness of the liberal elements of the bourgeoisie was illustrated in the failed revolution of 1905, which also witnessed the spontaneous development of local democratic councils (soviets) of soldiers and workers. The events of 1905 confirmed the weakness of Tsarism as a political system, the weakness of the liberal opposition, and the revolutionary strength of the small working class. Following the military defeat by Japan a revolution took place in Russia. It was eventually defeated, but not before real power in the cities had been exercised by spontaneously organised soviets. Trotsky, leader of the St. Petersburg Soviet, hailed them as the ideal democratic body, more accountable and representative than the parliamentary systems which had developed in the West.

The dreadful casualties incurred by Russian troops in the First World War undermined the Tsar's authority, and he was overthrown in February 1917. A Provisional Government was set up, headed first by Prince Lvov and then by Alexander Kerensky, and supported by the Kadet Party (liberals), the Mensheviks, and most of the Social Revolutionary Party, which represented the mass of the peasantry. Besides this 'official' government, a soviet system developed which operated as an effective alternative administration, and the Bolsheviks gradually gained a majority position   in the principal soviets. Trotsky, who had hitherto maintained an independent position, joined the Bolsheviks in July in response to Lenin's surprising call for a second revolution to install 'all power to the soviets' (D'Encausse, 1982: 61–3). Why did Lenin change his mind and adopt Trotsky's strategy? In the first place his mistrust of political compromise had been heightened by the behaviour of the leadership of the German Social Democrats in August 1914, when they unanimously voted in favour of the credits to finance the war, in return for promises of political reform. The collapse of the Second International impressed on Lenin the corrupting effects of integration into constitutional politics. Alone of the parties of the Second International, the Russians had no legal existence and had never been obliged to make the sorts of political compromise familiar to the other European parties (Wallerstein, 1988: 87). A second factor was the likelihood of revolutions in Europe brought on by the sheer horror of the war. Lenin, in exile in Switzerland, would have been well aware of the revulsion felt by the working class participants, and would have been well aware that a defeated power would face a revolutionary situation.

The Provisional Government lost most of its support by insisting on keeping the country involved in the war against Germany, and the Bolsheviks seized power with minimal resistance in October. Although the scheduled elections to the Constituent Assembly went ahead later that month, the Assembly was dissolved as soon at it met in January 1918. The Social Revolutionaries won 410 seats, the Bolsheviks 175, the Kadets 17 and the Mensheviks 16. The results showed that the Bolsheviks had gained widespread urban support, but that the rural areas were loyal to the SR's (Farber, 1990: 55–60; Liebman, 1985: 232–7).

A short–lived coalition with the Left SR's ended when the Bolsheviks agreed to a humiliating peace treaty with the Germans, giving away enormous stretches of land. For over two years the Bolsheviks fought off military attempts to unseat them which were backed by interventions from numerous foreign armies. In this period of civil war and foreign intervention Russia lost about 11 million people, and agriculture and industry were in ruins. The Bolsheviks retained power, but the international revolution on which their strategy had been based did not materialise, and they presided over a workers state in a country in which the workers comprised a very small portion of the population. Most of the territories of the former Russian Empire were incorporated into the Union of Soviet Socialist Republics, which was founded in December 1922 (Carr, 1983: 39–40), although Finland, Poland, Latvia, Lithuania and Estonia achieved independence. In order to consolidate international support and to encourage revolutionary activity elsewhere, Lenin instigated the Third International, a development which produced the formal division in European socialism between communist and social democratic parties. The revolutionaries now identified reformist socialists as part of the opposition, and this mirrored the situation inside the Soviet Union. Political opposition to Bolshevism was not tolerated, even when it was totally opposed to a restoration of the old order. Mensheviks, Anarchists and Social Revolutionaries were harrassed, imprisoned, and eventually banned (Farber, 1990: ch. 4; Broido, 1987).

The dissolution of the Constituent Assembly in 1918 marked a critical break with the democratic impulse which had been an unshakable part of European socialism. This point was made at the time by Rosa Luxemburg. The extent to which Lenin's ideas on democracy within the party and in society as a whole differed from other Marxists of the period is illustrated in the criticisms made by Luxemburg and Kautsky. Luxemburg criticised Lenin's authoritarian model of party organisation as early as 1904, and her remarks were to take on a prophetic force:

> To grant to the party leadership such absolute powers of a negative character as Lenin does is to artificially strengthen to a dangerous extent the conservatism inherent in the essence of that institution...The ultra–centralism which Lenin demands seems to us...essentially sterile and domineering (Luxemburg, 1971: 294–5).

Luxemburg needed no persuasion that political rights in liberal constitutional societies were limited or controlled. But like most socialists she recognised that the extension of the liberal principle of government by consent was a progressive development. Socialist democracy had to go beyond the narrow political limits of liberal democracy, but to reject the progressive element of constitutional democracy raised the danger of the dictatorship of a party (or more accurately its leadership) rather than the majority of the people. She warned of the danger of 'the mere transfer of authority from the hands of the bourgeoisie to that of the Social Democratic central committee' and demanded the uprooting of the slavish spirit of discipline of the workers, not its appropriation by revolutionaries (Luxemburg, 1971: 291). In her pamphlet on the Russian Revolution she warned that freedom only for the supporters of the government or the members of one party is no freedom at all, but 'freedom is always and exclusively the freedom for the one who thinks differently' (Luxemburg, 1970: 389).

Kautsky's criticism of the authoritarian traits of the Bolsheviks came in 1918 in The Dictatorship of the Proletariat. For many years his work drew little sympathy from Marxists because he had refused to take a stand against the war in 1914 and his criticisms of the Bolsheviks were openly hostile. It is understandable that Lenin's reply was addressed to the 'renegade' Kautsky and was extremely bitter. Nevertheless Kautsky makes some telling points against the Bolshevik dismissal of constitutional democracy as 'bourgeois', and Lenin's defence of an allegedly superior form of democracy is unconvincing. Kautsky argued that a class cannot govern because of its amorphous character (Kautsky, 1983: 110–6). Parties governed, but a single party could not claim to represent all class interests, and where it imposed a ban on other parties it was effectively imposing a dictatorship of one part of the proletariat over another:

> Socialism requires the organisational discipline of the broad masses of the people and presupposes numerous free organisations, both economic and political. It requires complete freedom of organisation. The socialist organisation of labour cannot be modelled on a military barracks (Kautsky, 1983: 100).

Kautsky cited a few instances in history where socialised labour had been organised from 'above', without democracy, as for example in the Jesuit state in Paraguay in the Eighteenth Century. But he protested that such a 'system of tutelage' was incompatible with a class striving for its freedom.

In his reply Lenin claimed that the revolutionary dictatorship of the proletariat was 'unrestricted by any laws', and that Soviet power was 'a million times more democratic than the most democratic bourgeois republic' (Lenin, 1977: 27, 33). As we have seen, however, lawless societies consolidate power in the hands of those who can maximise coercion. Despite suggestions that Lenin considered the legalisation of the Mensheviks late in his life, there is no evidence to support the idea that he considered political pluralism to be of any significance.

1921-2

The Tenth Party Congress in 1921 marked a decisive moment in the history of the Soviet Union, when a number of options faced the leadership. The party presided over a devastated country. The military struggle had been led by Trotsky, using authoritarian methods and a system of directed labour and forcible requisitioning of foodstuffs known as 'war communism'. In 1920 Trotsky had advocated a return to a regulated market, and although this suggestion was rejected, it was reintroduced by Lenin at the congress in the form of the New Economic Policy (NEP) (Deutscher, 1963: 496–8). Lenin also demanded party unity, which led to the suppression of dissent both outside and inside the party. The economic reform involved the restoration of markets for agricultural produce and small–scale manufacture, while the state retained its nationalisation of the commanding heights of industry and transport and its monopoly of foreign trade. The political decisions signalled the end of opposition parties and the banning of factions within the Bolsheviks (from 1918 called the Communist Party). The dissolution of the Constituent Assembly had been an ominous sign, but in 1918 it was still possible to claim that the soviet system offered a democratic alternative, and even during the civil war the other socialist groups were periodically permitted to operate (Farber, 1990: 194–5).

It has been argued that the political line adopted by the Bolsheviks in 1921 was mistaken and avoidable, and that Stalin's rise to power might have been checked in a more tolerant political climate (Farber, 1990: 206–8; Sirianni, 1982: 368). However, from the point of view of the Bolshevik leadership there were powerful reasons for imposing a political clampdown. At the same time that the congress met there was an insurrection of 15,000 workers, soldiers and sailors at Kronstadt, demanding an end to dictatorial methods and the restoration of power to the soviets; this was crushed by the government, with many congress delegates joining in the suppression (Liebman, 1985: 253–6: Avrich, 1967: 225–31: Cohn–Bendit, 1968: 234–45). It was a clear signal of working class discontent, and it emphasised the fragility of the communist hold on power. One of the principal complaints of the Kronstadt rebels was the repressive role of the secret police, the Cheka (later GPU and KGB), which had 'executed' over a quarter of a million political opponents between 1917 and 1921 (Andrew & Gordievsky, 1991: 82). If the communists were to countenance the surrender of power there was a real danger that a new government might treat them with the ruthlessness which they had displayed towards the other parties.

The Bolsheviks had lost the popular support which carried them to victory in 1917, and Lenin argued that they could not tolerate the activity of factions such as the Democratic Centralists and the Workers Opposition in such a desperate situation (Lenin, 1977: 522–5).

By 1921 the Bolsheviks, who had seized power with liberational ideals, clung to that power by suppressing political liberty. The success of the new economic policy might have led to a more liberal political policy, and Lenin was certainly preoccupied with schemes for combating the bureaucratisation of state and party life (Liebman, 1985: 420–1). However, he was barely active after the first of three strokes in May 1922 until his death in January 1924. Following the suppression of legal democratic institutions, power inevitably devolved upon the party and state administrators, and here was Stalin's great strength. General Secretary of the Party from 1922, he presided over a massive expansion of party membership, from half a million in January 1923 to 1,680,000 by January 1930 (Bettelheim, 1978: 332). He was also Commissar of the Workers and Peasants Inspectorate (Rabkrin), originally set up to scrutinize the officials inherited from Tsarist days, to ensure that no corruption or slacking took place. In practice it became the training ground for new civil servants loyal to the Party Secretariat. He was a member of the Orgburo, which appointed personnel throughout the country, and was ultimately at the helm of the Party Control Commission, which was in charge of hearing complaints against members and deciding on expulsions. Again the intention behind this body was to increase accountability, as the meetings were to be open to the public, but it was quickly transformed into a form of internal policing (Deutscher, 1974: 232–8). In addition Stalin was Commissar for Nationalities, which gave him unmatched knowledge of the details of Party and State affairs throughout the USSR. Lenin, who advocated national self–determination, had already clashed with Stalin over the latter's 'Great Russia' policy (Liebman, 1985: 421–3). Stalin, as a Georgian, was probably more aware of the power of nationalism and simply would not tolerate it. When it was eventually tolerated, in the late 1980s, the Union fell apart.

Could the progressive disappearance of democratic practices have been halted during Lenin's lifetime? The refusal to tolerate rival political parties which sought neither a restoration of the monarchy nor the private ownership of industry (SR's, Mensheviks, anarchists) became final at the Tenth Party Congress in 1921, and the ban on factions within the Communist Party heralded the beginning of the end of intra–party democracy. In practice the Bolsheviks could not have held power in any sort of democratic system at that time, but the ban on rival pro–revolutionary groups and factions could have been specifically limited in time with a requirement to justify what ought to have been considered as extraordinary measures. The claims by Trotsky and his followers that the ban on factions was intended to be a temporary measure undoubtedly conveyed the intentions of the delegates at the 1921 Congress, but the failure to specify this intention indicates the extent to which the party was uninterested in the use of formal legal rights as a means of preserving the emancipatory impulse of the revolution.

Stalin later justified his dictatorship by claiming to be the exemplar of Leninist orthodoxy, yet his own position was saved by the leadership's decision not to publish Lenin's 'testament', which advised them to remove Stalin from the post of General Secretary. Even Trotsky adopted a conciliatory position towards Stalin on this occasion (Lewin, 1970). Trotsky, who was one of the first to express concern about the emergence of a new elite in The New Course, written in 1923, nevertheless refrained from defending his position on a number of occasions between 1921 and 1925 in the interests of party unity, perhaps feeling an extra obligation to demonstrate his loyalty because he was a relative newcomer to the party and many old Bolsheviks held this against him. Some measure of political freedom might have developed in the 1920s had Lenin lived, but he had shown few signs of understanding the need to create institutions in which power became accountable and in which political differences could be expressed. There is no reason to doubt the sincerity of the libertarian aspirations expressed in *The State and Revolution*, written months before the October revolution, but the book is notable for its absence of discussion about political parties or how differences of political opinion might be institutionalised. He was indifferent to these important structural factors.

THE ADVENT OF STALINISM

The major policy issues between 1922 and 1928 were the related questions of the position of the peasantry and the pace of industrialisation. The Bolshevik leaders acknowledged that in a predominantly peasant country they needed to cement an alliance between the urban workers and the poorer peasants. In 1917 the Bolsheviks had accepted the spontaneous redistribution of land. The problem for the Bolsheviks was that this consolidated the material basis for an independent peasantry which had no interest in the development of a socialist system. Bolshevik theorists followed Lenin in suggesting that 'middle' and 'poor' peasants did have such an interest, in that they would benefit from a cooperative system and could gain material support from the state–controlled industrial sector. There was much wishful thinking here, for despite theoretical attempts to demarcate the middle and poor peasants from the kulaks, their common interests were considerable, and they often acted in concert in matters of production and marketing, without assistance from the state (Bettelheim, 1978: 332).

The kulaks were considered by most Bolsheviks to be an enemy class, but they were the most efficient producers in the countryside. The Left, headed by

Trotsky, wanted to tax them at a higher level than the poorer peasants and legally circumscribe their freedom to withhold produce in order to gain higher prices (Trotsky, 1973: 30–4). The Right, led by Bukharin, argued for 'quick accumulation' in the peasant economy in order to benefit the industrial sector, which would then have a market for its goods (Bukharin, 1982: 242). Bukharin's economic policies required a prosperous kulak class capable of applying the most modern and capital–intensive methods on large tracts of land. But they would have to be paid high prices to release food and then purchase goods made in the towns. The policy would therefore favour light–industrial and consumer goods rather than investment in heavy industry. In political and ideological terms, however, the enhancement of the kulak class ran against the grain of Bolshevik thinking. Bukharin had to argue, somewhat awkwardly, that the Communist monopoly of state power and control over industry guaranteed the socialist direction of the NEP (Bukharin, 1982: 285–94). Indeed the existence of classes (small traders and peasants) whose support was unreliable moved Bukharin to defend limitations on political rights (Bukharin, 1982: 268–9). He operated from three assumptions. First, the NEP was intended to last for a considerable duration, second, any alliance with the mass of the peasantry had to be based on persuasion, and third, that the party was incorruptible. Lenin had said that it would take a whole historical epoch to achieve collectivisation through the NEP, but he went on to suggest that this could be as little as a decade, in keeping with his voluntarist zeal to 'make history' despite the conditions (Lenin, 1977: 27). However, neither Lenin nor the Left Opposition contemplated the complete confiscation of peasant property.

The recriminations between the Right and Left were skilfully exploited by Stalin. By 1926, when Kamenev and Zinoviev finally realised that it was necessary to ally with Trotsky in order to defend some vestige of political discussion, opposition was virtually impossible. Ideological differences, combined with suspicion of Trotsky's ambitions, meant that no coalition could be formed that was strong enough to prevent Stalin's remorseless rise to power (Farber, 1990: 176–83). Stalin first steered the party behind Bukharin's enthusiastic support for the continuation of the NEP in its existing form, and used that majority to expel Trotsky, Zinoviev, Kamenev and the entire 'Joint Opposition'. He then stepped up the pace of industrialisation and unleashed his attack on the peasantry in the collectivisation campaign of 1929. He used this emergency to mobilise the party against Bukharin and his followers and to bring back into the fold some of the 'repentant' members of the Left Opposition, who then joined the 'fight' against an unwitting and unarmed 'enemy'. In fact the forced collectivisation went well beyond anything contemplated by the Left (Davies, 1980; Nove, 1972: ch. 7; Carr, 1983: ch. 16).

The 'system' which emerged from the industrialisation and collectivisation drive was held up by millions of people throughout the world as a model of socialism. Economically the whole economy was brought under a planning system and market exchange was greatly reduced. The targets of the first five year plan of 1928 were declared to have been fulfilled in four years, and the second five–year plan achieved impressive results. The country was electrified and industrialised and a modern transportation network was created. The Soviet industrial economy expanded massively at the same time as most of the capitalist economies stagnated in the great depression. This expansion was achieved by the forcible holding down of consumption of both the urban workers and the peasants. Much support was generated by the enthusiasm of party members and the use of mass communication, but ultimately it was a policy which relied on terror. Nevertheless, between 1928 and 1938 industrial production almost doubled in a decade in which some countries, e.g. the United States and France, experienced a fall (Bairoch, 1982: 294).

Collectivisation had a devastating effect on agriculture. It is impossible to sustain the argument, advanced by apologists, that the collectivisation campaign was necessary to avert a grain procurement crisis, or that it was an economic prerequisite for the industrialisation drive (Millar, 1976). More than half of the animals in the Soviet Union were destroyed in the early 1930s as peasants refused to take them into the collectives. The final blow to peasant resistance came in the winter of 1932–3, when perhaps ten million died in the famine. Food was deliberately withheld from certain areas which were considered to be politically suspect (Nove, 1989: 75). The control of information was so effective that the world was kept in ignorance of this calamity. The kulaks, numbering perhaps a million households, were not allowed into the collective farms and were deported with little hope of survival (McCauley, 1984: 24). Life for the peasants was deperately oppressive throughout Stalin's era. They were punished by high taxes on private plots, they lacked most of the social benefits available to urban dwellers, and were even denied internal passports, a hangover from Tsarist times. Indeed the level of consumption for all Soviet citizens was dreadfully low in comparison with the West. The economy was ravaged during the Second World War, and despite spectacular advances in production in the immediate postwar period (Munting, 1982: 126; Nove, 1972: ch. 11), there was a consistent neglect of consumer goods. It has been calculated that the standard of living of the Soviet worker did not reach its 1928 level until the early 1960s (Mandel, 1989: 61).

In administrative terms the planning apparatus which developed in the 1920s became a massive empire, and the whole economy functioned on 'material balances' worked out in detail on every item of production, each fixed with its price. In the absence of any other means for establishing 'needs', the planners decided what would be produced under the guidance of the party leadership, and all enterprises obeyed the 'command' to produce (Lane, 1982: ch. 9; Mandel, 1974: ch. 15). Leading positions in the state bureaucracy were filled by

Communist Party members, and the party Secretariat shadowed the work of the state. The party itself permitted no opposition outside or inside its ranks, and after 1934 the vestiges of democratic practices within the party disappeared. At the Seventeenth Party Congress in 1934 Stalin was triumphant, but many of the old Bolsheviks wanted to restrain his powers. It is estimated that Stalin gained 300 fewer votes than Kirov, the Leningrad party boss, in the elections for the Central Committee (Gill, 1990: 404; Conquest, 1990: 33), but such opposition was destined for oblivion. Later in the year Kirov was assassinated, possibly at the behest of Stalin, and for the next four years waves of purges took place, crowned by four major 'show' trials in which virtually the entire old Bolshevik leadership was killed (Medvedev, 1976: chs. 5, 6). Out of the 1966 delegates to the 1934 Congress, 1,108 were murdered, including 70 per cent of the Central Committee (Deutscher, 1974: 495). As early as 1931 Stalin set down the logic which was to prevail until his death and which was displayed in the show trials of the 1934–8 period which Communists the world over dutifully accepted as 'just'. The logic of 'objective' guilt dictated that because Trotsky opposed the regime and so did the world bourgeoisie, Trotsky was an ally of the world bourgeoisie and all those who sympathised with him were guilty of treachery (Stalin, 1970: 18). Trotsky was murdered in Mexico City in 1940.

Victory in the 'great patriotic war' lent a legitimacy to the regime which some thought might lead to an easing of repression, but the labour camps continued to fill and the purges also continued. Most soldiers who had managed to survive German imprisonment received ten year sentences immediately after their 'liberation'. Just before Stalin died another purge was planned on the pretext of an imagined 'doctors' plot' (Deutscher, 1974: 603–5; Conquest, 1990: 462). The party had long ceased to function according to its own statutes. There were only two Congresses in the 22 years which followed the fateful 1934 Congress. The Central Committee hardly ever met and the Politburo tended to function through individual meetings with Stalin rather than as a properly established committee (Löwenhardt, 1982: 33).

Soviet society was transformed by the industrialisation drive. In 1926 the USSR had a population of 147 million of which 18 per cent were urban dwellers, while in 1951 the population of the enlarged country was 182 million, of whom 40 per cent lived in towns (Munting, 1982: 168). Illiteracy was virtually a thing of the past by Stalin's death, and millions of people had read nothing else but material approved by the party, which operated a strict censorship. Newspapers and cinema became important means for conveying the party line and developing the 'cult' of worshiping of Stalin. All cultural products were controlled and even ordered by the party. 'Socialist realism' in art required artists to produce hortatory pictures of heroic workers looking proud and strong with the red flags in the background. Composers were ordered to eschew modern music and to produce 'uplifting' and positive works. Poets were told to avoid 'self-indulgent' themes of love and instead honour the working efforts of the people. Two of Russia's greatest poets, Sergei Yesenin and Vladimir Mayakovsky, committed suicide, while another, Osip Mandelstam, died in the camps after sending a satirical poem to Stalin. Scientific life was also strictly controlled according to political decisions.

The ideological edicts of Stalin became mandatory for communist party members throughout the world. Marxism was transformed from a critical–dialectical theory into a simplistic dogma. The theoretical basis of the second revolution was the doctrine of 'socialism in one country', first touted by Stalin late in 1924, although earlier in the year he had stated quite clearly that socialism in one country was not possible (Stalin, 1970a: 18, cf Stalin, 1970b: 9; Trotsky, 1967: appendix 2). The idea that socialism could be built in a single country was anathema to the ideas of Marx and Lenin, who had both stressed the universal scope of capitalism and the need to overcome it internationally. The idea that socialism could be built in a country in which the working class comprised a small minority was preposterous. But as an inspirational slogan it was far more positive than the position of the Left, which continued to rely on international salvation at a time when there were limited prospects for it. The theory of 'socialism in one country' was an expression of the contradictory position dictated by the isolation and backwardness of the first 'workers state'. When Stalin declared that socialism had been achieved in the Soviet Union in 1936 on the basis of the abolition of private productive property, the world was asked to accept that socialism involved no political freedom, no legal protections, coercive labour practices, abject poverty and complete cultural conformity.

What were the alternatives to Stalinism? Apologists have argued that the industrialisation drive was necessary to win the war, and that food supplies to the cities could only be assured by destroying the independent peasantry. The enormous damage done to agriculture makes a nonsense of the second argument, and the first argument conveniently forgets the inept war preparations of Stalin. The purges destroyed most of the officer corps of the Soviet army and navy, some 40,000 in all (Nove, 1989: 49, 86–7), and when the Red Army attacked Finland in 1939 it was initially repulsed with heavy losses. Stalin's faith in the German–Soviet pact of 1938 was so naive that the Soviet defences were not ready for the German offensive, and the air force was destroyed on the ground. Soviet rule was so unpopular in parts of the country that there was little resistance to the Germans, particularly in the Ukraine. Much of the country's industrial plant was destroyed as the Germans advanced towards Leningrad and Moscow (Munting, 1982: 114–8).

The NEP had been highly successful in regenerating economic life and meeting basic material requirements. It could have been extended, but the policy was more likely to encourage growth in light industry rather than the huge capital projects undertaken after 1928. Bukharin's programme was economically viable, for many of the problems experienced in marketing food in the late 1920s could have been avoided through better macro–economic management (Millar, 1976). The NEP was not socialist but it had succesfully brought about the recovery of the economy. The policy of the Left favoured industrialisation and the encouragment of collectivisation but was less convincing about how this could be achieved, apart from highly graduated taxation (Trotsky, 1973: ch. 3). But either programme was feasible, and all the Bolsheviks were well aware of the need to defend the country, especially Trotsky, founder of the Red Army. The claim that Stalin's policies helped the Soviet war effort is groundless, and there were viable alternatives to Stalin's policy which would have left the country in better shape to withstand the German attack. In practice, however, Stalin was in power because the party of 1928 was very much his own creation.

Given the minority position which the Bolsheviks held in the country as a whole, even at the height of their popularity in late 1917, they could only have held power exclusively by using undemocratic methods. In keeping with their mistrust of other socialist groups, they showed little enthusiasm for a broad coalition with the Left Social Revolutionaries and Mensheviks, despite the fact that the elections for the Constituent Assembly displayed a massive popular support for a socialist programme. There was a major difference, however, between the authoritarianism of Lenin's day and the unremitting terror of the Stalin years (Golubovic, 1981; Gerratana, 1977). Debates in areas of cultural, economic and scientific life were open and forceful in the early NEP period, but this openness decreased as the power of the party bureaucracy increased from 1921 onwards. The centralisation of political power had proceeded in stages, beginning with the dissolution of the Constituent Assembly, continuing with the ban on opposition parties and the ban on factions, and finally resulting in terror against frequently imagined opposition to the leadership within the Party itself. Stalin presided over a world of blind obedience and terroristic social control. It was a nightmare world in which its architects were themselves devoured by their creation, in which crushing conformity reduced the individual to 'a million divided by a million' (Koestler, 1979: 204).

Stalin created an image of socialism which millions around the world followed. It flattered the workers even though the workers were denied any power in decision making. The worker was portrayed as a heroic figure, capable of mastering nature and creating a new world. The omniscient party could use its collective intellect to plan production and conquer all material problems. At a time when the capitalist countries were in the throes of the most serious crisis of the capitalist system, the immense growth of the Soviet Union was a living proof of the superiority of the planned, state–owned economy. Sympathisers in the West saw it as an alternative to a decaying capitalism and the only power capable of standing up to fascism.

KHRUSHCHEV AND DE-STALINISATION

Stalin died in March 1953 and was succeeded by Malenkov as Prime Minister in charge of economic policy, and Khrushchev as party leader. Within two years Malenkov's position as supremo in economic affairs was captured by Khrushchev, taking advantage of economic uncertainties caused by Malenkov's 'new course', and using his control over the party apparatus to good effect. Khrushchev shook the Communist world with his 'secret speech' at the Twentieth Party Congress in 1956, when he denounced many of the crimes of Stalin and supplied details of the executions and imprisonments that had taken place. It is possible to interpret this startling intervention as a device to secure power by relieving the higher strata of the party of the fear of oppression, of purging it of fear and guilt in order to renew its morale. In his selection of Stalin's crimes he focused on the extent to which the party itself was a major victim, without calling into question the policy switch of 1928-9 or rehabilitating Trotsky or Bukharin (Medvedev, 1982: 88–91).

It has been estimated that in 1956-7 up to 8 million people returned from the camps (Medvedev & Medvedev, 1977: 19–20). These years of 'the thaw' were years of relief and hope at home, but the limitations of the process of de–Stalinisation were made brutally clear in foreign policy. When the Hungarian leader Imre Nagy declared that Hungary would adopt a multi–party system the Soviets sent in the tanks to overthrow him and install a puppet regime. Nagy was executed two years later. Thousands of party members in other parts of the world resigned in disillusionment after the invasion of Hungary. Their departure weakened the anti–Stalinist ranks, but the leaderships of most parties followed Khrushchev in admitting some of the 'errors' of the past. However, when Khrushchev stepped up his attacks on Stalin, the Albanians and the Chinese denounced Khrushchev as a revisionist. Although there was to be no letting go of the buffer states secured by Stalin's post–war policy, Soviet supremacy over the entire communist world could no longer be taken for granted.

Could Khrushchev's renunciation of the Stalinist past have led to a thorough reform of the system which Stalin had bequeathed? The answer revolves around two related issues. First, was it possible to modernise the economic system to make it competitive with the West in productivity and the quality of goods? Khrushchev promised that the Soviet Union would outstrip the United States in economic terms by 1970 (Crouch, 1989: 44). Second, could the political and administrative system be reformed in such a way as to encourage participation and motivation in the absence of terroristic methods? Again Khrushchev recognised this goal, promising that 'communism', the ideal of a self–regulated stateless society, would be achieved by 1980. In reality the economic position of the Soviet Union was at a crossroads. The command economy established under Stalin operated from a central planning commission which set targets for every aspect of economic activity, and these targets were processed through ministries and then through enterprises. The command system became less efficient as economic activity grew more varied and the number of goods and services grew into millions rather than thousands. The problems of coordination were immense, for deliveries ordered by one ministry had to be matched by goods from another ministry. Managers had a vested interest in underestimating the capacity of their enterprises so that they could be given low targets to achieve. As long as the terror existed there was good reason to avoid shirking, but when it was lifted the structural inefficiencies became more obvious. Khrushchev attempted to remedy the problems by taking power from the Ministries and handing it to regional economic councils, but the same problems were simply replicated on a different level, and new problems arose when it came to inter–regional production and trade. The administrative turmoil involved was immense, upsetting the stability craved by all bureaucracies, and this irked the leading State officials. This sweeping reform was proposed, discussed, and implemented in less than six months in 1957 (Löwenhardt, 1981: 40–3). Although the number of economic councils was cut by more than half in 1960 the reform was not successful, and it was clear by 1958 that economic targets were not being met (Nove, 1972: 354–9).

Khrushchev neither challenged the operation of the planned economy at the micro level nor paid sufficient attention to the possibilities of revolutionising the planning system itself. Towards the end of his period in office selected factories were permitted to adjust production, find their own outlets and set their own bonuses. Following the ideas of the economist Liberman, these reforms were introduced after Khrushchev's removal in 1964 (Munting, 1982: ch. 7). But as long as prices were not determined by the market and the State supplied everything, there were limits to what improvements could be made. The possibility of economic renewal was hindered by the political control of science that had prevailed under Stalin. The work of Leonid Kantorovitch, winner of the Nobel Prize in 1973, illustrates this point. He was a mathematical economist whose insights could have led to the early use of computer programming in economic planning. He began his major work, Economic Calculations for the Better Use of Resources, before the Second World War, but as the ideas sounded similar to those of the 'bourgois' Austrian School they were regarded with suspicion and accordingly suppressed. The book was not published until 1959, but the resistance to this work indicates the power of those who had a vested interest in protecting the old, inefficient methods of command planning (Aganbegyan, 1989: 140–58).

In terms of political change Khrushchev attempted renewal and renovation rather than the sort of changes which might have threatened the power of the party–state bureaucracy. He opened up policy formulation to non–party experts, who were sometimes invited to address the Central Committee, and policy proposals were publicised across the country for comment and amendment. Nonetheless, measures were often pushed through with little consultation or preparation, but there was still far more participation in decision making than in Stalin's time. Party Congresses met regularly (1956, 1959 and 1961) and the Central Committee functioned as a proper executive body. Indeed the Central Committee came to Khrushchev's rescue in 1957, when a group of leaders, worried that Khrushchev had gone too far in his denunciation of Stalin, succeeded in passing a Politburo motion supporting his replacement by eight votes to three (Medvedev, 1982: 116–20). Khrushchev insisted that only the Central Committee could take such a decision, and his supporters mobilised well enough to reject the proposal. The 'vanquished' were apparently frightened for their lives, but no drastic action was taken against them apart from the loss of high office. The defeat of what was termed the 'anti–party' group enabled Khrushchev to fill the Politburo with his own nominees, and this emboldened him to try to revitalise party life and shake the complacency of time–serving office holders. Two reforms were attempted, and they almost certainly lost Khrushchev some support in the higher party echelons (Medvedev & Medvedev, 1977: 152; Medvedev, 1982: ch. 17). The first was adopted in 1962 and required the rotation of party officers at all levels, one third of each committee standing down at each 'election'. This would help more members gain experience of office, but it was a distinct threat to long–serving Central Committee members. The other reform involved splitting the regional party committees into industrial and agricultural sectors. Again this diminished the power of existing office holders and caused administrative confusion. Both reforms were abolished after his removal.

In the light of spectacular changes which occurred in the Soviet Union under Mikhail Gorbachev, the reforms of the Khrushchev era appear modest. But it must be remembered that the whole society was conditioned to respond to a series of bureaucratic commands and could not easily adjust to the new appeals for lower level initiative. The case of Kantorovitch illustrates the debilitating effects of the strict system of control. A more notable case was that of Trofim Lysenko, who was in charge of agricultural science under Stalin and throughout the Khrushchev period. His theories fitted in with a crude Marxist pre–scientific view that genetics was 'bourgeois' and that everything could be environmentally determined. Many of the best scientists in the country lost their jobs in 1948, and the economic cost was enormous (Medvedev, 1971). Within the political structure itself, the practice of Stalinism bred 'survivors' rather than initiators. Stalin's most likely successor in 1948 was Voznesensky, who had been head of Gosplan, the planning body, for ten years, and could take the credit for the successful management of the war economy. He was the most appropriate person to undertake the management of the planned economy, but he was shot in 1949 with barely a pretext for the sentence (Medvedev, 1976: 481–2;

Deutscher, 1974: 598–9). While such practices ceased under Khrushchev, the entire political elite of his period in power had lived through such terror, and were conditioned to be cautious and secretive rather than innovative and open.

De–Stalinisation promised more than it was able to deliver. The lifting of the terror was an immense relief, and the denunciation of many of the crimes of the past gave many communists the hope that they could reconstruct a better society. A generation of party workers developed ideas of a socialism based on cooperation rather than coercion, among them Mikhail Gorbachev. Tremendous optimism was released when the world's first space satellite was sent into orbit in 1957, and when Yuri Gagarin became the first man in space in 1961. Culturally the transformation was enormous, symbolised by the publication in 1962 of Solzhenitsyn's harrowing account of life in the labour camps, *One Day in the Life of Ivan Denisovitch* (Medvedev, 1982: 134–6), although the liberalisation was not complete, and did not extend to the renowned novelist and poet Boris Pasternak (Yevtushenko, 1991: 330–44). Khrushchev fulminated against modern art, but did not consider that it needed to be suppressed. This toleration disappeared shortly after his ouster in 1964, the closure signalled by the sentencing of two novelists, Daniel and Sinyavsky, to five years hard labour in 1966 (Yevstushenko, 1991: 330–44).

Several factors contributed to Khrushchev's dismissal by votes taken in the Politburo and Central Committee. The economic and party reforms were unpopular with party and state officials, and economic targets were not being met. The climbdown over the Cuban nuclear missile crisis of October 1962 was unpopular with the military, who were also suspicious of Khrushchev's view that in the nuclear age there was no longer the same need for massive armies. Khrushchev was pensioned off and the party dictatorship reverted to a more stable and comfortable routine, initially under a collective leadership of Brezhnev, Kosygin and Podgorny, and later under Brezhnev's undisputed command. Khrushchev was condemned by the new leaders for developing a new 'cult of personality', the very accusation he had levelled at Stalin. The new regime began as it meant to continue, refusing to make public the political reasons for the change and forbidding discussion of the matter at party meetings (Medvedev, 1982: ch. 21). If Khrushchev was able to resist the attempt to overthrow him in 1957, why did he fail in 1964? Policy failures in economic planning and adventurism in foreign policy were significant, and there was a loss of support from key groups in the party apparatus, particularly the KGB (Tompson, 1991; Andrew & Gordievsky, 1991: 482). They did not want the system 'opened up' in ways which might damage their own power. The strength of this 'conservative' apparatus was the decisive barrier to real reform.

The Brezhnev years represented a consolidation of the power system through an accommodation of interests and a tight control of dissent. The economic reforms undertaken in 1965 gave a limited amount of power to enterprise managers, but there was no alteration of the price setting mechanism and the state apparatus maintained its monopoly on supplies, so the reforms were by no means fundamental. Abel Aganbegyan, economic advisor to Mikhail Gorbachev from 1985 till 1989, stated that when he and Kantorovitch met Kosygin in 1965 they emphasised the importance of reforming the price system to facilitate an effective economic reform, but Kosygin could not understand the relevance of prices (Aganbegyan, 1989: 151). More radical reform was ruled out for fear of offending the party–state elite, for this became the era of 'stability of cadres', in which the positions and privileges of the elite were preserved and extended (Sakwa, 1989: 86). Indeed corruption became common but it often served as an illegal mechanism for overcoming supply bottlenecks, or filling the gaps left by the inadequacy of the system of planning by material balances (Rutland, 1990: 171). The foreign policy of détente opened up the foreign market and the Soviet Union began to buy in technological assistance from the West to finance the expansion of consumption (Frank, 1980: 185–94).

Until the late 1970s it seemed that the Brezhnev leadership was able to satisfy the important groups in society. The military gained vastly improved resources which brought them approaching parity with the United States for the first time (Holloway, 1978). The real incomes of workers rose impressively, far more so than professional groups, and the shortening of the working week and the increased availability of consumer goods secured the compliance of the working class (Crouch, 1989: 53). Their 'official' representatives, the trade unions, stayed entirely loyal to the leadership, opposing the workers in 68 out of 70 disputes in the 1970s (Kagarlitsky, 1990a: 310). Although there was a tight control on dissent, professional groups such as lawyers and scientists were brought into policy–making through the standing commissions of the Supreme Soviet (White, 1986: 58–9; Hough, 1983). In agriculture, some of the restrictions on private plots imposed by Khrushchev were lifted, but results continued to disappoint, often largely because of lack of storage or processing facilities (Nove, 1978). The failure to improve the infrastructure of the country was one of the greatest economic weaknesses of the Brezhnev period.

The Brezhnev regime consolidated privilege among the party elite while apathy and cynicism developed in society at large. According to Kagarlitsky, the development of mass consumer goods, especially televisions, in the late 1960s and early 1970s, brought 'a new style of life, more akin to the West's' (Kagarlitsky, 1990a: 288), but it also raised expectations which were difficult to satisfy without a fundamental overhaul of the whole system of economic management. Yet Brezhnev's policy had strengthened this conservative pillar of Soviet society, and it proved more difficult to shift than Mikhail Gorbachev imagined. In Khrushchev's period in office it was by no means evident that the planned economy could not be reformed to match Western levels of productivity. In the Brezhnev years it became clear that the economy could not match Western performance in productivity or quality. Military expenditure, which had been reduced by Khrushchev, was expanded and became an enormous drain on the Soviet economy. The productivity gap widened considerably from the late 1970s. In the West the downturn marked by 1974 led to a renewed intensity in competitiveness. The mass application of new technology and the disarming of organised labour by the spread of mass unemployment ensured that despite reduced growth rates, productivity increased enormously. The command economies were completely unable to emulate this development.

GORBACHEV

A new constitution of the Soviet Union was adopted in 1977 which boasted that it was a 'society of true democracy' (Lane, 1982: 554), but article six guaranteed the 'leading and guiding force' of the CPSU in all public organisations. There was no provision for an open and regular leadership succession, and Brezhnev, having made himself President and Chairman of the Defence Council as well as General Secretary, protected his power by making sure that conservative and reformist tendencies were evenly balanced in the Politburo. He was virtually incapacitated for the final years of his life, but he held office until his death at the age of 76 in 1982, when he was succeeded by Yuri Andropov, aged 68, formerly head of the KGB. Andropov attacked corruption with punitive zeal, but when he died in 1984 the party leaders sought a quieter life by choosing as successor Konstantin Chernenko, aged 72, a Brezhnev disciple. He died in 1985 and was succeeded by Mikhail Gorbachev, who, at the age of 54, represented a new generation, the first leader to be born after the Russian Revolution. He reverted to the Andropov policy of changing the personnel of the leading party cadres before embarking on an escalating programme of economic, political and cultural reform soon to be known throughout the world by their Russian names, *perestroika*, or restructuring, and *glasnost*, or openness (White, 1990: ch. 1; Sakwa, 1990: 11–13).

The economy was not in ruins, but it was stagnant to the point at which breakdowns in supply were becoming frequent and more damaging. It was calculated by Aganbegyan that there had been no growth of per capita GNP during the 1981–5 plan period, with a decline in production in many sectors, including transport and agriculture (Aganbegyan, 1988: 89). The effects of this stagnation were visible, with low rates of housebuilding despite massive investment, poor diet, and declining standards in health and education (White, 1990: 86–8). Gorbachev's response in the first two years appeared to follow Andropov's, with an emphasis on investment in more capital intensive methods of production to increase productivity. Most of the new investment went on re–equiping the capital goods industries (Arnot, 1988; Rutland, 1990). A new body was set up to improve quality control. Prime Minister Nikolai Ryzhkov's speech at the 27th party congress in 1986 promised that the productivity of Soviet workers would exceed the world average by the year 2000 (Sakwa, 1990: 270; Aslund, 1991: 39–47). Along with the usual exhortations against corruption and laziness there was a campaign against vodka consumption which in fact severely hit state revenues (Aslund, 1991: 78–80). When this approach proved no more successful than that of his predecessors, moves were · made to decentralise the management of the economy. Small family businesses were allowed by law in 1987, but they were subject to heavy local taxation and legal control on hiring and firing labour (Arnot, 1988: 4); these 'cooperatives', as they were misleadingly titled, were very unpopular (Mandel, 1990: 262). After 60 years of official anti–capitalist ideology, the absence of enthusiasm for entrepeneurship was hardly surprising.

The centrepiece of the economic reform was the Law on State Enterprise, which came into effect at the beginning of 1988. It was intended to turn the majority of enterprises over to a 'profit and loss' system, with loss–making enterprises going to the wall if necessary. Worker–participation in electing managers was to be encouraged. Yet an examination of the Law shows many ambiguities or contradictions, reflecting the success of various 'interests' in different areas of concern rather than producing a coherent guide to action (Simon, 1990; Aslund, 1991: 107–8). There was to be less power for Gosplan, the state planning body, but the proper mechanisms for ensuring a self–regulating decentralised exchange system did not exist to replace its functions. There was still no thorough reform of the price system, and Gorbachev admitted at the 19th Party Conference in the summer of 1988 that this was holding back the whole reform process (Sakwa, 1990: 276). Without it, the calculation of profits and losses was unreliable, and there were so many enterprises declared to be making losses that it became impossible to allow them to go into liquidation.

The promised transfer to market prices never arrived, and the projected date when the rouble would become a convertible world currency was constantly postponed. There was no 'half–way house' between the command economy and the market economy, and the problem of money was central (Ticktin, 1991: 21–2). If prices were to reflect costs of production and vary according to supply and demand, the rouble could be convertible and the Soviet Union fully integrated into the world economy. But if that was to happen then the whole administrative panoply of the planned economy would be swept away. The bulk of the 18 million Soviet bureaucrats had a short–term functional interest in opposing reform. In order to overcome this opposition the leadership would have had to persuade sections of the bureaucracy that there would be a future role for them in a different sort of system, whether as administrators in regulatory bodies, in research institutes, or in new management functions which would develop with market mechanisms. Enterprise managers were not necessarily time–serving conduits in the planning mechanism, and there were undoubtedly many who welcomed the promise of decentralised decision–making.

The failure to mobilise support in key administrative groups was decisive, for there was little social basis for reform anywhere else. Professional and cultural workers certainly welcomed the liberalisation, but they were unable to do much about the condition of the economy. The workers had much to lose in the short term if subsidies were lifted and enterprises allowed to go to the wall. The twin spectres of high prices and unemployment were not offset by the promise of worker participation and the right to strike, while the argument that in the long term the reforms would lead to a rise in living standards was treated with understandable scepticism. Workers staged large–scale strikes, particularly the strike of 400,000 miners in 1989. It was not clear whether the strike was directed against the ideas emanating from the Gorbachev leadership or the continued implementation of 'ministerial' management (Mandel, 1990; Friedgut & Siegelbaum, 1990; Kagarlitsky, 1990b: ch. 11). The Soviet government talked incessantly about radical economic reform but did not enact it.

The economic crisis came to a head in the winter of 1990–1, when food supplies to the cities became irregular. Since 1985 the budget deficit had quadrupled, the foreign debt had doubled to 50 billion dollars, and low growth had turned into negative growth (Aslund, 1991: ch. 7). The centrally planned economy had seen its coordinating centre weakened without being replaced by market mechanisms, and the situation was seriously worsened by the breakdown of inter–republican trade. The proposed shift to a market economy, based on the plan for a 500 day transition written by Stanislav Shatalin in the summer of 1990, was suspended, and two of the leading liberal supporters of Gorbachev, Alexander Yakovlev and Yevgeny Primakov, resigned in January 1991. Perhaps the most serious problem was the dreadful state of the infrastructure, which ensured that over half the produce simply did not find its way into retail outlets. Faced with this crisis, Gorbachev turned to the only groups who had the authority to deliver a life–saving package, the bureaucracy, the KGB and the Army (Aslund, 1991: 222). This 'retreat' contributed greatly to a sharp loss of public confidence in Gorbachev, as recorded in nationwide opinion polls (White, 1991: 16). But Gorbachev insisted that these were emergency measures, and talk about price–reform resumed in the spring of 1991.

By 1991 Gorbachev's chief difficulty was in preserving the political integrity of the Soviet Union, and he continued to waver over the pace of projected market reforms. For five years he had supported Ryzhkov as Prime Minister despite his poor record. He was replaced by Valentin Pavlov in January 1991, but Pavlov had worked with Gosplan between 1979 and 1986 and was not inclined to dismantle the command economy. He was one of the leaders of the abortive coup in August 1991 which attempted to strip Gorbachev of the Presidency and restore the command economy backed by force (Odom, 1991).

The inability to devise and implement a plan was linked to the pivotal role in the running of the economy played by the CPSU, and Gorbachev's unwavering loyalty to it in its existing form proved to be his undoing. When Gorbachev came to power in 1985, those watching for the seriousness of his reforming intentions looked for an initiative on the continued presence of Soviet troops in Afghanistan, the possible reintroduction of some of the intra-party reforms attempted by Khrushchev, and greater tolerance in culture and information. In fact the changes surpassed all these expectations and went beyond the controllable 'limited democracy' envisaged in Gorbachev's speeches and writings from the 1985-89 period (Gorbachev, 1988). Political 'clubs' began to proliferate throughout the Soviet Union from 1986 on, including nationalist groups in most of the Republics (Afanasyev, 1988: 85). Yet until early 1990 Gorbachev insisted that there would be no multi-party system. It was the sort of compromise briefly attempted in Czechoslovakia in 1968, but the political openness which exploded was too dynamic to be controlled. The openness quickly spread to the party itself, with rivalries between the conservatives and reformers scarcely concealed.

The conservatives retained much of their strength at Central Committee level because the 1986 Party Congress met before the reformers had been able to secure a comfortable majority. Gorbachev did not always support the reformers, most notably when he accepted the dismissmal of Boris Yeltsin, the Moscow party leader, in November 1987. The rift in the party became official in January 1990 when the first faction for sixty years, the Democratic Platform, was launched. The Platform berated the leadership for blocking perestroika, but when it failed to achieve success at the 28th Congress in the summer of 1990 the decision was taken to leave the CPSU, and the founding Congress of the Republican Party of Russia took place in November 1990. The emergence of parties had become possible when article six of the constitution was repealed in March 1990. Elections to the new Congress of Peoples Deputies in March 1989 had revealed the extent of popular hostility to 'old guard' communists, yet Gorbachev never unreservedly sided with the reformers within the CPSU, seeking to maintain an impossible unity.

The control of formal political decision-making was moved away from the CPSU following the election of the Congress of Peoples Deputies. The Congress had 2,250 Deputies, 750 of whom occupied places 'reserved' for the CPSU and other official bodies. In turn they elected a Supreme Soviet of 542 members. The Congress was the supreme legislative body and the Supreme Soviet was a full-time working body. The spring election of 1990 to republican and local soviets created working local councils which were no longer dominated by the

CPSU. However, the existence of rival and frequently hostile power centres had a disabling effect. The CPSU was still strong enough to obstruct reform (Sakwa, 1990: 194). Although millions of members resigned in 1990, it still had over 14 million members at the time of the coup. The new legislative bodies gave the Soviet Union a more democratic system than ever before, but the absence of proper party politics, or agreed parameters within which disagreements might be accommodated, persuaded Gorbachev to increase his own powers as President. He had been elected President by the Congress of Peoples Deputies in 1989, but now many of his original supporters grew worried that this was creating a new form of dictatorship.

A major factor, then, in the obstruction of reform was the tenacity of the conservatives within the party–state hierarchy, defending the *nomenklatura* system of political–administrative control as long as the Soviet Union continued to exist. An even greater factor in paralysing the reform process was the explosion of nationalist sentiment which swept across the USSR in 1988 (Sakwa, 1990: ch. 6; White, 1990: ch. 5). The Union had been put together by force and held together by coercion, and almost seventy years of frustration was expressed with uncompromising vehemence. The Baltic republics claimed independence, as they had been forcibly integrated in 1939 in accordance with a secret clause in the Soviet–German Treaty. Gorbachev tried to prevaricate by suggesting procedures for gradual secession. The nationalist tide extended to most of the other republics, and there was intense fighting in the enclave of Nagorno–Karabakh, where control was disputed by Armenia and Azerbaijan. Gorbachev sought to defuse these nationalist sentiments by promising greater autonomy within a looser federation, but few republics saw any benefit in submitting to rule from Moscow. The national rivalries disrupted trade within the Soviet Union and fuelled the economic crisis.

The political crisis finally came to a head with the coup in August 1991, led by the Vice–President, Gennadiy Yanayev, who headed a State Emergency Committee staffed by politicians who had all been promoted by Gorbachev. The leaders who defied the usurpers were Yeltsin, who had been elected President of Russia in June 1990, and the Mayor of St. Petersburg, Anatoli Sobchak. Both men had left the CPSU in July 1990, and both were prepared to accept the dissolution of the party and of the Soviet Union itself. Only after the collapse of the coup did Gorbachev resign from the leadership of the CPSU, which was then suspended. Shortly afterwards the leaders of the various Soviet Republics agreed to dissolve the Union, and in December 1991 a new Commonwealth of Independent States was set up to coordinate economic affairs between the former Republics, with the exception of the Baltic states. Gorbachev was stranded, without a state or a party to preside over. The new countries of the former Soviet Union were propelled along a free market path by the price liberalisation declared by President Yeltsin in January 1992. Its first year brought predictable economic and social disruption, with very few of the promised signals of stability or recovery.

Gorbachev admitted in 1991 that he had erred in failing to synchronise his reforms (White, 1991: 16). It appears that he wished to adopt a marketised economy with safeguards such as subsidies on basic goods, and that he favoured public ownership of various sorts to privatisation. The hardliners in the party opposed this. Their opposition can be interpreted either as a crude defence of vested self-interest or a principled opposition to the return of capitalism. The liberal reformers wanted a rapid transformation to the market, accepting the pain in the short term and also accepting the possible break-up of the Union. One option did not appear to have much support, and that was the Chinese option of market reform and political dictatorship. As long as his power-base resided in the CPSU, Gorbachev was obliged to persuade the leading party echelons that their interests could be protected in a radically reformed economy. Alternatively, he could make clear his differences with his opponents, legalise either the existence of factions or the existence of political parties, and dare the hardliners to place the issues to the vote or go down the path of illegality. Support for radical candidates was very strong in the elections to the Congress of Peoples Deputies in 1989, and in the republic and local elections of 1989-90 (Sakwa, 1990: 134-42). Gorbachev's attachment to the united CPSU and his opposition to a multi-party system placed him in an impossible position, a victim of what the poet Yevtushenko (1989: vi) called 'fatal half measures':

'With every half-effective

          half measure

half the people

          remain half pleased.

The half sated

          are half hungry.

The half free

          are half enslaved.'

The break-up of the country, the collapse of its economy and the improverishment of its people, as well as the nationalist fighting which broke out in Georgia, Moldova, Azerbaijan and Armenia, added up to a disastrous conclusion to a period which started with such great hopes.

CONCLUSION

The huge bureaucratic monolith created in Stalin's time proved itself resistant to attempted reform. Its power was so entrenched and its scope so universal that fundamental economic and political reform required two important preconditions, first, coherence, and second, the mobilisation of considerable social support. Khrushchev's attempts at reform were relatively mild but altogether too much for the party–state elite. If anything the situation for Gorbachev was more difficult. True, he did not have to succeed Stalin and the country was eager for some sort of reform, but the bureaucracy was even more entrenched after almost two decades of the Brezhnev policy of 'stability of cadres'. In both cases the reforms were neither coherent nor supported by major social forces. It is perhaps not surprising after decades of authoritarian rule that social forces have expressed themselves in negative ways. However, in the case of Gorbachev we can only speculate what support he might have generated if he had distanced himself from the opponents of reform and formalised the political differences between reformers and the 'old guard'.

In locating the origin of the Soviet system with Stalin, and in particular with the creation of the command economy after 1929, there is a tendency to exempt Lenin, Trotsky, and the 'old' Bolshveiks from criticism, and to defend the liberational ideals of the Russian Revolution. In Trotsky's phrase, Stalinism 'betrayed' the Revolution. However, the smoothness of Stalin's accession to dictatorship should draw attention to the weaknesses in Bolshevik practice. It is true that Lenin called for his dismissal, but this demand completely failed to address the problem of the institutional processes which were choking all political life (Deutscher, 1974: 250–5). The question of democracy is of crucial importance. Both Lenin and Trotsky had little respect for parliamentary democracy. Did they have a model of a superior form of democracy? First Trotsky and later Lenin praised the model of soviet democracy which first emerged in the Russian Revolution of 1905, and which appeared to offer the advantages of greater accountability and less bureaucracy. But soviet democracy was a spontaneous development in an emergency situation. When institutionalised, how would it differ from a parliamentary system? The soviets initially comprised of delegates from factories and military units, but this form of functional representation excluded many people, including the unemployed, the retired, and those who worked at home. In fact the soviets soon ceased to have any independent political power, and in Stalin's time the representatives were selected from approved lists without competitive election. It is apparent that the soviets were favoured because they gave a disproportionate strength to the urban areas where the Bolsheviks were strongest, but this relegation of the interests of the vast majority of the population could not be justified on egalitarian or emancipatory grounds. The workers could not speak for all the peasants any more than the Bolsheviks could speak for all the workers. The Marxist idea of 'self emancipation' was flatly contradicted.

The NEP was an opportunity to compromise, to buy time and to earn some legitimacy within the country, but it was jettisoned in favour of the drive towards 'socialism in one country'. The alternative of gradual development with the restoration of some political and social liberties was rejected in favour of a frenzied push to catch up and surpass the leading capitalist countries. This continued to be the aim of successive leaderships, but they found it difficult to maintain high net growth and even more difficult to raise productivity to anything close to Western standards. The Soviet Union ended its life as a semi-peripheral country in the world economy, just as Russia had been in 1913 (Arrighi, 1991: 52-7).

9 The Failure of Reform Communism

The defining features of the Soviet administrative and economic system were 'exported' to the countries of its 'sphere of influence' after 1948. Absolute political power was wielded by communist parties, organised as hierarchical monoliths under the principle of democratic centralism. State terrorism was used against any potential opposition, and even against party members in the Stalin years. In those countries where other parties were permitted a formal existence in 'national front' coalitions they were completely subservient to the wishes of the communist leaders. Independent pressure group activity was forbidden. Industry and trade were brought into full public ownership under a central plan, and agriculture was collectivised, except in Poland (Lovenduski & Woodall, 1987: ch. 4). The economic emphasis was on rapid industrial growth and the fulfilment of plan targets, as it had been in the Soviet Union since 1928. While this could claim some success, concerns for relatively low levels of productivity, poor quality of goods and restricted consumption were expressed by economists as early as the 1950s, and the reform debate was ongoing in one or other of the states. As political power was directly and inextricably linked to economic power in these countries, the question of political reform was never far away.

In this chapter we shall examine three attempts to reform the model. The first attempt occurred in Yugoslavia after the split between Stalin and Tito in 1948. Although the single–party system was retained, the Yugoslav model of workers' self–management was quite different from the politico–economic systems followed by the countries still under Soviet sway. The second example is Hungary, where the Soviet invasion of 1956 was followed by a long period of rule by János Kádár, under whose leadership a major economic reform was undertaken in 1968. It was the boldest attempt by any of the countries in the Soviet 'zone' to introduce market mechanisms into the economy, although it was not accompanied by a political reform. The third example lasted for only a few months, in Czechoslovakia in 1968, when the reform leadership of the Czechoslovak Communist Party embarked on its attempt to introduce 'socialism with a human face', only to see it crushed by the invasion of Warsaw Pact forces. The brevity of the experiment makes it difficult to assess the likely outcome of its unhindered progress, but Czechoslovakia at that moment certainly provided the most favourable conditions for political and economic reform. Most of the communist countries attempted to make their economies more efficient through the use of limited market mechanisms, but these attempts failed to prevent them falling behind the advanced industrial countries in productivity levels, especially after 1974. The communist economies became more integrated into the world economy on terms which reduced them to the hapless debtor status of so many of the world's semi–peripheral states. Was there really no alternative? What implications does their fate have for the claims made by socialists that it is possible to develop a more rational system of economic relations than the capitalist model?

YUGOSLAVIA.

At the time of Yugoslavia's expulsion from the Cominform the country was following the Soviet 'command economy' model (Dyker, 1991: 13–26). In 1950 Tito made the remarkable announcement that the workers were in future to manage their own factories, and the Basic Law on Workers Self–Management was introduced (Wilson, 1980: 68–72). The architects of the new system had strong economic and ideological reasons for the adoption of a system of radically de–centralised power (Djilas, 1969: 157–8). The most obvious economical reason was the blockade imposed by the Soviet Union and its allies, for most of Yugoslavia's trade had been with the Soviet bloc before the rift of 1948, and trade did not resume until 1955 (Bícanić, 1973: ch. 8). Yugoslavia was forced to turn to the West for credits, and the economy required all the stimuli it could get. Ideologically, key politicians such as Djilas and Kardelj were now free to express their revulsion at the degeneration of socialism in the Soviet Union, which Kardelj described as despotic and 'not socialist at all' (McFarlane, 1988: 33). They now had an opportunity to tap a resource which had been unavailable to Russia and most of the other East European countries at the outset of their communist dictatorships – a wide measure of popular support. The extent of this popular support is hotly disputed, and there were no free elections to measure it, but the communists had gained great respect through the success of the Partisans in the war of liberation. In addition to workers' self–management, administrative power was decentralised from Federal to Republican and District level, and although the communists constituted the only party, changes were adopted in 1952 which distinguished the party (henceforward called the League of Communists) from its Soviet–bloc counterparts. It swapped its 'leading role' for a 'guiding role', separated the party from government at local level, reduced party bureaucracy and instigated some degree of internal democracy (Gruenwald, 1983: ch. 3). In comparison with the Soviet Union and its satellites in the dark final years of Stalin's life, Yugoslavia was less coercive and more open in terms of freedom of speech and movement (Wilson, 1980: 77).

The system of workers' councils evolved over two decades. Their legal powers changed greatly over the years, with significant relinquishment of Federal economic and political controls over enterprises occurring in the mid–1960s and again with the 1974 Constitution. In general the councils had between 20 and 120 members, elected annually, with the power to appoint and dismiss directors, who served for four years. The councils decided on annual plans, bonuses, work practices, and they also had the power to veto suggestions from the Federal government on such issues as mergers (Horvat, 1976: chs. 4, 7). Dyker has argued that research on attitudes to the system indicated that workers did not feel 'in control', but on the other hand they strongly supported the ideals behind the system (Dyker, 1991: 53–4). In economic terms the results of the self–managed system appeared impressive until the late 1970s. Rates of growth were remarkably high in the 1950s and remained high in the 1960s and 1970s. Growth tended to be extensive rather than intensive, and productivity growth was slower than most West European economies (Dyker, 1991: 43–5, 92). The drive to increase productivity was clearly not as great as in capitalist economies. This was sharply revealed in the responses to the great oil price rises (1973–82) when the industries of leading western economies lowered their energy intakes by 31 per cent while Yugoslavia's increased their intakes by 1 per cent (Dyker, 1991: 93). Although prices were not set by 'the centre' and a market of sorts existed, the market mechanism was distorted by various forms of collusion, regulation and protection exercised by political and administrative elites and the enterprises themselves. When the world economic crisis came to a head in 1980 it heralded an economic disaster for Yugoslavia. The workers' councils continued in operation until the disintegration of the country, although in the final years the trade unions began to re–emerge as conventional western–style representatives of workers' interests as the powers of the managers were increased (Warner, 1990; McFarlane, 1988: 198, 148–50).

Unlike the states within the Soviet bloc, the elites which wielded power in Yugoslavia were local rather than central, due to the decentralised economic and political system. In 1953 major constitutional amendments declared the aim of the withering away of the state, and local, republican, and federal chambers representing economic producers were created alongside territorial chambers. In 1963 the new constitution set up four functional chambers alongside territorial chambers in all assemblies, established a Constitutional Court, and introduced the rotation of government posts and parliamentary seats. But by the early 1970s the Federal government was virtually immobilised by inter–republican rivalry, and populist nationalism developed, particularly in Croatia. Tito reasserted the central power of the League of Communists with a number of purges, first against the nationalists and then against liberals who had suggested political pluralism (Carter, 1982: 218–24; Wilson, 1980: chs. 15, 16). However, the centrifugal tendencies in the country were acknowledged in the 1974 new constitution, which gave immense power to the Republics. All elections to Republics and the Federation were based on a delegate system rather than by direct election. At Communal and Republican level there were three chambers, one representing citizens in their geographical locations, one representing workers, and one representing 'socio–political groups'. The latter ensured that communists would maintain control. At the Federal level there were two chambers, the Federal Chamber and the Chamber of Republics and Provinces. The nine person Presidency was elected every five years by Republican Assemblies, and it elected a President of the Republic. Despite the use of local referenda and the operation of the principle of recalling delegates, the complexity of the system and the continuing power of the League of Communists led to widespread apathy and hierarchical decision making (Gruenwald, 1983: ch. 7).

The 1974 Constitution left the Federal authorities with limited power (Barrett Brown, 1993: 152–4). Most of its revenues were used to finance the armed forces. Although 'the centre' maintained responsibility for the currency, it was extremely difficult to promote redistributive investment or indicative planning. In 1982 the Central Committee of the League of Communists admitted that it did not have all the details of its foreign debt obligations, because these were entered into separately by republics, or even by enterprises using the services of banks (Burg, 1986: 174). The decentralisation of investment to banks and enterprises had begun in 1965, and the banks increasingly played a decisive role in determining what enterprises could or could not do (Supek, 1979: 258–9). The most notable example of corrupt collusion between bankers, local politicians and enterprise managers was the Agro–Commerc scandal in Bosnia in 1987 when it was discovered that $200 million had been stolen (McFarlane, 1988: 171–2). Political elites ensured that banks lent large amounts to loss–making enterprises to keep them open, a practice which contributed to an inflation figure of 400 per cent by 1989. The material basis for the collapse of Yugoslavia was its inability to overcome the problem of massive indebtedness which developed in the 1970s and which was compounded by balance–of–payments deficits triggered by the oil price rises (Barrett Brown, 1993: 155–6). Yugoslavia's situation was similar to other semi–peripheral countries with markedly different economic systems, such as Brazil, Mexico, and Algeria (Dyker, 1991: 126). The external debt was in the region of $20 billion throughout the 1980s, or over $800 per head. By the late 1980s real incomes had been declining for a decade. There were over a million unemployed, or about 17 per cent of the working population (Lee, 1988: 43). Eighty per cent of them were under 30 and over half were highly skilled or had received higher education (Seroka, 1988: 85). In addition there were about one million Yugoslavs working abroad.

The decentralised system undoubtedly made it more difficult to manage the economic crisis. It magnified regional disparities and caused both relatively rich and relatively poor republics to see independence as a solution (Hashi, 1992). Two major attempts to reform the system, the Kraigher Commission and the Critical Analysis, were ignored. Both criticised the power given to elites because of low participation rates in elections at all levels. The Kraigher Commission argued for stabilisation led by the centre, and although it was adopted in 1983 by the League of Communists and the Federal Parliament, after one wage and price freeze its programme was abandoned (Burg, 1986; Shoup, 1989). The Critical Analysis reported in November 1985. It criticised the failings of the complex system of electing delegates, the way in which legislatures were subordinate to the power of political and financial elites, and the lack of coooperation and coordination between assemblies. It suggested accountability standards, 'opening up' of the socio–political chambers, and direct elections for the Federal Assembly, but although the Federal Presidency suggested constitutional changes along these lines, inter–Republican rivalry produced an impasse (Seroka, 1988). Perhaps the 'last chance' for agreement on economic reform came when Federal Prime Minister Ante Marković succeeded in stabilising prices in 1990, but the 'solution' was destroyed by the theft of $730 million from the Yugoslav National Bank by the Serbian government in January 1991. This was a prelude to the collapse of the federation.

Opinions differ on the extent to which the system of self–management gave real power to the workers. Pavlowitch dismisses it as a 'charade of workers' participation, effectively controlled by political coteries' (Pavlowitch, 1988: 152). Yet other writers such as Gruenwald (1983), Carter (1982) and Pateman (1970) have considered that the system at least offered the possibility of a development towards democratic socialism. It is clear that the domination of important decision making in economic and political matters by the communists and other technocratic elites acted as a major obstacle to democratisation. And although Yugoslavia may have enjoyed a greater degree of freedom than the countries of the Soviet bloc, the Yugolslav communists were reluctant to relinquish their monopoly of political power. The collapse of communism elsewhere in Eastern Europe led to elections in the various republics, a process which precipitated the break–up of the federation. The self–management system led to some noteworthy contributions to socialist theory from the Praxis Group, whose work became internationally respected. The ideals on which the system was premised served as a springboard for the development of critical analyses of the diffusion of power in society and discussions about advancing genuine participatory democracy (Marković, 1982; Crocker, 1983). However, the inter–communal carnage which has accompanied the disintegration of Yugoslavia has removed such considerations from the political agenda.

HUNGARY

Following the Soviet invasion of 1956, communist power in Hungary was restored under the leadership of Kádár and a reconstructed party, the Socialist Workers Party (HSWP). There was widespread repression against those who had fought for national independence, involving an estimated 2,000 executions, including the former Prime Minister, Imre Nagy (Heinrich, 1986: 39; Molnár, 1990). The agricultural sector was collectivised between 1959 and 1962, and around that time the leadership adopted more liberal and reconciliatory policies which culminated in the New Economic Mechanism, which came into effect in January 1968 (Berend, 1990; Nove, 1983: 123–32). In some respects this radical attempt to decentralise economic decision taking became a prototype for other communist regimes to study. It did not involve substantial fundamental political reforms, although in the discussions leading up to the adoption and early implementation of the reform a considerable freedom of expression was granted to the humanist Marxist writers of the Budapest School, followers of philosopher Geörgy Lukács. Agnes Heller, Ferenc Feher, Mihaly Vajda, Geörgy Markus and Mária Markus published works calling for the empowerment of citizens in all aspects of life (Hegedus, Heller, Markus & Vajda, 1976; Hegedus, 1976). However, when some of the most radical elements of the economic reform were rescinded in 1972 and 1973, the Hungarian authorities deemed such critical work to be unacceptable. Many academics were dismissed from their posts and encouraged to emigrate, among them Feher, Heller and Győrgy Markus, who in 1983 published a withering analysis of East European societies, *Dictatorship Over Needs*, which ruled out any possibility that the system could be reformed from within (Feher, Heller & Markus, 1983).

The New Economic Mechanism ended the central specification of production and the central allocation of material inputs. It replaced detailed annual plans with five year indicative plans, and declared profitablity to be the chief objective in economic life. The price system was reformed in such a way as to suggest a gradual transition to world market prices, but this involved a combination of centrally fixed prices, prices which could vary between fixed limits, and free prices (Berend & Ranki, 1985: 242). Investment was decentralised to some extent, although only firms requiring no external finance or imported materials were entirely free of the planning mechanism (Hare, 1981). In political terms the only concession from the party was to permit a plurality of candidates for parliamentary elections, but the nomination process was still controlled. As in other communist countries parliament met only for a few short sessions and carried no real power. It is very important to note that the economic reform was diluted significantly by the reimposition of central allocative planning on 50 large enterprises in 1973. Some leading communists complained that the new system had increased income differentials to an unacceptable degree, but of course the bureaucracy had a vested interest in maintaining central control of the economy (Berend & Ranki, 1985: 245–6; Richet, 1981: 33).

Perhaps the most distinctive feature of the Hungarian economy was the rapid development and acceptance of the 'second' economy, in which it is estimated that a majority of Hungarian workers operated second jobs on an untaxed, free–market basis (Kemeny, 1982). It became common for workers to save their energy in their official job in order to maximise their opportunities on the free market, and the effects on state–controlled industry and public services were quickly felt (Vajda, 1982: 185–9). Not only did the proliferation of the second economy lead to wide income differentials, but in forcing up prices it created real poverty among those who remained on 'official' incomes. Another departure was the way in which the economy was opened up to the West. This developed apace in a 'second phase of reform' in the early 1980s, and unlike the Polish experience under Gierek, the business was largely conducted at enterprise or industry level. Hungary joined GATT (General Agreement on Tariff and Trade) in 1973 and became a full member of the International Monetary Fund and the World Bank in 1982. Much of Hungary's economic relations were still with countries of the Soviet–bloc, which were transacted in roubles with no relation to world prices. However, firms which could export to the West were encouraged to do so, and in order to survive they needed to import technology from the West. The relative openness of the Hungarian economy was not accompanied by a dramatic increase in productivity, in part at least because so much economic activity was not exposed to the harsh reality of the world market. The result was a developing debt crisis of astonishing and unmanageable proportions, and this was the underlying reason behind the decision to voluntarily relinquish power following the removal of Kadar in 1988 (Swain, 1989; Batt, 1991: 9–16; Fagan, 1991). The foreign debt increased from $8.8 billion in 1984 to $17.3 billion in 1988. In a country of less than 11 million people this meant a per capita debt of $1600, one of the highest in the world (Swain, 1989: 15). The country also suffered from high inflation and high unemployment.

Hungary was applauded by many Western commentators in the early 1980s for the way in which it had liberalised its economy. There was a far greater supply of goods available in the shops than in other East European states, and a wider range of available services if the money could be found to pay for them.

But behind this appearance, the economy produced by the liberalised trade policies produced an economy which simply sucked in imports and lacked the ability to create the exports to pay for them. When the government decided to turn a blind eye to the second economy it effectively consigned the official economy to a slow death. If the regime had moved to legalise and tax the second economy there would have been widespread social unrest. If the whole economy had been opened to the world market they would have divorced themselves from the other countries in the CMEA bloc and created social and economic ruin at home. This was the quandary which faced a political elite which had never enjoyed widespread support.

The party under Kádár had always controlled the major differences of opinion about the management of the economy through personnel changes. Károly Grósz thought that the party could resolve the economic difficulties by bringing in more expert advice, and he used the hitherto unimportant role of Prime Minister to do this and generate the support to unseat Kádár. Imre Pozsgay used another innocuous role to push for a more thoroughgoing pluralism. He was head of the Patriotic Peoples Front, an umbrella organisation designed to develop general support for the regime, but used by Poszgay to develop opposition to one–party rule (Batt, 1991: 10–13, 64–8). A direct outcome of this was the formation in 1987 of the Hungarian Democratic Forum (HDF), which later won Hungary's first free election in May 1990. The majority of communists re–formed as the Hungarian Socialist Party, but despite the orderly surrender of power it won only 8.5 per cent of the party–list vote. The hardliners of the Hungarian Socialist Workers Party polled 3.7 per cent and failed to pass the 4 per cent threshold for representation, and the Hungarian Social Democratic Party polled only 3.5 per cent. The M.D.F led a three–party coalition after the elections, and although it was ostensibly right–wing it has been obliged to maintain a significant public sector in the economy to avoid economic and social calamity.

CZECHOSLOVAKIA

The period of communist reform in Czechoslovakia was short and dramatic, and in many respects it encapsulated all the dilemmas facing socialists who wished to promote a democratic socialism in the shadow of the Soviet Union (Skilling, 1976: Golan, 1973). Alexander Dubček succeeded Antonin Novotny as First Secretary of the Czechoslovak Communist Party in January 1968. He was not an obvious choice, and some regarded him as a compromise candidate between the conservative followers of Novotny and the more liberal reformers. However, even before his promotion he had denounced 'coercive and despotic methods', and he was soon calling for the development of a participatory democracy (Ello, 1968; Dubček, 1993). Within months there was an explosion of free expression as censorship was lifted for the first time in a communist state, a situation which prompted Jean–Paul Sartre to claim that 'no press or radio has ever been freer than in Czechoslovakia during the spring of 1968' (Sartre, 1974: 113). The 'Prague Spring', as it instantly became known, witnessed an explosion of debate and preparation for what became known to the world as 'socialism with a human face'. The experiment ended on August 20 when the armed forces of the Warsaw Pact invaded Czechoslovakia, arrested the leadership of the Czechoslovak Communist Party, took them to Moscow and induced them to sign a protocol committing them to rescind the freedoms of the brief reform period (Mlynár, 1980: ch. 3). Although the leaders agreed to resume their posts, within a year there had been a wholesale change in the leadership and a massive purge of the party (Kusin, 1978: parts 1, 2). Dubček was replaced by Gustáv Husák, who remained President until replaced by Vaclav Havel in the 'Velvet Revolution' of 1989. Ironically, the chief organiser of the purges was Miloš Jakeš, who was party leader when the communists were swept from office in 1989.

Why was there a reform movement led 'from above' in 1968? This is a complex question. Despite the talk of a socio–economic 'crisis', Czechoslovakia was, with East Germany, the most prosperous country in the Soviet bloc, and its growth since the war was on a par with most of the economies of Western Europe (Bairoch, 1981: 10). Economic reformers such as Ota Sik recognised that the economy would have to move quickly from labour–intensive methods to a more varied capital–intensive mode if it was to maintain competiveness. There were already signs that productivity was not increasing at a sufficiently high rate (Fejto, 1974: 214–5). A modest attempt at giving enterprises increased responsibility was undertaken by Novotny at the beginning of 1967, but despite its grand name the 'new economic model' was little different from the limited reforms which were being promoted at the same time by Kosygin in the Soviet Union. But the frustration which economic reformers within the party felt under Novotny was only part of a wider political and cultural frustration. It was manifested in the sardonic style of writers such as Milan Kundera, Ivan Klíma, Josef Skoverecký, and Václav Havel, and in the films of internationally renowned directors Miloš Foreman and Jiri Menzel. The Writers Congress of June 1967 marked a sudden deterioration in relations between an increasingly frustrated intelligentsia and an increasingly anxious and conservative leadership (Pelikan, 1972: 16; Simmons, 1991: 74–8). In political terms, the reformists had spent a long time in 'loyal opposition' and had developed an impatient desire to amend the mistakes of the previous twenty years.

It has been argued that there were three main groups in the party following the purges which ended in 1954. Jancar has claimed that the first group comprised of those who had consolidated their positions and who were directly implicated in the purges. The second group were the victims, some of whom were rehabilitated by the three commissions called between 1955 and 1966 to investigate the purges. The third group were those members who joined after 1954 or who were rank–and–file members in the immediate post–war period (Jancar, 1971: 102–7). Mlynář, who was on the Secretariat of the Central Committee in 1968, has also described three groups, somewhat differently, as Stalinists, reformers who largely followed Khrushchev's more liberal line, and waverers (Mlynář, 1980: 29–30). In 1963 Novotny dismissed the last of those directly implicated in the purges, and he remained the last of the leadership who had been directly involved in the political trials. Isolated and wavering on the issue of economic reform, the party decided it needed renewal at the top, and the Brezhnev–Kosygin leadership of the CPSU were content to accept such a change. What made the liberals so bold when they achieved power? There may be an instructive comparison with the other notable 'departure', Yugoslavia. The Yugoslav leadership had the confidence of those who had won a genuine revolutionary struggle. The Czechoslovak Communist Party was part of a very strong Marxist tradition in the country, which reached its peak when it won almost forty per cent of the vote in the 1946 election (Bloomfield, 1979: 50). The memory of the *de facto* social democracy which existed between 1945 and February 1948 served as a reminder of an alternative course which might have been taken had it not been for the imposition of the Stalinist model (Pelikan, 1972: 15; Mlynář, 1988: 35; Myant, 1981). Unlike Poland and Hungary, where communism was always a minor force, in Czechoslovakia the communists had some grounds for believing that there was a 'natural constituency' for a more pluralist form of socialism.

From the moment of Dubček's elevation the rhetoric revolved around renewal, reform, and democracy. Novotny resigned as President and was replaced by Ludvík Svoboda, and soon after the party revealed its 'Action Programme' (Ello, 1968). The programme lamented the ossification of the old system and declared a range of new political rights, including freedom of assembly and voluntary organisation, and freedom of the media. People would have the right to emigrate or travel abroad. The independence of the courts was assured and the role of the security apparatus was to be strictly limited. The victims of the purge period would be rehabilitated. In the economic sphere there was to be decentralisation of decision–making to enterprise level and the restoration of works councils which had last operated in the 1945–48 period. Trade unions were to act as defenders of workers' rights rather than transmission belts for party policy. The programme promised that work would begin on a new constitution, but in advance of this Slovakia was offered semi–autonomy within the federation. There was a strong feeling among the five million Slovaks that they had been treated as second–class citizens, outnumbered as they were by ten million Czechs. Indeed the national issue was for many Slovaks the most important factor at stake in 1968 (Kusin, 1972: 148). Ironically, the introduction of devolved administration was the only reform that was permitted after the invasion, but without the other political reforms it was of little significance. The programme broke sharply from normal communist practice in espousing an avowedly pluralist line, recognising the 'manifold interests of the social groups and individuals' and calling for a 'new model of socialist democracy'. However, the limitations of this pluralism were left rather unclear in the programme. Voluntary organisations were permitted, but not new political parties, and the emphasis on the role of the 'National Front' as a genuine representative of different interests was ambiguous. The Front was a bogus coalition including two nominally independent parties which operated in practice as puppets of the regime, but it had been a genuine coalition in the 1945–8 period. The Action Programme indicated that the Front could be renewed and used as a means to developing full political pluralism. The new chairman of the National Front was one of the most radical reformers, Frantisek Kriegel. Finally, in order to assuage conservative elements at home and abroad, the programme reaffirmed the 'leading role' of the Communist Party and made the usual obligatory expressions of gratitude and friendship towards the Soviet Union.

The popular response was wildly enthusiastic. The atmosphere of free speech was particularly attractive to the intelligentsia, students, and youth in general (Kusin, 1972: chs. 3, 4). The manual working class was not the prime–mover of the reform process, but it soon displayed its support. The trade unions were still expected to play a dual role, as independent defenders of workers' interests and as constructive partners in the National Front. Ota Sik's plans for workers councils to have supervisory powers over management were welcomed, although only a minority of enterprises had functioning councils by August. Attempts were made to extend the system after the invasion, but such initiatives were terminated by the Husák regime in 1969 (Kusin, 1972: ch. 1). After 1969 the economy was recentralised, the workers' councils were scrapped, and tens of thousands of trade union officials were removed from office (Kusin, 1978: 124–34). Organised groups began to emerge, and the most significant were the Club of Committed Non–Party People (KAN) and K231, a club for former political prisoners which took its name from the number of the article in the legal code under which prosecutions had taken place (Kusin, 1972; Pravda, 1973). There were many rumours that the Social Democratic Party was in the process of re–forming. It had been fused with the Communist Party in 1948 but a majority of its members stayed outside the new structure. The leaders of the Social Democrats in 1968 were divided over the question of how far to go in re–establishing an openly independent party. Some recognised that it would provoke the Soviets and lead to the end of the reform process, and others considered that the gradualist strategy employed by communist reformers was moving in the right direction. A large minority apparently wanted open action. There were a number of meetings between leaders of the Social Democratic

The Failure of Reform 151

Party and Communist Party leaders, with the latter pleading for restraint. In July, just before the Czechoslovak leaders met the leadership of the CPSU at Cierna, the Social Democrats agreed to suspend public meetings and cease issuing statements. But just before the invasion three Social Democratic leaders visited Kriegel and demanded recognition (Kusin, 1972: 170–91).

The accommodation of political groupings was a difficult task for the reform communists, and the existence of political pluralism was a major cause of the invasion. Mlynář, one of the architects of the reforms, subsequently argued that only a gradual shift to full political pluralism was possible under the circumstances. He envisaged full democratisation occurring over a ten year period. Within two years there would be elections with a plurality of candidates under the banner of the National Front, and a new constitution would be adopted. Self-management and free trade unions would be developed in this period (Mlynář, 1980: 144–5). In retrospect, Mlynář argued that if elections had been held and the Party Congress brought forward to the spring of 1968, the political situation would have been stabilised. Certainly it was a commonly held view that the popular movement was racing ahead of the leadership's intentions (Tigrid, 1971: 17, 43–4). One publication which the Soviet leaders took to be a clear sign of political instability was the 'Two Thousand Words' manifesto, which appeared in June. Written by Ludvik Vaculik, a writer, it called for full democratisation through citizens' committees and commissions, and it was signed by many communists, some of whom were on the Central Committee. It was officially opposed by the leadership, many of whom were worried that it would provoke armed intervention (Smrkovsky, 1984: 399–401; Mlynář, 1980: 144–5). Even after the invasion, at the hastily convened clandestine Party Congress, the delegates approved freedom of political activity only within the framework of the National Front, and they proposed elections with a choice of candidates from a single, preselected list (Pelikan, 1971; 235–7).

As early as March, Dubček had been warned by leaders of the Warsaw Pact at Dresden that a situation of 'disintegration' existed in Czechoslovakia. The warnings were repeated at Moscow meetings in May and June, and then again at Cierna at the end of July. The possibility of intervention was never mentioned in public by Dubček, and apparently it was hardly discussed in the leading echelons of the party. No consistent foreign policy was conducted to try to gain the support of countries such as Yugoslavia, Romania (which showed some independence in foreign policy), China, or the large communist parties of France and Italy (Mlynář, 1980: 175). The Chairman of the National Assembly, Josef Smrkovsky, has left an account of the Cierna meeting which conveys the gulf between the Czechoslovak reformers and a Soviet leadership still wedded to neo-Stalinist methods and discourse (Smrkovsky, 1984: 408–10). The demands made by the Brezhnev team were quite specific. Two individuals were singled out for dismissal, Kriegel from his post as Chair of the National Front, and Cisar from his post as Secretary of the Party Praesidium. KAN and K231 were to be banned, and there was to be no legalisation of the Social Democratic Party. Finally, the freedom of the media was to be ended. The meeting ended with some reconciliatory gestures, but apparently Brezhnev was on the telephone daily in the following week demanding to know why immediate action had not been taken. Dubček tried in vain to explain that the issues had to be discussed at the Central Committee meeting at the end of August, and that the whole course of future action was to be discussed at the Party Congress called for September.

The imminence of the Congress probably decided the timing of the invasion, and the constitution of the preparatory committee of the Social Democratic Party in mid–August was also a factor (Tigrid, 1971: 73). Why did they invade? Pelikan is surely correct to ascribe it to 'the fear of the Soviet bureaucracy that the Czechoslovakian experiment would overcome its difficulties and succeed in creating a different kind of socialist society' (Pelikan, 1972: 24). To which it should be added that Gomulka in Poland and Ulbricht in East Germany also had much to fear of the success of the Czechoslovak reform movement. In neither country could the communists expect to hold on to power in a pluralist system. The Soviet reason was given in the joint Soviet–Czechoslovak declaration in October, 1969, when the invasion was justified as an 'act of international solidarity which helped to stop the anti–socialist counterrevolutionary forces'. There is no doubt that tensions would have developed about the pace and extent of democratisation if the invasion had not taken place. But opinion polls consistently showed that a large majority of Czechoslovak citizens were enthusiatic supporters of the reform process and had confidence in the leadership of the Communist Party (Piekalkiewicz, 1972). The public demonstration of support for Dubček at the time of the invasion was immense. Given the relative strength of the economy and the clarity of the ideas on economic reform formulated by Sik (Sik, 1976), the internal situation was uniquely propitious for communist reform, but even here it has been estimated that there were about 400,000 hardline opponents of the reform process, those who survived the purges of 1969–71 and who controlled the 'normalisation' process (Kusin, 1978: 88–9) The invasion marked not only the end of the possiblity of reform socialism 'from above' in Czechoslovakia, but everywhere else in Eastern Europe.

CONCLUSION

Brus has pointed out that communist governments have felt the need to decentralise economic decision making to enterprise level at least since the mid–1950s, but that these attempts have generally been unsuccessful (Brus,

1988). Only in the Soviet Union during the NEP, and in Hungary and China more recently, has a measure of entrepeneurship been consolidated under communist rule. In persistently attempting to introduce market mechanisms in countries with little private ownership of the means of production, the communists were acknowledging the superior efficiency of those mechanisms in allocating resources and satisfying consumer demand compared with the system of central allocative planning. European communist regimes apart from Albania accepted the need to find a competitive niche within the world system, and in so doing they were drawn into the compelling logic of that system. Brus has commented that it is theoretically possible to imagine that a conscious preference could be expressed for other economic goals besides those aided by the market, such as full employment, low income differentials and stability (Brus, 1988: 107–8). However, not only does this presuppose a considerable shift in political opinion, it amounts to an acceptance that capitalism is still able to develop the forces of production more efficiently than any alternative, i.e. that in Marx's own terms capitalism was not yet 'ripe' for replacement. Communism had rested its whole strategy since the Russian Revolution on demonstrating that the planned economy could 'out accumulate' its capitalist foes. In the 1950s and 1960s the economies struggled to keep up with the West in terms of output, and from the mid–1970s they were unable to make the switch from extensive to intensive production to maintain competitiveness in the world economy. The productivity gap widened, with palpable consequences.

There are many reasons for the failure of economic reforms, and they are inextricably linked to the political system. The material basis of communist power was the control over the planned economy by the political elite, and plans to supplement this economic structure with market mechanisms threatened that power. As long as the communists insisted on full control of economic and political life, this contradiction was bound to surface. The populations of Eastern Europe had an image of an alternative political system in the West which they found far more desirable than their own bureaucratic despotism. Attempts at mixing command planning and market economics without an accompanying political reform failed in Hungary, which fell into heavy international debt with astonishing rapidity. The communists simply surrendered power, but the years of their rule have left very little public support for the idea of socialism. It could be argued that in economic terms the mix of plan and market has worked in China, but the comparison is misleading, both economically and politically. China is at a far lower level of economic development, and is not integrated into the world economy to the same extent as the East European countries. The market reforms adopted in 1978 have created deep divisions in society which contributed to the attempt to wrest political reforms from the communist leadership in 1989. The democracy movement was violently smashed in Tiananmen Square in June 1989 and throughout the country in the weeks and months that followed (Whyte, 1992; Ure, 1989).

It is possible that if central planning had been introduced only in those areas of economic activity where and when it was clearly advantageous, then the economies of Eastern Europe would have fared better. Only in Czechoslovakia and perhaps East Germany could this path have been taken, but in both cases the consolidation of communist dictatorship entailed the imposition of the full command model. This was a clear disregard for Marx's view that 'new superior relations of production never replace older ones before the material conditions for their existence have matured within the framework of the old society' (Marx, 1969: 21). The communist model flowed from the premature abandonment of the New Economic Policy in the Soviet Union in 1928, and it was premised on the conviction that socialism could be reduced to the abolition of private ownership and separated from its democratic component. The experience of the communist regimes does not prove that there is no alternative to capitalism, let alone that capitalism as a system is triumphant. The new economic structures of Eastern Europe are likely to be under severe strain for years to come, and will inevitably require considerable state intervention to maintain production and ameliorate poverty. Similarly, the major problems which beset the capitalist world economy also demand considerable public intervention. 'Mixed' economies are an unavoidable reality, despite the revival of free market rhetoric in recent years, and the nature of the 'mix' will form an important part of the political and economic debates of the new Europe.

10 Revolution and Transition:
Poland and Czechoslovakia

Nineteen eighty nine was a year of revolution to rank with 1848 in European history. In Romania a thousand died as the Ceausescu regime resisted its fate, but in East Germany, Hungary, Poland, Czechoslovakia and Bulgaria, the collapse of communist dictatorship was largely peaceful. This chapter will focus on the transfer of power in Poland and Czechoslovakia and the subsequent development of socialist politics there until the constitutional break between the Czech and Slovak republics at the end of 1992. Why were the communists forced to relinquish power? How have they regrouped in the aftermath? What role did democratic socialists play in the opposition to communist rule? How have they fared since 1989? Can socialism survive the experience of communism in the new Eastern Europe?

POLAND

Poland was the only country in Eastern Europe in which an organised mass movement engaged in protracted and finally victorious struggle against the communist regime. The free trade union, Solidarity, emerged in the summer of 1980 and quickly recruited 10 million members. The immensity of its support forced the government to agree to its legalisation, an unprecedented concession, but it was banned in December 1981 (Ash, 1991: Potel, 1982; Ascherson, 1981; Ruane, 1982). After seven years of failing to revive a stagnant and indebted economy, the communists were forced to negotiate at the 'round table' talks with the leaders of Solidarity early in 1989, the prelude to the peaceful transfer of power (Glenny, 1990: ch. 2; Batt, 1991: 31–3, 83–7; Staniszkis, 1991).

Communist rule was imposed on Poland following the Second World War, as the Soviet Union considered it strategically imperative as a buffer against German revival. As a largely rural and devoutly Catholic country it was hardly fertile territory for communist rule. Communism was associated with Russia, which had ruled Poland until 1918, and whose leaders collaborated with Germany in the dismemberment of the country in 1939. Stalin had shown his contempt for Poland in 1937–8 by having most of the leaders of the Polish Communist Party executed and the party formally dissolved (Conquest, 1990: 405–7). Perhaps the one moment when Polish communism had a chance to earn a measure of popular support was when Gomulka came to power in October 1956 against the opposition of the Stalinists within the communist Polish United Workers Party – the PZPR (Syrop, 1976; Davies, 1982). Gomulka enjoyed the reputation of being able to act independently of the Soviet leadership, and his popularly acclaimed victory promised a more liberal future for the country. However, no major political reforms were sustained, and the only significant economic consequence was that Poland did not press ahead with collectivisation of agriculture. The extent of the regime's descent into reaction was shown by the anti–semitic campaign of 1968, the support for the invasion of Czechsolovakia in the same year, and finally, the shooting dead of over 100 workers in the Baltic ports in 1970 (Fejtö, 1974: 490–7; Walesa, 1987: 60–87; Krajewski, 1982). The violence of December 1970 led to the removal of Gomulka and his replacement by Eduard Gierek, who pursued a modernisation strategy based on the import of western capital goods and technology (Kaminski, 1991: 101–6; Sanford, 1983: 27–35). Heavy investment in selected industries was supposed to generate export–led growth, but the export prospects of these industries were poor and were finally demolished by the restructuring which took place in the world economy after 1974. The Polish debt grew from $1.8 billion in 1970 to 8.4 billion in 1975, and then rose to $25 billion by 1980 (Kaminski, 1991: 237–44). Forced by their own mismanagement to raise prices sharply in 1980, Gierek's government confronted a similar reaction to that which had toppled Gomulka, again in the Baltic ports. This time the opposition was better prepared, led by experienced workers and supported by many academics and other intellectuals. Many of the workers had been involved in the strikes of 1970, and the protests against price rises in 1976. They were well aware that the regime needed their labour to preserve its power, but they were also acutely aware of the danger of applying the 'workers veto', for communist governments had not hesitated to shoot demonstrators in Poland in 1956, 1970, and 1976.

Intellectual support came from a number of sources (Zielonka, 1989). Direct assistance came from the Workers Defence Committee, founded in 1976 by 14 dissidents, most of them democratic socialists. It brought legal aid to workers who were victims of arbitrary state action, and it published information bulletins and a newspaper for workers. It possessed the expertise to identify the weaknesses in the regime and expose the ultimate dependence of the regime on the compliance if not cooperation of the people. Its boldness in publishing signed statements condemning government policy ensured that it was known to large sections of the population. Another organisation of intellectuals came to prominence in 1977, the Movement in Defence of Human and Citizens Rights (ROPCiO), which attempted to put into practice some of the guarantees embodied in the 1975 Helsinki Agreement, which Poland had signed. From ROPCiO came the idea of free trade unions (Walesa, 1987: 97–8), and in 1977 and 1978 the first free trades union bodies were secretly founded. The Catholic Church was a source of of ideological and moral support for the opposition. The Club of Catholic Intellingstia (KIK) was particularly important in launching criticisms of the conditions faced by working people and the lack of civil liberties. Notable dissidents such as the historian Adam Michnik strove to forge a common front containing democratic socialist and anti–socialist Catholics against the communists. And the election of Wojtyla as Pope in 1978 gave a feeling of empowerment to workers disaffected with an oppressive regime (MacDonald, 1984: 469–70).

The strike which triggered the development of a mass free trade union began in August at the Lenin shipyard in Gdansk, and it spread spontaneously throughout the country. It took the form of 'one big union' to present a united front against its powerful opponent. Even after the government had capitulated in signing the Szczecin and Gdansk agreements at the end of August it was several months before the Supreme Court accepted the validity of the statutes of the new union (Touraine, 1983: 196–201). It is estimated that about a million communists joined Solidarity, approximately one third of the membership of the PZPR (MacDonald, 1984: 477). This high level of support from PZPR members revealed the extent to which disillusionment with the Gierek leadership had developed, but it also pointed to the authentically working class nature of the new movement and the democratic socialist nature of the original 21 demands. The key one was for the acceptance of a free trade union movement, but there were also demands for widespread participation in the discussion of a reform programme, an end to privileges enjoyed by the PZPR, an end to political appointments in industry, the release of political prisoners, freedom of the press, an improvement of the health service, reduction of working hours, lowering of the retirement age, extension of nursery provision, and three years maternity leave (Potel, 1982: 219–20). The demands did not reflect anti–socialist aspirations, but the communists regarded every attempt to establish the free articulation of groups in civil society as a threat to socialism.

The period of Solidarity's first legal existence was one of deep economic crisis with shortages of basic material goods, a situation as bad as anything witnessed in Europe in the previous 30 years. The PZPR reacted quickly by replacing Gierek with the more conciliatory Stanislaw Kania, but the party was divided to the point of paralysis (Sanford, 1983; MacDonald, 1984: 484–7).

Although some hardliners wanted the immediate suppression of Solidarity, Kania and the centre of the party wished to accept the existence of the union and bring them into a controlled corporatist management of the economic crisis, thereby preserving the political power of the PZPR. There were also groups of reformists, such as Tadeusz Fiszbach, who wanted to promote a socialist pluralism along the lines of the Czecholsovak experiment in 1968. However, the reformers were defeated at the Party Congress in July 1981, following which four army generals were appointed to the government. It may have been possible for Solidarity to promote closer links with the reformist wing of the PZPR, but there was a strong reluctance from many quarters to such involvement (MacDonald, 1984: 508–9; Arato, 1982: 32–40). It ran counter to the 'self–limiting strategy' consistently adopted by the Solidarity leadership, whereby the union kept a discrete distance from 'political' decision making. The early calling and meticulous management of the Congress ensured that no such alliance could take place, and from that point on it became evident that the apparatus's will to resist had stiffened.

At the first Solidarity National Congress in September and October 1981 there were calls for free elections and steadfast pursuit of self–management of the economy to replace the nomenklatura system. Although Walesa was elected President of the Union, his 'moderate' line was supported by only 55 per cent of the delegates (Sanford, 1990). The PZPR now moved decisively. General Wojciech Jaruzelski, who had been appointed Prime Minister in February, replaced Kania as Party Secretary, martial law was declared, and thousands of worker–activists and intellectuals were arrested (Sanford, 1986: ch. 4; Swidlicki, 1988). Preparations for the suppression of Solidarity had been underway for many months, and the Brezhnev leadership in the Soviet Union was actively involved (Kaminski, 1991: 152–4; Ash, 1991: 358). The ultimate veto of Soviet force was something that had to be considered by all the groups. The Soviet Union had become embroiled in Afghanistan in 1979, and some considered that it would be prepared to permit Poland to follow the path of Finland, i.e. 'friendly' neutrality within a liberal democratic framework. This was not, however, a real possibility, for the implication was a dissolution of the whole Warsaw Pact 'zone'. As long as Brezhnev was at the helm, his 'doctrine', enforced on Czechoslovakia in 1968, would prevail.

The imposition of martial law hardened the hostility felt by the vast majority of the population towards the regime. Although martial law was lifted in the summer of 1983, the last of the political prisoners were not released until 1986. Coercion ensured that Jaruzelski could never hope to gain the social cooperation required to introduce the limited market mechanisms in the economic field which he desired. There was a slight recovery in production in 1983 and 1984 following the adoption of an economic policy similar to the one suggested in Solidarity's programme in 1981; instead of importing investment goods the emphasis was switched to importing supplies for current production. However, the foreign debt grew larger, from $17 billion in 1979 to $39 billion in 1989. The Jaruzelski leadership consistently spoke of the need to reform the economy, but in the context of the debt and severe shortages it was difficult to reform the price system and move enterprises over to market mechanisms. There was also resistance from the conservative wing of the PZPR (Batt, 1991: 10). Finally, Jaruzelski attempted a direct appeal to the people in the form of a referendum in November 1987, asking the people if they supported economic reforms even if it meant two or three years of austerity, and also asking if they favoured the 'deep democratisation of political life', as well as industrial self–management. Although the government gained majorities on both questions, the low turnout of 67 per cent meant that it did not receive the 50 per cent of registered voters required by the electoral law (Holland, 1988: 24). In 1988 waves of strikes hammered home the message to the government that there could be no cooperation from society without the legalisation of Solidarity, and by the end of the year Jaruzelski agreed to hold talks with Walesa and his colleagues. If the terms of these talks were similar to those held between the union and the government in 1981, there were two important differences this time. First, the government could not even pretend to have an answer to the economic crisis, and second, the threat of Soviet invasion had receded.

The election in 1989 which toppled the communists had been designed by the rulers to concede a voice in the political system to the representatives of Solidarity, but because only 35 per cent of the seats in the Sejm were freely contested, it was expected that the communists would retain power. In effect the rulers were trying to cling to power by adopting a 'state corporatist' compromise, but the tactic misfired when Solidarity, at that time maintaining a united front, won all 35 per cent of the seats on offer, as well as all but one of the hundred seats in the free election for the Senate, the Upper House. This would not have been sufficient to remove the communists from government but for the unexpected rebellion by the representatives of the Democrat and Peasant Parties, which had been no more than puppet parties controlled by the PZPR since 1948. After a parliamentary impasse lasting two months, the representatives of these parties agreed to form a coalition with Solidarity under Tadeusz Mazowiecki as Prime Minister. Jaruzelski held on to the post of President.

It took more than two years before fully free elections for the Sejm were held, a delay which did nothing to encourage the development of open party politics. The local elections of May 1990 cleared out the communists from local government, but the turnout of 42 per cent indicated the extent to which the Polish people had grown disillusioned with politics in the face of a severe drop in living standards. Soon after taking power the Finance Minister, Leszek Balcerowicz, reached a deal with the International Monetary Fund for a staged transformation to a privatised market economy, involving massive price increases until the currency found its natural convertible level. The result was a thirty per cent fall in real wages in the first half of 1990, combined with soaring unemployment (Kowalik, 1991: 261–5).

These measures were intended to 'kick start' the economy into competitiveness, but this did not happen in the short–term for a number of reasons. The monopolistic character of much Polish production meant that prices could rise without increasing efficiency because the penalties which normally prevail in a competitive domestic market did not exist. In addition, the collapse of the important Soviet market in the wake of the disintegration of the Soviet Union was a heavy blow. In terms of trade with the European Community, new agreements failed to remove quotas and tariffs on potentially high–earning Polish exports in agriculture, coal, textiles and steel (Gowan, 1990: 69; Gowan, 1993). Ironically, the first sector to be hit by the reforms was agriculture, which had been left in private hands. The final act of the communist government in the summer of 1989 had been to lift agricultural subsidies, which instantly revealed the uncompetitiveness of the labyrinthine system of tiny private farms. Soaring food prices led to reduced sales and severely eroded living standards in town and country alike.

Having achieved the primary objective of the overthrow of communist political power, Solidarity began to fall apart. Walesa, standing outside the government, was ruthlessly opportunistic in criticising his former allies. Matters came to a head during the 1990 Presidential election campaign, when anti–semitic innuendoes and personal abuse were used by Walesa supporters against those who had done so much to bring about the end of the dictatorship. Walesa won the Presidency after a second ballot in December 1990, and the new government under Jan Bielecki continued to implement the IMF policies with sufficient zeal to encourage the Western governments to halve the official foreign debt in March 1991. The depth of the crisis led to a revival of the former 'official' trade union organisation, the OPZZ, which claimed a higher membership than Solidarity by 1993. It was now Solidarity, reduced to less than two million members, which was in the difficult position of being associated with an unpopular government (Kloc, 1993).

The formation and development of political parties was remarkably slow. The leading members of the old Solidarity organisation divided between the right–wing Centre Civic Alliance, faithful to Walesa, and the more centrist Democratic Union, led by Mazowiecki, which contained some democratic socialist elements. The Polish Left comprised the former communists and a variety of small organisations, including the Polish Socialist Party (PPS) and 'Labour Solidarity' (Wilde, 1991). The old Polish Socialist Workers Party was dissolved in January 1990 and re–formed into the Social Democracy of the Republic of Poland (SdRP), led by Aleksander Kwasnieski and Leszek Miller (Hawkes, 1990: 33–4). It claimed by far the largest membership (60,000) of any of the new parties, and declared its rejection of democratic centralism and the dictatorial practices of the past. At the same time it used its new name and constitution to distance itself from responsibility for four decades of communist rule. It accepted the necessity of some market reforms, provided that jobs were protected and welfare maintained, and it quickly took advantage of the alarming social consequences of the lifting of subsidies and the freeing of prices. The Polish Socialist Party, revived in 1987, found it difficult to recruit members, and its prospects were hampered by the death of its veteran leader, Jan Jozef Lipski, just before the 1991 election. The party was still not strong enough by the time of the 1993 election to be granted full membership of the Socialist International.

In the election of October 1991 the people of Poland passed their judgement on the economic disaster that had befallen them since the IMF economic plan was adopted in 1989. The turnout, at 43 per cent, was the lowest in a European general election this century. The three leading parties were all critical of the social consequences of the introduction of the free market. There was no 'winner' in this election, but the Democratic Union headed the poll with 12.1 per cent of the vote. The former Communists, running under the banner of the Left Democratic Alliance, secured 11.7 per cent support. The Polish Peasants' Party, formerly a communist puppet organisation, came third with 8.9 per cent. The next five parties, all of them right–wing, polled between five and nine per cent. They included the Catholic Election Alliance, whose ultra–conservative social programme attracted only 8.7 per cent of the vote, and the group closest to Walesa, the Centre Civic Alliance, which polled 8.5 per cent. The Liberal Democrats, the party of the outgoing Prime Minister, Bielecki, polled only 7.1 per cent of the vote. An uneasy and short–lived right–of–centre coalition was formed under a new Prime Minister, Jan Olszewski. For democratic socialists the result was dismal. Although some of the representatives of the Democratic Union may be regarded as socialist, the Polish Socialist Party and Labour Solidarity stood in alliance and polled only two per cent, less even than the 3.2 per cent support given to the Polish Beerlovers' Party. Solidarity Trade Union, which contained left–wing elements in some parts of the country, gained only 4.8 per cent. Because of the strict proportionality of the electoral system, eighteen parties gained representation in the Sejm. Although Democratic Union did not participate in the first coalition, Mazowiecki had made it clear that he wanted to see 'responsibility' from the Solidarity–bred groups. The leader of the Democratic Left Alliance, Kwasniewski, argued for a 'left coalition' after the election (*Warsaw Voice*, 29 October 1991), clearly reflecting the former communists' long–term strategy to break out of their isolation.

The Democratic Union entered a broader, pro–reform coalition in 1992, with one of its members, Hanna Suchocka, as Prime Minister. Although the market reforms continued and the first signs of growth emerged, it appeared that corporatist–style compromises would emerge in order to avoid to mitigate the socio–economic damage which accompanied untrammelled market forces. Early in 1993 the Democractic Union Labour Minister, Jacek Kuroń, once a revolutionary socialist, signed agreements with the unions and employers governing the privatisation of state enterprises, involving workers' participation on company boards and workers' share ownership. The painful social cost of transition took its toll on the parties in the ruling coalition, resulting in the sensational return to power of the former communists after the election of September 1993. Their Democratic Left Alliance won 20.4 per cent of the vote, and formed a coalition with their former allies the Polish Peasant Party (15.4 per cent). As a 5 per cent threshold had been introduced into the electoral system in order to encourage stable coalitions, the two parties controlled 301 of the 460–seat Sejm. Democratic Union was reduced to 10.6 per cent, while the recently formed Labour Union achieved 7.2 per cent. In October, President Walesa swallowed the bitter pill of swearing in the new government, comprised of many of his old arch enemies, with the Peasant Party's Waldemar Pawlak as the new Prime Minister. Walesa may have reflected that Jaruzelski's "surrender" of power had turned out to be a skilfully managed transition which had preserved the material interests of large sections of the old ruling elite. In the early stages of market reforms, existing managers had taken advantage of their position to acquire private title to state property, a process labelled as 'political capitalism' or 'making owners out of nomenklatura' (Staniszkis, 1991). It is likely that the new administration will pursue a national consensus through corporatist practices, while moderating the influence of the Church in social affairs. However, the democratic credentials of the Democratic Left Alliance will continue to be viewed sceptically within Poland by socialists who resisted the old regime, and elsewhere in Europe by socialists affiliated to the Socialist International.

CZECHOSLOVAKIA

The leaders of post–1968 'normalisation' avoided the deep indebtedness which beset the Polish communists. By 1989 the foreign debt was just short of eight billion dollars (Glenny, 1990: 33), about one third of the per capita debt borne by Hungary and less than a half that of Poland. Czechoslovakia, along with East Germany, had the highest living standards in the Soviet bloc. However, comparisons with other countries in Eastern Europe are somewhat misleading, since the historical and cultural comparison more frequently drawn by the people in both Czechoslovakia and East Germany lay with their affluent German–speaking neighbours, West Germany and Austria. With a sizable number of emigrants from 1968–69 letting people at home realise the disparity between living standards, and with the availablity of West German and Austrian television, the mere absence of shortages of basic goods could not placate a population which was simultaneously cowed and resentful. The external debt was controlled but the deterioration of working conditions, services and environment constituted a formidable 'internal debt' (Urban, 1990: 111). The horrific pollution pumped out by Czechoslovak industry led to a reduction in life expectancy and a sharp increase in infant mortality in northern Bohemia (Glenny, 1990: 31–2).

If the backbone of the resistance to communist rule in Poland was provided by the manual working class, the principal source of resistance in Czechoslovakia was the dissident intellectual group associated with Charter 77. One of the reasons for this was that the immense purge which took place in the years following the invasion created a mass of 'displaced' intellectuals (educators, writers, artists) and former reform communists. Urban has pointed out that in a comparison of the Writers' Union membership lists of 1968 and 1970 only ten out of several hundred were common to both (Urban, 1990: 106). Thousands of former high-ranking artists, teachers and administrators were reallocated to unskilled manual labour. Throughout the 1970s oppositionists were placed under surveillance, dismissed from posts, periodically arrested and imprisoned, and unauthorised publications were completely banned (Simecka, 1984; Kusin, 1978). An attempt to rally the reform communists, the Socialist Movement of Czechoslovak Citizens, was set up in 1970 but was effectively broken two years later when 47 members were imprisoned (Kusin, 1978: 152–60). One of the features of the resistance was its international dimension. Former political leaders of the Prague Spring such as Zdeněk Mlynář and Jiří Hajek, and prominent dissidents such as the playwright Václav Havel and the philosopher Karol Kosik managed to publish abroad or give interviews to western media (Simmons, 1991: chs. 5–7). Many of those who emigrated continued to supply the opposition with material support of various sorts. Josef Smrkovsky released his account of how the Prague Spring was crushed in an interview in Prague in 1973 which was smuggled out and printed by the Australian Communist Party in 1976 (Smrkovsky, 1984). The Eurocommunist perspective was sympathetic to the ideals of the Prague Spring. When Smrkovsky died in 1974, Dubček, confined to an administrative position with the forestry commission after 1970, wrote letters protesting about represssion in Czechoslovakia which were published abroad (Dubček, 1993: 263).

This use of international pressure ensured that the Husák leadership had to restrain the severity of the sentences meted out to the opposition, particularly as Brezhnev was set on establishing détente with the Western powers in order to develop trade with the West. The Helsinki Agreement of 1975 committed its signatories to respect human rights, and dissidents throughout Eastern Europe used this opportunity to set up monitoring groups. The strategy was to expose the arbitrary nature of communist rule by claiming that activities which were banned were in fact perfectly legal. Charter 77 came to symbolise this struggle for civil rights, and its leaders made contact with the Polish KOR organisation and sympathetic Western groups such as European Nuclear Disarmament. It outlined the areas in which the authorities were denying the rights that they had subscribed to at Helsinki and also in United Nations accords. Initially signed by 242 people, with Havel as one of the spokespersons (Kusin, 1978: 304–25), it was intended for simultaneous delivery to a number of public bodies, but the police intercepted the documents and arrested the carriers. Teachers and other public servants were then required to sign a document denouncing the Charter, which they had not read. While the majority complied, others found themselves thrown out of work and into the area of active opposition (Urban, 1990: 109–13). Hundreds more signed the Charter over the next 12 years, and hundreds were harrassed and imprisoned for their actions. Havel himself was jailed on four occasions, including a nine–month sentence early in 1989 after attempting to lay flowers at the place in Wenceslas Square where Jan Palach had burned himself to death in January 1969. Few Czechoslovak citizens had read a word from Havel's pen, yet all knew of the moral strength and persistence of his opposition, and they demanded his Presidency during the revolutionary days of November and December 1989.

The accession to power of Gorbachev in the Soviet Union gave some hope of a thaw in Czechoslovakia. A statement from Charter 77 in 1988 offered the hope that 'the current social motion in the Soviet Union might evolve into a wider impulse' (Dawisha, 1988: 109). Gorbachev had been a fellow student of Mlynár, one of the initial signatories of Charter 77. It seemed to many that after 1987 Gorbachev was adopting a similar strategy to that pursued by the reform communists in Czechoslovakia in 1968. Nevertheless, on his visit to Czechoslovakia in April 1987 Gorbachev was careful to distance himself from the Prague Spring without explicitly justifying the invasion; the official pronouncements of the Husák leadership remained unswerving and valedictory (Dawisha, 1988: 167–70). Husák was replaced as party leader by Miloš Jakeš in 1987, but this signalled no major change of direction. Batt has argued that in retrospect the defeat of the conservatives in the Soviet Politburo and the reorganisation of the foreign policy apparatus at the CPSU Central Committee plenum of September 1988 marked the death of the 'Brezhnev doctrine' whereby Soviet force could be used to ensure the 'loyalty' of its Warsaw Pact allies. However, she points out that it was not until the autumn of 1989 that the East Europeans could be certain that if they abandoned communism there would be no invasion (Batt, 1991: 22–7). The caution displayed in Czechoslovakia was entirely understandable.

Waves of emigrating East Germans brought the crisis in Eastern Europe to a head in the summer of 1989. Their presence in Prague prepared the way for the collapse of communist rule in Czechoslovakia in what became known as the 'velvet revolution' (Hawkes, 1990: 100–23). Poland had already replaced its communist government and in Hungary the communists had announced their acceptance of political pluralism. The breech of the Berlin Wall on 9 November quickly led to the promise of free elections in East Germany. In Prague, a peaceful demonstration of 50,000 students on 17 November was violently dispersed. It has since become clear that the violence was orchestrated by the elements within the party in collusion with the KGB in order to discredit the Jakes leadership and replace it with party 'reformers' (Urban, 1990: 116–7n), but it was too late for the communists to cling to power. The opposition formed a broad organisation, Civic Forum, comprising Charter 77 supporters, Christian oppositionists, independent socialists and former reform communists of the 'Obroda' group. The unity and discipline of the opposition was decisive in breaking the nerve of the ruling party. Actors and students staged a nation–wide strike and peaceful demonstrations involving hundreds of thousands made it clear that the people would not be satisfied with anything less than a complete surrender of power by the communists. A two–hour general strike throughout the country dismissed the lingering communist illusions that the workers were not behind the revolution. The new non–communist government was sworn in on 10 December, and three weeks later Havel replaced Husák as President. Havel immediately made it clear that he wished the country to revert to the pluralist political culture established by the first president, Thomas Masaryk. This was symbolised by the selection of Marian Calfa, a former communist, as Prime Minister; he retained his position after the general election in June 1990.

Civic Forum and its Slovak counterpart, Public Against Violence, decided to stand as a united front against the old regime and gained a notable victory in an election with a 96 per cent turnout. Civic Forum secured 53 per cent of the vote in the Czech republic and PAV secured 33 per cent in Slovakia. The Communist Party, the only one in the former Soviet bloc prepared to retain its name, scored over 13 per cent across the republic, beating the Christian Democrats into third place (Wightman, 1991). The government comprised of a broad coalition excluding the communists, and set about the twin processes of restoring a market economy and investigating the extent of collaboration with the communist secret police (St.B), a process which became known as 'lustration'. Under this system investigative committees are able to bar people from public office and public employment for up to six years if they were deeply implicated with the old regime. Unfortunately most of the evidence was taken from secret police files and was therefore dubious. Civic Forum was always too broad an organisation to preserve its unity, and in February 1991 it formally split. The free market enthusiasts under Finance Minister Václav Klaus formed the Civic Democratic Party, and those inclined to ensuring a measure of social protection during the transition to capitalism formed the Civic Movement. The split resulted in five deputies elected on the Civic Forum ticket joining the Social

Democratic Party and forming a broader parliamentary group. The Social Democrats failed to secure the necessary 5 per cent of the vote to gain representation in the 1990 election, but they continued to build up their organisation and attract support on the basis of opposing the social damage suffered by many as the guarantees of full employment and cheap housing were withdrawn. Initially the Social Democrats were active only in the Czech Republic, but the organisation in Slovakia received an enormous boost when Dubcek became a member.

The problem for democratic socialists in Czecholsovakia is shared by all those who operate in the old Soviet bloc. The concepts and language of socialism are automatically associated with the old totalitarian regime. In addition there is the problem of dealing with membership applications from those who were formerly in the Communist Party. How is it possible to distinguish between those who genuinely disavow the past and those who may be seeking to use the party to work towards some sort of left–coalition sometime in the future? One Social–Democratic deputy, Pavel Dostal, adopted a positive view:

> Our society should in good time rid itself of primitive anti–communist attitudes and people should be able to distinguish between the Communists and the democratic left. I think that within three or four years we will have an integration of all the elements of the democratic left, regardless of who was in the Communist Party or not (Wilde, 1992).

Like many other socialist dissidents, Dostal suffered discrimination for two decades after the Prague Spring. Is his optimism justified? Czechoslovakia had the strongest democratic and socialist heritage of the former communist states and it is likely that a strong sentiment for social protection against the effects of the market will express itself. However, the pro–market forces have gained considerable support in the Czech Republic. In Slovakia there is a much stronger feeling for retaining many elements of the socialised economy.

The Social Democrats in Czechoslovakia were in a poor state of organisation for the elections of June 1990. Many activists who could be identified as part of the democratic socialist opposition to the dictatorship stood with Civic Forum. The party, a full member of the Socialist International, adopted a new constitution at its 1991 Congress and agreed on a new programme for the transition period. Under the leadership of Jiří Horák it began to enlarge its membership base and develop contact with the reconstituted trade unions. Its priority was to fight against the development of poverty. It argued that the privatisation process was leading to the mass transfer of property to foreign control before a proper system of taxation and regulation had been worked out. It claimed that only 15 per cent of the cash involved in the first round of privatisation – the small businesses – came from inside the country. The party programme called for a mixed economy with greater protection for producers and consumers, as well as support for cooperatives. The Social Democrats also proposed a scheme for Employee Stock Ownership (ESOP) as a more equitable way of disposing of state property. The party was in favour of early Czechoslovak entry into the European Community, but now that the federation has dissolved it is possible that the Czech Republic will be ready for entry before Slovakia.

The Communist Party of Czechoslovakia surpassed most expectations in the 1990 elections, and in the local elections in November 1990 it secured over 17 per cent support in the Czech Republic and over 13 per cent in Slovakia (Batt, 1991: 128–9). Shortly afterwards the Slovak wing re–founded itself as the Party of the Democratic Left. At its congress in March 1991 the Communist Party elected Jiri Svoboda as President, supported by a new young leadership team. Democratic centralism was renounced in favour of a new organisational structure which gave relative autonomy to eight different 'platforms', which were free to participate in initiatives involving non–party groups (Wilde, 1992). The party dramatically altered its programme in an attempt to secure the support of those who would oppose the effects of market reforms. Most of its property was confiscated in 1990, but it secured funding due to the state financing of political parties on the basis of the 1990 election results.

In 1991 the Communist Party claimed that there were over 200,000 active members (before the revolution there had been 1.8 million members, almost 20 per cent of the adult population). The new programme accepted the introduction of the market but wanted the widest possible dispersal of ownership, as well as co–decision making in enterprises. Like the Social Democrats, the Communist Party favoured Employee Stock Ownership Plans. The communists switched to opposing direct state ownership of property, and indeed all forms of state authoritarianism, and it accused the Calfa Government of imposing an economic policy in a dictatorial way without seeking the participation of ordinary people. However, it is difficult to judge to what extent this 'revision' is genuinely accepted by the membership or is simply regarded as a tactical necessity. The feeling of many observers, expressed by former Social Democratic leader Jirí Horák, was that the Slovak Party of the Democratic Left had made a 'genuine step in the direction of democratic socialism' (Horák, 1993).

The major issues which dominated politics in Czechoslovakia between the 1990 and 1992 elections were the national question, privatisation, and the issue of lustration. The vast majority of foreign investment went into the Czech Republic, where privatisation of small enterprises was managed in a successful and orderly fashion by Klaus, despite allegations that much of the property has ended up in foreign hands. The 'big' privatisation, started in January 1992, attracted a great deal of popular interest because a 'voucher' system enabled

Czechoslovak citizens to buy shares in newly privatised companies at a sizable discount. Certainly Klaus's competence and confidence has gained him and his Civic Democratic Party, which won 33 per cent of the vote in the general election of June 1992, easily the largest support in the Czech Republic. The Communists, campaigning as the Left Bloc, came second with 14 per cent, and the Social Democrats came third with 7 per cent.

The question posed by Slovaks was whether or not they wanted full independence or maximum autonomy within a Federal Republic. Most of the inefficient heavy industry and armaments factories were in Slovakia, and its unemployment increased at four times the rate of the Czech Republic. Not surprisingly the election in Slovakia produced widespread support for nationalist groupings. The Movement for a Democratic Slovakia (HZDS), led by former communist Vladimir Mečiarc, won 33 per cent, and the National Party won 9 per cent. The former communists, now the Party of the Democratic Left, gained 14 per cent. The Social Democrats gained 5 per cent. The Movement for a Democratic Slovakia favoured continued support for publicly owned industries and a much slower introduction of privatisation. Before the election most of the interest on the national question focused on what the Slovaks were going to demand, but after the election Klaus indicated that the Czechs, more populous and more prosperous, were not interested in negotiating a half–hearted federation. The implication was that the Slovaks would continue to blame the Czechs for their problems. Mečiarc and the HZDS–led Slovak government were thus given little choice but to follow through their nationalist rhetoric and agree to the creation of two separate republics from January 1993.

CONCLUSION

A number of factors were simultaneously present when the communist dictatorships were swept from power. The first two were discussed in the previous chapter, namely, the structural paralysis which prevented fundamental economic or political reform, and the dramatic worsening of the competitive position of the communist economies in the world system. In the cases of Poland and Czechoslovakia, the military suppression of previous reform movements made it clear that the communist system was supported by only a small minority, and this legitimation crisis ensured that there could be no solution based on exhortation or appeals for sacrifice. Only coercion or the threat of greater coercion remained, and that had always been underwritten by Soviet communism's unyielding interpretation of the Yalta division of Europe. Once the Soviet veto was ended, the pressure for change was irresistible. In all the countries concerned a broad political opposition emerged to capitalise on the weakness of the communists. In Poland it was a mass working class movement supported by the Church and intellectuals, many of whom were democratic socialists. In Czechoslovakia the initial opposition had come from within the party, but in the years following the invasion it was the dissident intellectuals linked with Charter 77 who kept the flame of resistance burning, and who emerged to form the Civic Forum/Public Against Violence movement. Once again democratic socialists played a leading role in bringing an end to the dictatorship.

It is pertinent to ask what sort of a revolution took place in Eastern Europe. Primarily it was a political revolution directed against regimes which lacked legitimacy. Agnes Heller argued convincingly in *Dictatorship Over Needs* that the regimes not only lacked popular support but that people saw in the West a model of the pluralist political system which they desired (Feher, Heller & Markus, 1983: part 2). But communist power was embedded in the productive and administrative apparatus which touched everybody's daily lives, so it was natural that the economic structure should also be challenged by the revolution. There was a strong desire not simply to adopt political pluralism but to break down the Yalta barriers and become full members of a new Europe; the restrictions on travel had previously been one of the chief sources of grievance. But this political and cultural 'opening' also involved an economic 'opening'. The ideology of the free market played no significant role in the anti–communist struggle in Eastern Europe, but it quickly swept all before it by its association with the 'free' world. The democratic socialist forces which played a leading role in resisting communism were quickly marginalised. Ironically, the chief beneficiaries of privatisation were those who had administrative access to potentially valuable capital and information, in other words, members of the former communist power elite.

There is no doubt that in general the economic management of the communist countries was poor and environmentally malign. However, to regard this as the decisive factor in their failure raises false hopes about the economic prospects of the new democracies. Some opponents of the communist regimes in Poland and Czechoslovakia who wished to maintain some of the social guarantees provided under communism in the postcommunist system looked with interest at Sweden and Austria as possible role models. The depth of the disparity between the economies has now dispelled such dreams. Gunder Frank has argued that the decisive factor in the collapse of the communist regimes was their vulnerable position in the world economy:

> In particular it was the world economic crisis that spelled the doom of the 'socialist' economies, much more than their 'socialist planning', 'command economy', which is now almost universally blamed for the same. Not unlike the 'third world' economies of Latin America and Africa, the 'second world' economies of the Soviet Union and Eastern Europe were

unable to bear the pace of accelerated competition in the world economy during this period of crisis (Frank, 1993).

While Frank is correct in stressing the significance of the global economic context, his judgement tends to deflect attention away from the structural paralysis which was specific to the communist model, and which defied all attempts at economic and political reform. Nevertheless, it is a sobering reminder of the magnitude of the external problems which now confront the new democracies, putting them in a more precarious position than the situation which faced Spain, Greece, and Portugal when they threw off their dictatorships in the 1970s. The condition of the economic infrastructure and the extent of international debt will ensure low living standards for the forseeable future, and without strict regulation, subsidies, and welfare support there will be extensive and severe poverty. This was apparent after three years of trying to implement a deregulated capitalist model, with the full encouragement of Western governments, the International Monetary Fund, and the World Bank. The possibility of unconditional aid to the East has been hindered by the difficulties faced by the European Community in moving towards political union. Although many of the former communist states wish to join the Community as soon as possible, there is clearly some way to travel before that can be achieved. Unfortunately the focus on the EC has meant that little attention has been paid to promoting an association of East European states which could deal with the Community as a bloc and rectify some of the unfair trading relationships which have developed since 1989 (Horák, 1993; Gowan, 1993). Moreover, the continued political instability of the countries of the former Soviet Union has further diminished the possibility of such an association.

The spectacular success of the former communists in Poland in 1993 was a strong indicator that the successor parties are capable of capitalising on public unrest at the high social cost of the transition to the market economy. The crucial test of their democratic sincerity will be their performance in power and their acceptance of the alternation of government. The other socialist parties have been justifiably suspicious of those former communists claiming to renounce their past mistakes, yet already there have been informal alliances in parliamentary votes on economic and social issues in both the countries reviewed in this chapter. Many old enmities will have to be overcome before the stage is reached when electoral alliances or governmental coalitions can be forged between socialists who were persecuted under communism and those who were implicated in the old regimes. It is clear, however, that there is a high degree of agreement between them on the need to provide welfare and employment rights to protect the vulnerable, and to regulate the economy in the interests of the whole of society. This is certainly a basis for the revival of a different form of socialism in Eastern Europe.

11 Conclusion: Towards a New Internationalism

> Nothing is harder, yet nothing is more necessary, than to speak of certain things whose existence is neither demonstrable nor probable. The very fact that serious and conscientious men treat them as things brings them a step closer to existence and to the possibility of being born (Hermann Hesse, *The Glass Bead Game*).

The revolutions of 1989 appeared to herald a new political era for Europe. For the first time, a system of free elections involving a plurality of parties was to become the accepted process for deciding political power throughout the continent. The European Community seemed geared to proceed towards a federal state, capable of incorporating the new democracies in the forseeable future. However, the disintegration of the Soviet Union and Yugoslavia has been followed by brutal conflicts and political and economic crises. Progress towards European integration has faltered in the face of accentuated economic problems. Stability remains elusive, yet the hope remains that democratic processes will prevail in the new Europe. What problems confront the socialist movements at this volatile juncture? What is their potential? A century ago Friedrich Engels unequivocally pinned his hopes for world socialism on the advent of universal franchise (Marx & Engels, 1973: 649–56), but the electoral strategy was seriously damaged by the division of the socialist movement into communist and social democratic camps in 1919–20. Threequarters of a century later, the collapse of the communist dictatorships and the abandonment of the doctrine of Marxism–Leninism has opened the possibility of reconstructing a new unity around the ideals of democratic socialism. However, the cyclical crisis in the world economy brought unbearable pressure not only on the communist regimes, but also on social democratic economic strategies in Western Europe. Where does this leave socialism?

In assessing the strength of socialism in the former communist states, a number of difficulties arise. Most of the states have had only one or two elections since the end of communist rule, the first elections being 'foundation' events in which broad anti–communist movements subsumed a range of ideological positions. Nationalist formations have also obscured the ideological picture. Some states which have emerged from the former Soviet Union had not held free elections by the end of 1993. In most of the countries the old communist parties have dissolved and reconstituted themselves, ostensibly rejecting democratic centralism and pledging respect for political pluralism. Early election results indicated that these parties were stronger in the poorer countries in the east of the region (Bulgaria, Romania, Serbia, Montenegro and Albania) than in the countries seeking rapidly to establish close links with the West (Hungary, the Czech Republic, Poland, Slovenia, the Baltic Republics). However, the pattern was altered by the victories of the former communists in Lithuania (1992) and Poland (1993). Although social democratic parties have made little impact as yet in the postcommunist countries (Wolchik, 1992), it appears that there is a strong constituency for parties of the Left which are prepared to argue for policies to cushion the impact of market reforms.

In Western Europe there has been a decline in popular support for most of the social democratic parties. The following table indicates the share of the vote of a selection of parties affiliated to the Socialist International up to October 1993:

ELECTORAL PERFORMANCE OF SELECTED S.I. PARTIES

Country	Most recent	Previous	Best result
Austria	42.8 (1990)	43.1 (1986)	51.0 (1979)
France	20.3 (1993)	35.9 (1988)	37.5 (1981)
Germany	33.5 (1990)	37.0 (1987)	45.8 (1972)
Spain	38.7 (1993)	39.6 (1989)	48.4 (1982)
Sweden	38.2 (1991)	43.7 (1987)	50.1 (1968)
U. K.	34.2 (1992)	30.8 (1987)	48.8 (1951)

(Sources; *Socialist Affairs 4*, 1991, pp. 64–5, S. Padgett & W. Paterson, *A History of Social Democracy in Postwar Europe* (1991b: ch. 3), and *The Guardian*).

Following the defeat of the French Socialist Party in March 1993, Spain was the only large country in Western Europe to retain a social democratic government. Despite winning places in government following elections in 1992 and 1993 in Ireland, Denmark, Spain, Norway and Greece, social democrats are removed from the main levers of power in Europe, and have struggled to convince electorates that they have an answer to the pivotal question of mass unemployment. The communist parties, once capable of gaining massive support in France (20 per cent in 1978) and Italy (34 per cent in 1976), now secure around 10 per cent of the vote in France, Spain, and Portugal. 'Left libertarian' parties representing the new social movements have found it difficult to attract more than 6 per cent support, with the exception of the Danish Socialist People's Party (Kitschelt, 1990: 183).

Can the socialist project renew itself and command the support required to resolve the issues of mass unemployment, poverty, and civil strife in Europe, and to address the ecological and economic problems which beset the world as a whole? An assessment of the prospects for renewal has to address three major problems which have always been present in the history of socialist movements, and which have become acute in recent years. The first is the focus on the state as the instrument for achieving social change. The second is the social basis of support for socialism, which now assumes serious proportions with the relative shrinking of the size of the manual working class as a result of changing patterns of accumulation. The third is the question of socialist internationalism.

THE STATE

Socialist and communist parties have consistently placed great emphasis on using the machinery of the central state to take control of their economies and to ensure high levels of social provision. What else could they do? And yet in 1871 Marx warned that 'the working class cannot simply lay hold of the ready-made state machinery, and wield it for its own purposes' (Marx, 1974: 206). Viewing the state apparatus as an expression of ruling class interest, Marx saw the difficulty of using it to further socialist goals. As part of a competitive inter-state system, the state is obliged to provide the most favourable conditions for accumulation. This was true for the communist states, even though private productive property had been largely abolished. Until the collapse of the postwar boom, it was widely accepted by socialists and liberals alike that an increasingly high degree of state intervention was a rational and inexorable development. The experience of the depression in the 1930s provided strong evidence for this, for the countries which overcame unemployment and recovered quickest were the ones with the most vigorous state intervention. The strict state economic management of the war effort provided further evidence that the market could not be relied upon to meet social requirements. In the postwar period the public sector of the economy grew considerably in all the major European countries, and this seemed to offer the degree of economic control needed to conquer cyclical crises. 'Planning' became synonymous with economic rationality and progress. Even communist theorists admitted this possibility when they produced the ideas of 'general crisis' and 'state monopoly capitalism' to explain the sustained growth and relatively full employment of the long postwar boom (Jessop, 1982: 40–53).

Social democracy used the state in a variety of ways, as we have seen, but in the 1970s many began to question whether the existing 'mix' of the economy was leading to a more egalitarian distribution of power and wealth. The programmes of the Left in Britain and France suggested a major transfer of ownership from the private to the public sector, while in Sweden the wage earner funds idea promised the transfer of ownership directly to organised labour. Capitalism, however, reasserted its cyclical volatility in the mid–1970s. Not only was state management of the economy insufficient to prevent the return of mass unemployment, but the state budgets were squeezed severely by the international deflation. States unwilling to cut public expenditure and taxes risked capital flight, investment strikes, and the refusal of credit from the International Monetary Fund. The social democratic commitment to full employment ran up against the capitalist requirement to weaken the power of organised labour. The attack on union power was used to force through changes in the labour process designed to ease the swift introduction of new technology and achieve increased productivity.

The communist states, occupying a semi–peripheral position in the world economy, fell further behind the advanced economies. Encouraged to borrow money to modernise their production, they were unable to generate the exports to pay their rapidly increasing debts. Their position was exacerbated by the inflexible nature of their command economies and the commitment to full employment. The threat of bankruptcy and the presence of a large reserve army of unemployed enabled firms in the West to extract high productivity gains. In the communist countries this could not happen, although Hungary was resorting to it in the late 1980s. All these states saw the need to introduce market mechanisms into their economies, but all attempts at reform stalled at the point at which the stability of the party–state apparatus was threatened. The economic disintegration of these states has had a wider effect, calling into question the whole idea that socialism is compatible with efficiency. The conclusions are inescapable: the idea of socialism in one country (and later one zone) was a theoretical nonsense and a practical disaster, and the undemocratic nature of these states contributed greatly to their inability to respond to the pressures.

If it were true that the neo–liberal policies which have been executed in Western Europe were efficient in resolving problems of low growth, debt, pollution, mass unemployment and the attendant social problems of poverty, homelessness and crime, then socialism would indeed be in terminal decline. However, it is evident that they have failed to resolve these problems, and indeed that they have prolonged them. It should also be noted that despite the 'rolling back the state' rhetoric of the New Right, the state continues to consume high levels of Gross Domestic Product even where socialists have not been in government for many years, as in Britain and Germany. The framework of the welfare state is still in place, despite cuts in provision, and it seems to be something that even the New Right ideologues have been unable to dispense with (Pierson, 1991: ch. 6; Offe, 1984: ch. 6). In Britain, after 13 years of Conservative Government, public expenditure was still a high 42 per cent of Gross Domestic Product, while the tax burden actually increased slightly between 1979 and 1992.

The social democratic governments in Sweden and Austria handled their economies much more successfully than those within the European Community during the 1980s, in terms of the trade off between inflation and unemployment and the maintenance of growth (Leborgne & Lipietz, 1990), although by the end of the decade the pressures to dance to the laissez faire tune had grown harder to resist. The creation of the single market for goods and services in the European Community and the commitment to price stability through semi–fixed exchange rates are factors which have further diminished what relative autonomy the member states once enjoyed. At the same time this de facto loss of sovereignty has not been compensated by the creation of a proper European state with the power to make the sort of interventions needed to remedy the social costs of the play of free market forces (Godley, 1993). It is not the case that socialists have been bereft of ideas which, if implemented, might combine economic efficiency with egalitarian goals, e.g. the wage earner funds and the renewal funds in Sweden, social partnership in Austria, competitive state–owned companies in France, and even the National Enterprise Board in Britain. What should be clear from the cases examined in this book is that it is no longer possible to implement socialist policies in an isolated nation state in the modern world economy.

Socialist forms of state intervention in the past were frequently bureaucratic, unresponsive and ineffective, and there is no doubt that in the future socialist movements will have to rethink state intervention to make it less centralised, more accountable and more flexible in regard to labour processes, management systems, working hours and location. The demand for accountability does not need to stop at the public sector, and if extended to all aspects of decision–making and remuneration in society it would represent a significant advance in democratic control. There are, of course, major economic and social problems which can be resolved by state intervention only at 'levels' where the state (as a formal public body) barely exists, or exists with little public accountability, in Europe and the world. This is another aspect of 'democratic loss'. At the moment when virtually the whole continent has the right to vote in free elections for the first time, the governments they elect have less power than ever before. If socialists are to aspire to use political power to attenuate the power of transnational capital, they will have to think beyond the nation state.

SOCIAL SUPPORT

The working class has always been the natural constituency of communist and socialist movements. In the early days of socialism those who depended on the sale of their labour power were in a majority only in Britain, but it was assumed that this class would predominate in most European societies as capitalism developed. As the class was exploited in the process of capital accumulation, it had an 'objective' interest in achieving socialism. Brought together in the workplace and in communities, the working class developed a certain stability and homogeneity, and provided the socialist and labour movements with mass memberships.

The development of new technology has meant that fewer manual workers are required in the production process. There has been a large increase in the numbers involved in clerical work, services, and professions. There has been a large increase in part-time work, with a preponderance of women in this category. The strength of organised labour has been severely weakened by the persistence of mass unemployment, the pressure to deregulate the labour market and make the labour process more 'flexible'. The creation of mass unemployment has led to an increase in poverty for millions while the working 'working' class have seen their real incomes rise. All these changes have produced fragmentation (Therborn, 1992: 22–4). Unions and socialist parties have suffered declining membership, communities have been destroyed through shifts in the pattern of production and the demand for greater job mobility. In addition, the development of the mass sale of consumer durables has carried with it an ideology of individual acquisitiveness. Crosland, writing in 1956, believed that the establishment of the welfare state had led to a change of values away from 'self help or aggressive individualism' and a trend 'towards equality' (Crosland, 1968: 64, 284). In reality, the welfare state provided the social wage which served as the basis for the growth of consumerism. Whatever the material benefits, the values which this development carried were the opposite of those forecast by Crosland.

Even if the working class is defined in such a way as to embrace all those dependent on the sale of their labour power (Meiksins, 1986; Wilde, 1990), it cannot be assumed that the various interests of this fragmented class can be mobilised in anti–systemic movements. In the chapter on Sweden it was noted that rivalries between different groups of workers had destroyed the solidaristic wage bargaining system and contributed to the defeat of the Social Democrats. Sweden has the most highly unionised workforce in the world, and only a decade before it was pushing for some of the most radical reforms yet attempted in a capitalist democracy. The ethos of individual acquisitiveness has been aggressively promoted in recent years, and social democratic parties have trembled to challenge it for fear of losing the support of those who prioritise personal wealth above all else. This acquiescence has made it more difficult to mount the counter arguments concerning the alarming social effects of widespread poverty and hopelessness, and the increasing disavowal by government of responsibility for problems begging for collective action such as homelessness, pollution, urban decay and traffic pollution.

Socialist parties in Europe have little choice but to pursue coalitions and alliances with groups within the broad working class who do not necessarily see their interests in class terms, but whose demands are broadly in line with socialism's historical project of taming the power of capital and pursuing egalitarian goals (Esping–Andersen, 1985: 321–2). Alliances or coalitions have often been regarded with suspicion by socialists, who see their radical aspirations blunted by expediency. But the new social movements have mobilised enormous support at a time when social democratic and communist politics have been in retreat, and often their agendas introduce more radical options than those of the traditional Left parties (Müller–Rommel, 1990). New social movements perhaps offer a new and alternative sense of community, but in general they lack the muscle to effect the collective action which their demands require. It could well be through such alliances that the question of mass unemployment could be tackled. The social democratic acceptance of mass unemployment has been its greatest weakness, and a contradiction of everything it stood for when it was at its electoral peak. 'Growth–led' strategies from isolated social democratic government have failed to make an impression, but ideas for work–sharing could be more successful. Campaigns on reduced working hours, extended education, earlier retirement, flexible working hours and working life 'breaks' could attract widespread support across the European Community (Gorz, 189: part 3; Scott, 1993). Similarly, concrete initiatives on the environment could create new jobs and provide visible results.

However, millions of largely young activists have been justifiably unimpressed by the attempts of social democratic parties to simultaneously incorporate and marginalise their demands. There has always been a 'totalising' tendency in both social democracy and communism, whereby attempts are made to embrace all radical demands but ultimately to reduce them to the discipline and priorities of party leaders. The mass protests of 1968 were in part directed against this ossification of the old Left. However, there are signs in Germany, France, Denmark and Holland that pluralist arrangements involving coalitions or alliances are being seen by many socialists as not simply as an expediency but as a desirable and democratic process of negotiating priorities (Bronner, 1991: 161–4; Lafontaine, 1992). Above all this will involve a redefinition of what politics ought to be about, involving a consideration of the nature and future of society, the quality of life, civil rights and social responsibilities. These are the 'grand' questions which challenge the individualist assumptions of liberals and conservatives. They threaten to break the discursive closure which has accompanied the apparently irresistible power of global economic forces. But for socialists to change the agenda of political debate they would have to demonstrate ways of resisting that power. Strategies for tackling poverty, pollution, discrimination quickly run up against the barrier of the limited autonomy of the nation state, and there are some signs that socialists are recognising the need to develop effective forms of international action (Bronner, 1991: 177–87; Denitch, 1990, ch. 6; Picciotto, 1991).

INTERNATIONALISM

Socialism has always been proud of its commitment to internationalism, expressed in its famous songs, *The Internationale* and *The Red Flag*, but in practice socialist internationalism has been less than impressive. The failure to mount an effective resistance to the carnage of the First World War dealt the deathblow to the Second International. The Third International quickly turned into an extension of Soviet foreign policy and involved the blind obedience to Stalin's definitions of what was required to promote the world proletarian revolution. It also involved the murder of many of its members. After the Second World War the Soviet army invaded Hungary and the armies of the Warsaw Pact invaded Czechoslovakia in the name of 'proletarian internationalism'. The social democratic parties meanwhile threw in their lot with the Americans by supporting the North Atlantic Treaty Organisation, a nuclear alliance armed to the teeth against the communist threat and quite prepared to tolerate neo–fascist allies. The Socialist International was not re–formed until 1951 at Frankfurt. Not surprisingly it was totally opposed to the communists, for the social democratic parties of Eastern Europe had been eliminated during the communist takeovers. The British Labour Party, the largest member, was completely uninterested in the idea of European unity, and so the Socialist International became an information and discussion group with few concrete achievements. There was no shortage of statements to the effect that only a united Europe led by social democrats could find the fabled third way between Russian communism and American capitalism, but the parties remained wedded to their national strategies (Featherstone, 1988). For the millions of young Europeans protesting against the US war in Vietnam in the late 1960s and early 1970s, the 'say nothing' attitude of social democracy was unacceptable. The British Labour Party was willing to go to great lengths to preserve the 'special relationship' with the United States, and the German SPD leader Helmut Schmidt actually inititiated the 'dual track' NATO policy which brought a new range of nuclear weapons on to European territory in the early 1980s.

The end of the cold war has provided an opening for a new form of socialist internationalism. There will continue to be major differences about the scope and pace of reforms designed to mitigate the worst effects of the market, but there might be agreement on two premises for future action. First, it is no longer conceivable to think of the successful implementation of a strong socialist programme, such as that of British Labour in 1973 or the French Project of 1981, at the level of the nation state. Second, the European Community is developing into a political union which will be the main locus of power for all Europeans, and will be a major player on the world stage.

Whose Europe? Whose World?

It has often been stated that the Common Market, set up by the Treaty of Rome in 1957, was a 'capitalist club', and that the accelerated integration announced by the Single European Act of 1986 has fulfilled a largely 'neo–liberal agenda' (Grahl & Teague, 1989). The Europe of '1992' which flowed from this Act was a decisive step away from national sovereignty, but because it was largely 'economic' in character, the traditional liberal separation between the economic and political spheres ensured that the process developed as an administrative exercise rather than a political debate. The completion of the single market among the 12 states of the European Community permitted the free movement of goods, services, capital and people, and the savings for European capital are clear. Some commentators have argued that 'European integration is antithetical to social democracy' (Lemke & Marks, 1991: 15–16). However, Jacques Delors, the President of the European Commission, disagrees, arguing that Europe could be 'the theatre in which social democracy accomplishes its mission' (Delors, 1989: 32).

In order to understand the potential for social democracy in a new form of European Union we have to consider the implications of agreements reached at the Maastricht Summit in December 1991. Despite the fact that the words 'federal union' were left out of the treaty at the insistence of the British government, the general direction indicated by the agreements pointed to just such an outcome. Full economic union was to be sealed with a single currency by 1999, although the British Government negotiated a clause to enable it to opt out of this arrangement. In preparation for this it was agreed to set up a European Central Bank, probably by the end of 1996. The priority of stable prices was reflected in limitations on borrowing and deficits which reflected the predominance of neo–liberal economics in the 1980s and which, if implemented, would guarantee the continuation of low growth and unemployment. Nevertheless, the proposed Bank will also be required by statute to support the Community aims of high levels of employment, social protection, sustainable growth and environmental protection (Holland, 1993: 71–3). All governments except Britain's agreed to sign the Social Chapter, with a range of guarantees on maximum hours and health and safety measures. In terms of decision making there was still a considerable 'democratic deficit', as it has become known, with strict limitations placed on the powers of the European Parliament. All power of initiation lies with the unelected Commission, while the Council of Ministers has a final say on legislation, either by unanimous or majority voting, depending on the scope of the issue at hand. The principle of subsidiarity means that the Community is limited to acting in areas where it has 'exclusive competence', and all other matters should be left to the nation states. While this implies a rather weaker centre than most modern federation, it also opens the possiblity that subsidiarity could be used by regions or cities to claim decision–making power from their central governments, and to deal directly with the European authorities. The Community comprises approximately 345 million people, and it surpassed the United States in gross domestic product in 1990 (Somers, 1991: 16). There is already a free trade arrangement between the Community and the seven members of the European Free Trade Association. It has been envisaged that by 1995 the Community will be expanded to include Sweden and Austria, and possibly Finland and Norway. It is possible that some of the former communist states may join at a later stage.

The Socialists formed the largest group in the European Parliament at Strasbourg following the 1989 elections. If the various 'green', 'rainbow' and communist groups are counted as potential allies, there is the possibility of a progressive coalition. Four countries at the front of the queue for membership, Sweden, Austria, Norway and Finland, all have strong social democratic movements. In ideological terms, the socialists have an advantage over conservative rivals on the issue of nationalism. Socialism has always espoused internationalism, but in practice socialist parties have had to fight for reforms through national parliaments, and have had to represent themselves as responsible guardians of the national interest. The right–wing parties consistently claimed to be the unswerving upholders of the national interest, and it was easier for them to do so, as the political institutions and traditions were largely the creations of their ruling elites. Although the fighting in Eastern Europe reminds us of the enduring mobilising power of nationalism, it is clear that it has nothing to deliver in the new Europe.

It would suit some business interests if the new Europe was restricted to little more than a de–regulated trading zone, leaving a loose collection of nation states in which the scope for radical reform or even the defence of welfare provision is severely restricted by the power of multi–national capital and the financial arrangements of the Community. This lends new meaning to the phrase 'democratic deficit', which has hitherto primarily referred to the restrictions placed on the powers of the European Parliament. This vision of a 'minimal state' Europe would render citizens virtually powerless in the face of business interests. This is one possible direction pointed to by Maastricht, with Britain's opt-out from the Social Chapter removing the guarantee that all states will face similar duties to their citizens. In addition, the restrictions on the level of public borrowing pose a threat to traditional Keynesian means of reflating the economy. The assimilation of more and more countries, particularly the poorer ones of Eastern Europe, may limit the extent to which 'best practices' in social provision, workers' rights and regional support could be enacted across the continent.

The opposition to Maastricht was an understandable response to the 'railroading' of public opinion which has been associated with this continental-wide corporatist compromise. Yet Maastricht probably offers the best chance for the Left to push for developing the strongest possible United States of Europe with full powers to the European Parliament and effective regional decentralisation to give citizens a variety of arenas in which to counter the dominant economic powers. An added complication is that some of the left-wing opposition to the Treaty does not emanate from a feeling that it does not offer sufficient democracy or social rights, but from an outdated commitment to pursuing 'national roads' to socialism. The conclusions drawn from the cases studied in this book indicate that this is a flawed scenario. However, socialist suspicions about accelerated integration have been fuelled by the administrative nature of what is, after all, potentially the most significant developement in the continent's history. The Delors strategy of a two-stage leap to a federal Europe was promoted with great expertise in committee rooms throughout the continent. Doubters were occasionally treated to a more public justification, such as Delors' great success in winning over the British TUC to the idea when he spoke to the 1988 Congress. The whole 'Social Europe' strategy has been conducted in a familiar social democratic 'executive' style, without mobilising popular support.

In both economic and political spheres, the internationalisation of labour lags well behind the internationalisation of capital. A good example was provided by the respective responses to the 'Vredeling Directive' of 1982 which emanated from the European Commission and which offered workers in multinational firms the right to information on future policies which affected them. The proposals were rendered harmless after the most intensive lobbying from American and European business (DeVos, 1989). The representatives of capital have put far greater financial resources into the lobbying process, and they represent interests which are consciously international. The nation-state remains the focus for labour movement activity, and there have been few examples of international industrial action. Because the European Parliament has been a parliament in name only with no legislative powers, the labour movements have been unable to benefit from the strength of the Socialist Group. MacShane has outlined a number of areas in which labour movement activity might develop across Europe, in particular in the struggle for a shorter working year and on environmental protection (MacShane, 1990). In both of these areas the potential for linkages with the new social movements is strong. Many of the 'new politics' parties in Europe have already framed their programmes in terms of the need for European–wide policies (Lambert, 1991: 22).

The proposed monetary union will end a defining aspect of national sovereignty, an independent currency, and it will hasten the recognition that sovereignty has shifted to the European centre. Yet in recent national elections the debates continue to focus on the small number of national issues that national governments can affect only marginally. The development of coordinated policies by the Left has been confined to the Socialist Group in the European Parliament. Bjorn Engholm, when leader of the German SPD, commented that 'at every party Congress in Europe we talk about global inter–dependencies in terms of the economy, the environment and other issues, yet our social–democratic parties are organised in a classically national manner'. He also notes how 'ludicrous' it is that the European Parliament has less power than did the Reichstag before the First World War (Engholm, 1991). The formal announcement of the creation of The Party of European Socialists at the annual congress of the Confederation of Socialist Parties in the European Community in the Hague in November 1992 was long overdue. Its membership was extended beyond the Community to include the major socialist parties in Austria, Sweden and Finland. Under the Presidency of Belgian Foreign Minister Willy Claes, the new party pledged to create a common manifesto by the end of 1993, but it was clear that the party's 'organic development' was to be left to national parties (Claes, 1993: 9–12). The comments of four leading socialist politicians, Andras Papandreou, Michel Rocard, Poul Nyrup Rasmussen and Mario Soares, made it clear that the new party is likely to be no more than a consultative vehicle for selected representatives of the various national executives (European Labour Forum, 10, 1993: 13–7). It was clearly not envisaged that the new party would claim some measure of organisational independence so that it could recruit in all the major cities and regions, although this might well mobilise support from those disillusioned with the performance of their national parties. Such a development would reverse a trend dating back more than a century, since the disintegration of the First International and the founding of the socialist or labour parties.

The potential of a united Europe is immense, but so too are the problems which face the continent in the closing decade of the century. It has been estimated that with growth of 1.5 per cent and low levels of 'cohesion expenditure' from the European budget, unemployment in the Community will average over 14 per cent in the year 2000, with levels of 24 or 25 per cent in Spain and Ireland (Coates, 1993: 12). Cohesion and social funds are designed to help the poorer regions offset the market losses suffered as a result of economic integration. But the Community budget is planned to be only 3 per cent of the public expenditure of the member states by 1997 (Delors, 1993: 46), and as long as it is so small the cohesion and social funds will be inadequate to offset the market losses suffered by the poorest regions. A European Recovery Programme involving widespread redistribution, public investement, large–scale training and research programmes and a substantial downward revision of working hours is imperative if the destructive tendencies of the recent past are to be reversed. It is an imperative for the re–establishment of the practical relevance of European socialism.

If we stay with the scenario of a strong European state with a Red–Green political leadership, exciting possibilities open which have global implications. Europe could emerge as the new hegemonic power in the world, the first one pledged to the creation of a more egalitarian world economy. Barrett Brown has argued that the new Europe could pursue those aspects of Keynesian policy which were not implemented after the Second World War due to the power of American capital:

> What was established was the Bretton Woods complex of financial institutions – the World Bank, IMF and GATT. These fell very short of what Keynes proposed – a world money, managed by an international bank and an international trade organisation. Bretton Woods became an instrument of United States hegemony and the dollar became the world's money (Barrett Brown, 1992: 9).

The problem is that no single power is prepared to take the lead to build such a cooperative system. Despite the fact that the economy of the European Community is now the largest in the world, its lack of full statehood means that 'it has no more power than its weakest member' (Barrett Brown, 1992: 10). This weakness was noted in the protracted Uruguay round of the GATT negotiations to liberalise trade.

The international debt disaster constitutes one of the world's most pressing problems, and only international cooperation at the highest level will resolve it. The gap between the rich 'core' countries and the semi–peripheral and peripheral countries has grown wider (Chase–Dunn, 1991: 266–8; Arrighi, 1991). In the 1970s the banks were flush with funds invested from high oil revenues, and they loaned on a massive scale to countries who attempted to modernise their economies and improve their position through export–led growth. The resultant debt crisis is of such enormity that the third world is impoverished and the world economy is finding it extremely difficult to climb out of depression (MacEwan, 1990; Gill & Law, 1988: 182–8). To write off the debts of the world's poorest countries and to reduce the others to manageable proportions would require a new international banking system and world currency which could only be set up by agreement between Europe, Japan and the United States of America. Only with the support of the United Nations could there be an element of democratic control. The evolution of such institutions could pave the way to a more progressive management of the terms of trade, in the long–term advantage of all participants. Such a solution is highly interventionist, and, along with the emergence of monopoly production in major trading blocs, challenges the logic of capitalist development.

Accountable international institutions with executive powers could provide the means to resolve the world's pressing ecological problems. There has been a widespread acknowledgement that these major problems need to be resolved by international agreement, but the lack of decisive action at the Earth Summit in Rio de Janeiro in June 1992 indicated the extent to which such globally rational cooperation is thwarted by the short–term profit interests of the major trading blocs. It is another indication of the pressing need to control the power of multinational capital through international political control. Arrighi has pointed out that decisions of supreme importance are increasingly taken by institutions such as the World Bank, the Group of Seven, or the United Nations Security Council (Arrighi, 1991: 64–5; Picciotto, 1991). The instruments of world government are emerging. The political nature of such global power will be decided in the next century, but socialist movements and ideas will be involved in the contest (Wallerstein, 1988: 156–8; Chase–Dunn, 1991: 343–5). However, at the global level the problem of the 'democratic deficit' looms larger than in the European Community, which is going through a crisis of representation in which the citizens are turned into quietistic subjects. At the world level this situation is replicated, with faceless institutions dictating the ways of life of millions of people (Wood, 1989).

There are many obstacles for those seeking to renew socialism in the framework of a federal Europe. The first is the danger of what has been described as 'Fortress Europe', which not only involves an unwillingness to take the initiative on the problems of the world economy, but daily demonstrates its Eurocentrism in its treatment of immigrant workers (Barrett Brown, 1991). A powerful Europe exerting an aggressive Euro–nationalism is a frightening thought for socialists and supporters of the new social movements. Socialists are pledged by their links in the Socialist International to combat this impulse to a 'new isolationism'. And there is a widespread awareness that in a world trade war there would be no winners. In economic terms, what is to prevent the world market logic, which has thwarted Keynesianism at the level of the nation state, prevailing at the European level? The sheer size of the new European market will be sufficient to ensure that threats by companies to leave such a market would lack credibility. In terms of opposition to a shorter working life, minimum wages and better social provision, the arguments are already being made from some sections of business (particularly the Confederation of British Industry) that this will reduce competitivess *vis-a-vis* the United States and Japan. However, the size of the internal market and the pressures faced by the American economy makes the argument of international competitiveness far less compelling than when it has been trotted out in medium–sized nation states. It is important to remember that Europe is virtually economically self–sufficient (Leborgne & Lipietz, 1990: 183). Indeed, capital largely based in Germany should be wary of capital based in poorer countries of Europe taking advantage of lower wages and looser regulations. The isolation of the British on the Social Chapter indicates that the majority of business interests represented in the Union of Employers' Confederations of Europe are keen to avoid 'social dumping'.

In political terms, if the parties of the Right can win appeals for 'cheap government' at national level, why not at the European level? For example, recovery programmes and debt repudiations are costly and necessitate high taxation; would this deter the voters? In this respect the consistency and determination of European socialism will meet a stern test, and its ability to forge close alliances with the new social movements will be vital if success is to be secured. The conservative forces will face two immense difficulties. The first is their historic affiliation to the nation, which is particularly pronounced in Britain and France. Right–wing nationalist groups are likely to split the support for conservatism for many years to come. The second is that conservative opposition to viable programmes for combatting mass unemployment and poverty would leave them to vindicate an increasingly indefensible *status quo*, the effects of which will not simply be confined to the 'new poor'. The success of the socialists is largely dependent on their capacity to develop and publicise recovery programmes, and to show some tangible signs that they are achievable even within the limitations of the nation–state. Perhaps the most difficult factor to estimate is the effect which the postcommunist states will have on the political disposition of the new Europe. Support for socialist movements has been small since 1989, but the egalitarian impulses are still strong and there is sure to be a strong public sector in the new democracies.

If the socialist movements can make a campaigning reality out of their commitment to internationalism they will establish a powerful opposition to the power of international capital. The Socialist International, once dominated by Europe, is now a world–wide body. It has produced or sponsored a number of reports and initiatives on North–South relations, debt and dependency, and the need for global agreements to protect the environment. Taken separately, the policies suggested may not appear to be revolutionary, but their implementation would refute the dynamics of neo–liberal world capitalism. A renewed socialist internationalism would have to seek democratic control over the new power centres of international finance and transnational capital. It is an illusion to think that these powers can be effectively controlled at the level of the nation–state, but the development of a democratic European state could create the context in which socialist politics recovers its relevance. But would this politics be restricted to a 'weak' form of socialism, seeking only to redress the worst effects of capitalism without threatening its existence as a mode of production? In 1950 Wilfred Fienburgh wrote that the internationalisation of basic industries provided the best form of control over economic activity to ensure the fulfilment of social goals. He added that the idea would be resisted 'until the ideal of a West European Community has been accepted and has been given some political and parliamentary significance' (Fienburgh, 1950: 9). Over 40 years later the majority of the European nations are on the verge of a new political union, but the development of international common ownership is nowhere discussed. The need to regulate the global and domestic economies is even greater now than it was then, and the drive towards monopoly production has continued remorselessly. As long as capitalism continues to demonstrate its inability to deliver security and prosperity in its world system, the question of the ownership and control of the means of production and exchange will remain open.

References

Abse, T. (1985) 'Judging the PCI' in *New Left Review* 153.

Afanasyev, Y. (1988), 'The 19th Conference of the CPSU' in *New Left Review* 171.

Aganbegyan, A. (1989), *Moving the Mountain: Inside the Perestroika Revolution*, (Bantam, London).

Aganbegyan, A. (1988), 'New Directions in Soviet Economics' in *New Left Review* 169.

Ambler, J. (1985), (ed), *The French Socialist Experiment* (Institute for the Study of Human Issues, Philadelphia).

Ambos, K., (1988), 'The Greens and the West German Federal Election of 1987: The New 'Third Party'?' in *Politics* 8 (1).

Amin, S. (1990), *Maldevelopment: Anatomy of a Global Failure* (Zed, London).

Amyot, G. (1981), *The Italian Communist Party: The Crisis of the Popular Front Strategy* (Croom Helm, London).

Andrew, C. & Gordievsky, O. (1991), *K.G.B.: The Insider Story of its Foreign Operations from Lenin to Gorbachev* (Spectre, London).

Arato, A. (1982), 'Empire versus Civil Society: Poland 1981–82' in *Telos* 50.

Armstrong, P., Glyn, A., Harrison, J. (1984), *Capitalism Since World War Two: The Making and Breakup of the Great Boom* (Fontana, London, 1984).

Arnot, B. (1988), 'Gorbachev's Industrial and Economic Policies: Continuity or Change?' in *Politics* 8 (1).

Arrighi, G. (1991), 'World Income Inequalities and the Future of Socialism' in *New Left Review* 189.

Arrighi, G., Hopkins, A., Wallerstein, I. (1989), *Antisystemic Movements* (Verso, London).

Ascherson, N. (1981), *The Polish August* (Penguin, Harmondsworth).

Ash, T. G. (1991), *The Polish Revolution: Solidarity* (Granta, London).

Aslund, A. (1991), *Gorbachev's Struggle for Economic Reform* (Pinter, London).

Avrich, P. (1967), *The Russian Anarchists* (Princeton University Press, New Jersey).

Bahro, R. (1984), *The Alternative in Eastern Europe* (Verso, London).

Bain, G. n.d. Papers, University of Warwick Modern Records Section.

Bairoch, P. (1981), 'The Main Trends in National Economic Disparities Since the Industrial Revolution' in P. Bairoch & M. Levy–Leboyer (eds) *Disparities in Economic Development Since the Industrial Revolution* (Macmillan, London).

Bairoch, P. (1982), 'International Industrialisation Levels From 1750 to 1980' in *The Journal of European Economic History* 11 (2).

Balibar, E. (1977), *On the Dictatorship of the Proletariat* (New Left Books, London).

Ball, K. (1988), 'Reaffirming the Limits' in *Labour Focus on Eastern Europe* 10 (1).

Barjonet, A. (1968), 'CGT 1968: Subjectivism to the Rescue of the Status Quo', in Posner, C. (ed), *Reflections on the Revolution in France: 1968* (Penguin, Harmondsworth).

Barrett–Brown, M. (1979), 'The Growth and Distribution of Income and Wealth' in Coates, K. (ed), *What Went Wrong: Explaining the Fall of the Labour Government* (Spokesman, Nottingham).

Barratt Brown, M. (1990), 'Only One World' in *European Labour Forum* 1.

Barrett Brown, M. (1991), *European Union: Fortress or Democracy?* (Spokesman, Nottingham).

Barratt Brown, M. (1992) 'Beyond Marx and Keynes' in *European Labour Forum* 7.

Barratt Brown, M. (1993a), 'The War in Yugoslavia and the Debt Burden' in *Capital and Class* 50.

Barratt Brown, M. (1993b) 'Money, Debt and Slump' in Coates, K. & Barrett Brown, M. eds, *A European Recovery Programme* (Spokesman, Nottingham).

Barrett, M. (1980), *Women's Oppression Today: Problems in Marxist–Feminist Analysis* (Verso, London).

Batt, J. (1991), *East Central Europe from Reform to Transformation* (Royal Institute of International Affairs/Pinter, London).

Baumann, B. (1977), *Wie Alles Anfing: How It All Began* (Pulp Press, Vancouver).

Bell, D. & Criddle, B. (1988), *The French Socialist Party: The Emergence of a Party of Government* (Clarendon Press, Oxford).

Bell, D., *The Coming of Post–Industrial Society* (Basic Books, New York, 1973).

Bell, D. & Criddle, B, (1989), 'The Decline of the French Communist Party' in the *British Journal of Political Science* 19 (4).

Benn, T. (1974), *Speeches by Tony Benn* (Spokesman Books, Nottingham).

Benn, T. (1982), *Parliament, People and Power: Agenda for A Free Society* (New Left Books, London).

Benn, T. (1989), *Against The Tide: Diaries, 1973–76* (Hutchinson, London).

Benn, T. (1979), *Arguments for Socialism* (Jonathan Cape, London).

Berend, I. (1990), *The Hungarian Economic Reforms, 1953–1988* (Cambridge University Press, Cambridge).

Berend, I. & Ranki, G. (1985), *The Hungarian Economy in the Twentieth Century* (Croom Helm, London).

Berghahn, V. R. (1988), 'Corporatism in Germany in Historical Perspective' in Cox, A. & O'Sullivan, N. (eds) *The Corporate State: Corporatism and the State Tradition in Western Europe* (Edward Elgar, Aldershot).

Berki, R. N. (1975) *Socialism* (Dent, London).

Bettelheim, C. (1978), *Class Struggles in the USSR, Second Period, 1924–30,* trans. B. Pearce (Harvester, Sussex).

Bicunic, R. (1973), *Economic Policy in Socialist Yugoslavia* (Cambridge University Press, Cambridge).

Birnbaum, P. (1985), 'The Socialist Elite, "Les Gros" and the State' in Cerny, P. & Schain, M. (eds) *Socialism, the State and Public Policy in France* (Pinter, London).

Block, F. (1980), 'Eurocommunism and the Stalemate of European Capitalism' in Boggs, C. & Plotke, D., (eds) *The Politics of Eurocommunism: Socialism in Transition* (Macmillan, London).

Bloomfield, J.(1979), *Passive Revolution: Politics and the Czechoslovak Working Class, 1945–1948* (Alison & Busby, London).

Botella, J. (1988), 'Spanish Communism in Crisis: The Communist Party of Spain' in Waller & Meindert (eds), *Communist Parties in Western Europe.*

Camiller, P. (1984), 'The Eclipse of Spanish Communism' in *New Left Review* 147.

Bramwell, A. (1989), *Ecology in the 20th Century: A History* (Yale University Press, New Haven and London).

Brandt, W. (1978), *People and Politics: The Years 1960 –1975* (Collins, London).

Brandt Commission (1983), *Common Crisis – North–South: Cooperation for World Recovery* (Pan, London).

Brandt Commission (1980), *North–South: A Programme For Survival* (Pan, London).

Braunthal, G. (1983), *The West German Social Democrats, 1969–82: Profile of a Party in Power* (Westview Press, Boulder).

Braunthal, G. (1989), 'Public Order and Civil Liberties' in Smith, G., Paterson,

W. & Merkl, P. (eds), *Developments in West German Politics* (Macmillan, Basingstoke).

Brett, E. A. (1985), *The World Economy Since the War: The Politics of Uneven Development* (Macmillan, Basingstoke).

Broido, V. (1987), *Lenin and the Mensheviks: The Persecution of Socialists under Bolshevism* (Gower, Aldershot).

Bronner, S. (1991), *Socialism Unbound* (Routledge, New York and London).

Brooks, R., Eagle, A. & Short, C. (1990), 'Quotas Now: Women in the Labour Party', Fabian Tract 541.

Brus, W. (1988), 'Enterprise and Socialism – Are They Compatible? Lessons From Eastern Europe and China' in *Praxis International* 8 (1).

Bukharin, N. (1982), *Selected Writings on the State and Transition to Socialism* (M. E. Sharpe, New York).

Bull, M. (1991), 'Whatever Happened to Italian Communism? Explaining the Dissolution of the Largest Communist Party in the West' in *West European Politics* 14 (4).

Burg, S. (1986) 'Elite Conflict in Post–Tito Yugoslavia' in *Soviet Studies* 38 (2).

Burk, K. & Cairncross, A. (1992), *'Goodbye Great Britain': The 1976 IMF Crisis* (Yale University Press, London).

Burns, R. & Van der Will, W. (1988), *Protest and Democracy in West Germany: Extra Parliamentary Opposition and the Democratic Agenda* (Macmillan, London).

Buttafuoco, A. (1980), 'Italy, The Feminist Challenge' in Boggs, C. & Plotke, D. (eds), *The Politics of Eurocommunism, Socialism in Transition* (Macmillan, London).

Callaghan, J. (1988), *Time and Chance* (Collins/Fontana, London).

Carew, A. (1987), *Labour Under the Marshall Plan: The Politics of Productivity and the Marketing of Management Science* (Manchester University Press, Manchester).

Carr, W. (1987), 'German Social Democracy Since 1945' in R. Fletcher (ed), *Bernstein to Brandt: A Short History of German Social Democracy* (Edward Arnold, London).

Carr, E. H. (1983), *The Russian Revolution from Lenin to Stalin, 1917–1929* (Macmillan, London).

Carrillo, S. (1977), *Eurocommunism and the State* (Lawrence & Wishart, London).

Carter, B. (1985), *Capitalism, Class Conflict and the New Middle Class* (Routledge Kegan Paul, London).

Carter, A. (1982), *Democratic Reform in Yugoslavia: The Changing Role of the Party* (Pinter, London).

Carver, T. (1987), *A Marx Dictionary* (Polity Press, Cambridge).

Casini, S. (1991), 'Refondazione Communista' in *Labour Focus on Eastern Europe* 1992 (1).

Castle, B. (1980), *The Castle Diaries 1974–76*, (Weidenfeld & Nicolson, London).

Chase–Dunn, C. (1989), *Global Formation: Structures of the World–Economy* (Blackwell, Oxford).

Cheles, L., Ferguson, R., Vaughan, M. (1991), *Neo–fascism in Europe* (Longman, London).

Childs, D. (1966), *From Schumacher to Brandt: The Story of German Socialism*, 1945–1965 (Pergamon, Oxford).

Childs, D. (1982), *The GDR: Moscow's German Ally* (Allen & Unwin, London).

Churchill, W. (1988a), *The Second World War*, volume five (Penguin, Harmondsworth).

Churchill, W. (1988b), *The Second World War*, volume six (Penguin, Harmondsworth).

Claes, W. (1993), 'What's in a Name?' in *European Labour Forum* 10.

Claudin, F. (1975), *The Communist Movement; From Comintern to Cominform* (Penguin, Harmondsworth).

Claudin, F. (1978), *Eurocommunism and Socialism*, (New Left Books, London).

Coates, D. (1975), *The Labour Party and the Struggle for Socialism* (Cambridge University Press, Cambridge).

Coates, K. (1979) (ed), *What Went Wrong: Explaining the Fall of the Labour Government* (Spokesman, Nottingham).

Coates, K. (1993), 'The Dimensions of Recovery' in Coates, K. & Barrett Brown, M., *A European Recovery Programme* (Spokesman, Nottingham).

Cobler, S. (1978), *Law, Order and Politics in West Germany* (Penguin, Harmondsworth).

Cohn–Bendit, D. (1968), *Obsolete Communism: The Left Wing Alternative* (Deutsch, London).

Cole, G. D. H. (1978), 'What is Socialism?' in de Crespigny, A. & Cronin, J., (eds), *Ideologies of Politics* (Oxford University Press, Oxford).

Corrin, C. (1992), 'Women in Eastern Europe' in *Labour Focus on Eastern Europe* (1).

Courtois, S. & Peschanski, D. (1988), 'From Decline to Marginalisation: the PCF Breaks With French Society' in Waller, M. & Fennema, M., (eds), *Communist Parties in Western Europe: Decline or Adaptation* (Basil Blackwell, Oxford).

Cox, R. (1991), 'Real Socialism in Historical Perspective' in R. Miliband & L. Panitch, (eds), *Socialist Register 1991* (Merlin, London, 1991).

Horak, J. (1993), 'Democratic Options in Central and Eastern Europe' in *Socialist Affairs* 1.

Craig, F. W. S. (1975), *British General Election Manifestos 1900–1974*

(Macmillan, London).

Crocker, D. (1983), *Praxis and Democratic Socialism: The Critical Social Theory of Markovic and Stojanovic* (Harvester, Sussex).

Cronin, J.(1984), *Labour and Society in Britain, 1918–1979* (Batsford, London).

Crosland, C. A. R. (1968), *The Future of Socialism*, (Cape, London).

Crosland, S. (1982), *Tony Crosland* (Cape, London).

Crouch, C. (1989), *Revolution and Evolution: Gorbachev and Soviet Politics* (Philip Allan, Hemel Hempstead).

D'Encausse, H. C. (1982), *A History of the Soviet Union, 1917–1953, volume one, Lenin: Revolution and Power*, (Longman, London).

Dahlberg, A. & Tuijman, A. (1991), 'Development of Human Resources in Internal Labour Markets' in *Economic and Industrial Democracy* (12) 2.

Dalton, R. & Kuechler, M. (1990), (eds), *Challenging the Political Order: New Social and Political Movements in Western Democracies* (Polity, Cambridge).

Daniels, R. (1985), (ed), *A Documentary History of Communism*, vol 2, (I. B. Tauris, London).

Dankelman, I., & Davidson, J. (1988), *Women and Environment in the Third World: Alliance for the Future* (Earthscan, London).

Dankert, P. & Kooyman, A. (1989), (eds), *Europe Without Frontiers: Socialists on the Future of the European Economic Community* (Cassell, London).

Davies, N. (1981), *God's Playground: A History of Poland* (Oxford University Press, Oxford).

Davies, R. W. (1980), *The Industrialisation of Soviet Russia, volume one, The Socialist Offensive: The Collectivisation of Soviet Agriculture 1929–30* (Macmillan, London).

Dawisha, K. (1988), *Eastern Europe, Gorbachev, and Reform: The Great Challenge* (Cambridge University Press, Cambridge).

de Beauvoir, S. (1984), *The Mandarins* (Fontana, London).

Delors, J. (1989), 'A New Frontier For Social Democracy?' in Dankert, P. & Kooyman, A., (eds), *Europe Without Frontiers: Socialists on the Future of the European Community* (Mansell/Cassell, London & New York).

Delors, J. (1993), 'The Scope and Limits of Community Action' in Coates, K. & Barrett Brown, M.,(eds), *A European Recovery Programme* (Spokesman, Nottingham).

Denitch, B. (1990), *The End of the Cold War: European Unity, Socialism, and the Shift in Global Power* (Verso, London).

Deutscher, I. (1963), *The Prophet Armed – Trotsky: 1879 – 1921* (Oxford University Press, Oxford).

Deutscher, I. (1974), *Stalin* (Penguin, Harmondsworth).

DeVos, T. (1989), *Multinational Corporations in Democratic Host Countries: U.S. Multinationals and the Vredeling Proposal* (Gower, Aldershot).

Di Scala, S.(1988), *Renewing Italian Socialism: Nenni to Craxi* (Oxford University Press, Oxford).

Djilas, M. (1969), *The Unperfect Society* (Methuen, London).

Dobson, A. (1991), *Green Political Thought* (Harper Collins, London).

Donoghue, B. (1987), *Prime Minister: The Conduct of Policy under Harold Wilson and James Callaghan*, (Jonathan Cape, London).

Dorril, S., & Ramsay, R. (1991), *Smear: Wilson and the Secret State* (Fourth Estate, London).

Dubcek, A. (1993), *Hope Dies Last* (Harper Collins, London).

DuBois, E. C. (1991), 'Woman Suffrage and the Left: An International Socialist–Feminist Perspective' in *New Left Review* 186.

Dunn, J. (1984), *The Politics of Socialism: An Essay in Political Theory* (Cambridge University Press, Cambridge).

Dyker, D. (1991), *Yugoslavia: Socialism, Development and Debt* (Routledge, London).

Dyson, K. (1989), 'Economic Policy' in Smith, G., Paterson, W. & Merkl, P. (eds), *Developments in West German Politics* (Macmillan, Basingstoke).

Edinger, L. (1965), *Kurt Schumacher: A Study in Personality and Political Behaviour* (Stanford University Press, California).

Eduards, M. (1991), 'The Swedish Gender Model: Productivity, Pragmatism and Paternalism' in *West European Politics* 14 (3).

Elder, N. (1988), 'Corporatism in Sweden' in Cox, A. & O'Sullivan, N.,(eds), *Corporatism and the State Tradition in Western Europe* (Elgar, London).

Gerlich, P. (1988), with Grande, E. & Müller, W., 'Corporatism in Crisis: Stability and Change of Social Partnership in Austria' in *Political Studies* XXXVI (2)

Ello, P. (1968), (ed), *Czechoslovakia's Blueprint for Freedom* (Acropolis, Washington).

Engholm, B. (1991), 'New Tests – New Opportunities' in *Socialist Affairs* (2).

Esping–Andersen, G. (1985), *Politics Against Markets: The Social–Democratic Road to Power* (Princeton University Press, New Jersey).

Fagan, G. (1991), 'Hungary: The Collapse of Kadarism' in Labour Focus on *Eastern Europe*, June.

Fanon, F. (1985), *The Wretched of the Earth* (Penguin, Harmondsworth).

Farber, S. (1990), *Before Stalinism: The Rise and Fall of Soviet Democracy* (Polity, Cambridge).

Featherstone, K. (1988), *Socialist Parties and European Integration: A Comparative History* (Manchester University Press, Manchester).

Feher, F., Heller, A., Markus, G. (1983), *Dictatorship Over Needs* (Blackwell, Oxford).

Fejto, F. (1974), *A History of the People's Democracies* (Penguin,

Harmondsworth).

Femia, J. V. (1981), *Gramsci's Political Thought* (Clarendon, Oxford).

Fienburgh, W. (1950), *International Control of Basic Industries* (British Labour Party for the International Socialist Conference).

Firestone, S. (1971), *The Dialectic of Sex* (Bantam, New York).

Fitoussi, J–P. (1985), comments on J. McCormick, 'Apprenticeship for Governing' in Machin, H. and Wright, V., (eds), *Economic Policy and Policy–Making Under Mitterand* (Pinter, London).

Fitzmaurice, J. (1991), *Austrian Politics and Society Today* (Macmillan, Basingstoke).

Fletcher, R. (1987), 'The Life and Work of Eduard Bernstein' in Fletcher, R. (ed) *Bernstein to Brandt: A Short History of German Social Democracy* (Edward Arnold, London).

Ford, G. (1990), 'The Growth of Racism and Fascism in Europe' in *European Labour Forum* 1.

Forester, T. (1979), 'Neutralising the Industrial Strategy' in Coates, K. (ed), *What Went Wrong* (Spokesman, Nottingham).

Frank, A. G. (1980), *Crisis in the World Economy* (Heinemann, London).

Frank, A. G. (1993), 'A World Economic Interpretation of East–West European Politics' in Palan, R. & Gills, B., (eds), *Transcending the Global–State Divide* (Lynne Reinner, Boulder).

Freund, M. (1972), *From Cold War to Ostpolitik: Germany and the New Europe* (Oswald Wolff, London).

Friedgut, T. & Siegelbaum, L. (1990), 'Perestroika From Below: The Soviet Miners' Strike and its Aftermath' in *New Left Review* 181.

Gaffney, J. (1989), *The French Left and the Fifth Republic: The Discourses of Communism and Socialism in Contemporary France* (Macmillan, Basingstoke).

Gallie, D. (1985), 'Les Lois Auroux: The Reform of French Industrial Relations?' in Machin, H. & Wright, V., (eds), *Economic Policy and Policy–Making Under the Mitterand Presidency* (Pinter, London).

Gamble, A. (1988), *The Free Economy and the Strong State: The Politics of Thatcherism* (Macmillan, Basingstoke).

Gamble, A. (1985), *Britain in Decline* (Macmillan, Basingstoke).

Geoghegan, V. (1981), *Reason and Eros* (Pluto, London).

George, S. (1988), *A Fate Worse Than Debt: The World Financial Crisis and the Poor* (Penguin, Hamondsworth).

Gerlich, P. (1992), 'A Farewell to Corporatism' in *West European Politics* 15 (1) 1992.

Gerratana, V. (1977), 'Stalin, Lenin and "Leninism"' in *New Left Review* 103.

Gill, S. & Law, D. (1988), *The Global Political Economy: Perspectives, Problems, and Policies* (Harvester, Hemel Hempstead).

Gillespie, R. (1989), 'Spanish Socialism in the 1980s' in Gallagher, T. & Williams, A., (eds), *Southern European Socialism: Parties, Elections and the Challenge of Government* (Manchester University Press, Manchester).

Gillespie, R. (1993), 'Programma 2000: The Appearance and Reality of Socialist Renewal in Spain' in *West European Politics* 16 (1).

Gillespie, R. & Gallagher, T. (1989), 'Democracy and Authority in the Socialist Parties of Southern Europe' in Gallagher, T. & Williams, A., (eds), *Southern European Socialism* (Manchester University Press, Manchester).

Girvan, B. (1986), 'Social Change and Moral Politics: the Irish Constitutional Referendum 1983' in *Political Studies* 34 (1).

Glenny, M. (1990), *The Rebirth of History: Eastern Europe in the Age of Democracy* (Penguin, Harmondsworth).

Godley, W. (1993), 'A Federal Government?' in Coates, K. & Barrett Brown, M., (eds), *A European Recovery Programme* (Spokesman, Nottingham).

Golan, G. (1973), *Reform Rule in Czechoslovakia: The Dubcek Era, 1968–1969* (Cambridge University Press, Cambridge).

Golubovic, Z. (1981), 'Stalinism and Socialism' in *Praxis International* 1 (2).

Gorz, A. (1982), *Farewell to the Working Class: As Essay in Post–Industrial Socialism* (Pluto, London).

Gorz, A. (1983), *Ecology as Politics* (Pluto, London).

Gorz, A. (1985), *Paths to Paradise* (Pluto, London).

Gorz, A. (1989), *Critique of Economic Reason* (Verso, London).

Gould, C. (1988), *Rethinking Democracy* (Cambridge University Press, Cambridge).

Gowan, P. (1990), 'Western Economic Diplomacy and the New Eastern Europe' in *New Left Review* 182.

Gowan, P. (1993), 'The EC and its Eastern Neighbours' in *Labour Focus on Eastern Europe* 1.

Graf, W. (1976), *The German Left Since 1945* (Oleander, Cambridge).

Gramsci, A. (1971), *Selections From the Prison Notebooks*, (Lawrence & Wishart, London).

Gruenwald, O. (1983), *The Yugoslav Search For Man: Marxist Humanism in Contemporary Yugoslavia* (Bergin, Mass.).

Haines, J. (1977), *The Politics of Power* (Jonathan Cape, London).

Hall, P. (1987), 'The Evolution of Economic Policy Under Mitterand' in Ross, G., Hoffmann, S. & Malzacher, S., (eds), *The Mitterand Experiment: Continuity and Change in Modern France* (Polity, Cambridge).

Hall, P. (1990), 'The State and the Market' in Hall,P. Hayward, J. & Machin, H., *Developments in French Politics* (Macmillan, Basingstoke).

Hamilton, R. & Barrett, M. (1986), (eds), *The Politics of Diversity: Feminism, Marxism and Nationalism* (Verso, London).

Hamilton, M. (1989), *Democratic Socialism in Britain and Sweden* (Macmillan, London).

Hanley, D. (1986), *Keeping Left? Ceres and the French Socialist Party* (Manchester University Press, Manchester).

Hanley, D. L., Kerr, A. P., Waites, N. H. (1984), *Contemporary France: Politics and Society Since 1945* (Routledge & Kegan Paul, London).

Harding, N. (1977), *Lenin's Political Thought,* volume one, (Macmillan, London).

Hare, P. (1981), 'The Investment System in Hungary' in Paul Hare, Hugo Radice & Nigel Swain, (eds), *Hungary: A Decade of Economic Reform* (Allen & Unwin, London).

Hare, P., Radice, H., Swain, N. (1981), (eds), *Hungary: A Decade of Economic Reform* (Allen & Unwin, London).

Harris, G. (1990), *The Dark Side of Europe: The Extreme Right Today* (Edinburgh University Press, Edinburgh).

Hartmann, H. (1979), 'The Unhappy Marriage of Marxism and Feminism: Towards a More Progressive Union' in *Capital and Class* 8.

Haseler, S. (1969), *The Gaitskellites* (Macmillan, London).

Hashi, I. (1992), 'The Disintegration of Yugoslavia: Regional Disparities and the Nationalities Question' in *Capital and Class* 48.

Haug, Frigga (1992), *Beyond Female Masochism* (Verso, London).

Haug, F. (1986), 'The Women's Movement in West Germany' in *New Left Review* 155.

Hawkes, N. (1990), (ed), *Tearing Down the Curtain* (The Observer/Hodder & Stoughton, London).

Hayward, J. (1990), 'Ideological Change: The Exhaustion of the Revolutionary Impetus' in Hall, P, Hayward, J. & Machin, H.,(eds), *Developments in French Politics* (Macmillan, Basingstoke).

Healey, D. (1989), *The Time of My Life* (Michael Joseph, London).

Hegedus, A., Heller, A., Markus, M., Vajda, M. (1976), *The Humanisation of Socialism: Writings of the Budapest School* (Allison & Busby, London).

Hegedus, A. (1976), *Socialism and Bureaucracy* (Allison & Busby, London).

Heinrich, H. G. (1986), *Hungary: Politics, Economics and Society* (Pinter, London).

Himmelstrand, U., Ahrne, G., Lundberg, L., Lundberg, L. (1981), *Beyond Welfare Capitalism: Issues, Actors and Forces in Societal Change* (Heinemann, London).

Hodgson, G. (1981), *Labour At the Crossroads* (Martin Robertson).

Hogan, M. (1989), *The Marshall Plan: America, Britain, and the Reconstruction of Western Europe, 1947–52* (Cambridge University Press, Cambridge).

Holland, D. (1988), 'Poland After the Referendum' in *Labour Focus on Eastern*

Europe 10 (1).

Holland, S. (1993), 'Planning the Recovery Programme' in Coates, K. & Barrett Brown, M., *A European Recovery Programme* (Spokesman, Nottingham).

Holland, S. (1976) 'Capital, Labour and the State' in Coates, K., (ed), *What Went Wrong* (Spokesman, Nottingham).

Holland, S. (1975), *The Socialist Challenge* (Quartet Books, London).

Holloway, D. (1978), 'Foreign and Defence Policy' in Brown, A. & Kaser, M., (eds), *The Soviet Union Since the Fall of Khrushchev* (Macmillan, London).

Holmes, M. (1985), *The Labour Government, 1974–79: Political Aims and Economic Reality* (Macmillan, London).

Holmes, G., & Fawcett, P. (1983), *The Contemporary French Economy* (Macmillan, London).

Holton, R. (1986), 'Industrial Politics in France: Nationalisation under Mitterand' in *West European Politics* 9 (1).

Horvat, B. (1976), *The Yugoslav Economic System: The First Labor–Managed Economy in the Making* (Sharpe, New York).

Hough, J. R. (1982), *The French Economy* (Croom Helm, London).

Howarth, J. (1990), 'Foreign and Defence Policy: From Independence to Inter–dependence' in Hall, P., Hayward, J. & Machin, H., (eds), *Developments in French Politics* (Macmillan, Basingstoke).

Hughes, J. (1991), *The Social Charter and the Single European Market* (Spokesman, Nottingham).

Hülsberg, W. (1988), *The German Greens: A Social and Political Profile,* (Verso, London).

Hulse, J. (1964), *The Forming of the Communist International* (Stanford University Press, California).

Husted, S. & Melvin, M. (1990), *International Economics* (Harper & Row, New York).

Inglehart, R. (1977), *The Silent Revolution: Changing Values and Political Styles Among Western Publics* (Princeton University Press, New Jersey).

Inglehart, R. (1990), 'Values, Ideology, and Cognitive Mobilisation in New Social Movements' in Dalton, R. & Kuechler, M., (eds), *Challenging The Political Order* (Polity, Cambridge).

Jancar, B. W. (1971), *Czechoslovakia and the Absolute Monopoly of Power: A Study in Political Power in a Communist System* (Praeger, New York).

Jenkins, M. (1979), *Bevanism: Labour's High Tide* (Spokesman, Nottingham).

Jenson, J. (1990), 'Representations of Difference: The Varieties of French Feminism' in *New Left Review* 180.

Jenson. J. & Ross, G. (1984), *The View From Inside: A French Communist Cell in Crisis* (University of California Press, Berkeley).

Jessop, B. (1982), *The Capitalist State: Marxist Theories and Methods* (Martin

Robertson, Oxford).

Johnson, R. W. (1982), *The Long March of the French Left* (Macmillan, London).

Kagarlitsky, B. (1990a), *The Dialectic of Change*, (Verso, London).

Kagarlitsky, B. (1990b), *Farewell Perestroika* (Verso, London).

Kaminski, B. (1991), *The Collapse of State Socialism: The Case of Poland* (Princeton University Press, New Jersey).

Kautsky, K. (1983), *Selected Political Writings*, (Macmillan, London).

Keane, J. (1988), *Democracy and Civil Society* (Verso, London).

Kellner, D. (1984), *Herbert Marcuse and the Crisis of Marxism* (Macmillan, London).

Kemeny, I. (1982), 'The Unregistered Economy in Hungary' in *Soviet Studies* 34 (3).

Kendall, W. (1975), *The Labour Movement in Europe* (Allen Lane Penguin, London).

Kennedy, P. (1989), *The Rise and Fall of Great Powers: Economic Change and Military Conflict From 1500 to 2000* (Fontana, London).

Kesselman, M. (1985), 'The Tranquil Revolution at Clochemerle: Socialist Decentralisation in France' in Cerny, P. & Schain, M., (eds), *Socialism, the State and Public Policy in France* (Pinter, London).

Kindersley, R. (1981), (ed), *In Search of Eurocommunism* (Macmillan, London).

Kinnock, G., Lestor, J., Ruddock, J. (1988), (eds), *Voices For One World* (Fontana, London).

Kitching, G. (1983), *Re–thinking Socialism: A Theory for a Better Practice* (Methuen, London).

Kitschelt, H. (1990), 'New Social Movements and the Decline of Party Organisation' in Dalton, R. & Kuechler, M., (eds), *Challenging The Political Order* (Polity, Cambridge).

Kloc, K. (1993), 'Industrial Conflicts in Poland, 1990–92' in *Labour Focus on Eastern Europe*, 1.

Koestler, A. (1979), *Darkness At Noon* (Penguin, Harmondsworth).

Kogan, D. & Kogan, M. (1983), *The Battle for the Labour Party* (Kogan Page, London).

Kolinsky, E. (1986), 'Youth, Parties and Democracy in West Germany' in *Politics* 6 (1).

Korpi, W. (1978), *The Working Class Under Welfare Capitalism* (Routledge & Kegan Paul, London).

Korpi, W. (1983), *The Democratic Class Struggle* (Routledge & Kegan Paul, London).

Kowalik, T. (1991), 'Modernisation and Privatisation: The Polish Case' in R. Miliband & L. Panitch, (eds), *Socialist Register 1991* (Merlin, London).

Krajewski, W. (1982), 'The March Events of 1968 and Polish Philosophy' in *Praxis International* 2 (1).

Kriegel, A. (1977) *The French Communists* (University of Chicago Press, Chicago).

Kuisel, R. (1987), 'French Post–War Economic Growth' in Ross, G., Hoffmann, S. & Malzacher, S., (eds), The Mitterand Experiment: Continuity and Change in *Modern France* (Polity, Cambridge).

Kusin, V. (1972), *Political Groupings in the Czechoslovak Reform Movement* (Macmillan, London).

Kusin, V. (1978), *From Dubcek to Charter 77: A Study of 'Normalisation' in Czechoslovakia, 1968–1978* (Q Press, Edinburgh).

Ladrech, R. (1989), 'Social Movements and Party Systems: The French Socialist Party and New Social Movements' in *West European Politics*, 12 (2).

Lafontaine, O. (1992) 'Socialism and the Social Movements' in *Socialism of the Future* 1 (1).

Lambert, J. (1991), 'Europe: The Nation State Dies Hard' in *Capital and Class* 43.

Lancelot, A. & Lancelot, M–T. (1987), 'The Evolution of the French Electorate' in Ross, G., Hoffmann, S. & Malzacher, S., (eds), *The Mitterand Experiment: Continuity and Change in Modern France* (Polity Press, Cambridge).

Landauer, C. (1976), *European Socialism: A History of Ideas and Movements,* 2 vols., (Greenwood, Westport).

Lane, D. (1978), *Politics and Society in the U.S.S.R.* (Martin Robertson, Oxford).

Lange, P. & Vannicelli, M. (1981), (eds), *The Communist Parties of Italy, France, and Spain: Postwar Change and Continuity – A Casebook* (Allen & Unwin, London).

Lash, S. (1985), 'The End of Neo–Corporatism?: The Breakdown of Centralised Bargaining in Sweden' in *British Journal of Industrial Relations* 23 (2).

Lavau, G. (1987), 'The Left and Power' in Ross, G., Hoffmann, S. & Malzacher, S., (eds), *The Mitterand Experiment: Continuity and Change in Modern France* (Polity Press, Cambridge).

Leborgne, D. & Lipietz, A. (1990) 'How to Avoid A Two–Tier Europe' in *Labour and Society* 15 (2).

Lee, M. (1988), 'Awaiting the Future' in *Labour Focus on Eastern Europe* 10 (1).

Lefebvre, H., *The Explosion* (Monthly Review Press, New York, 1970).

Lemke, C. & Marks, G. (1992), 'From Decline to Demise? The Fate of Socialism in Europe' in Lemke, C. & Marks, G., (eds), *The Crisis of Socialism in Europe*, (Duke University Press, Durham & London).

Lenin, V. I., *The State and Revolution* (Progress, Moscow, 1972).

Lenin, V. I., *Selected Works*, three volumes (Progress, Moscow, 1977).

Lenin, V. I., *What Is To Be Done?* (Penguin, Harmondsworth, 1988).

Lewin, M. (1970), *Lenin's Last Struggle* (Vantage Books, New York).

Lewis, S. & Sferza, S. (1987), 'French Socialists Between State and Society' in Ross, G., Hoffman, S. & Malzacher, S., (eds), *The Mitterand Experiment: Continuity and Change in Modern France* (Polity, Cambridge).

Lichtheim, G. (1985), *A Short History of Socialism* (Fontana, London).

Liebman, M. (1985), *Leninism Under Lenin* (Merlin, London).

Lindemann, A. (1983), *A History of European Socialism* (Yale University Press, New Haven).

Lipietz, A. (1987), *Mirages and Miracles: The Crisis of Global Fordism* (Verso, London).

Loth, W. (1988), *The Division of the World 1941–1955* (Routledge, London).

Lovenduski, J. & Woodall, J. (1987), *Politics and Society in Eastern Europe* (Macmillan, London).

Löwenhardt, J. (1981), *Decision–Making in Soviet Politics* (Macmillan, London).

Löwenhardt, J. (1982), *The Soviet Politburo*, (Canongate, Edinburgh).

Luxemburg, R. (1970), *Rosa Luxemburg Speaks* (Pathfinder, New York).

Luxemburg, R. (1971), *Selected Political Writings*, ed. Dick Howard, (Monthly Review Press, New York).

Lyrintzis, C. (1989), 'PASOK in Power: The Loss of the "Third Road to Socialism" in Gallagher, T. & Williams, A., (eds), *Southern European Socialism* (Manchester University Press, Manchester).

McCauley, M. (1984), *Stalin and Stalinism* (Longman, Harlow).

McCauley, M. (1986), *The German Democratic Republic Since 1945* (Macmillan, London).

McCormick, J. (1985), 'Apprenticeship for Governing; An Assessment of French Socialism in Power' in Machin, H. & Wright, V., (eds), *Economic Policy and Policy–Making Under The Mitterand Presidency* (Pinter, London).

MacDonald, O. (1984), 'The Polish Vortex: Solidarity and Socialism' in Tariq Ali (ed), *The Stalinist Legacy: Its Impact on 20th Century World Politics* (Penguin, Harmondsworth).

MacEwan, A. & Tabb, W. (1989), (eds), *Instability and Change in the World Economy* (Monthly Review Press, New York).

MacEwan, A. (1990), *Debt and Disorder: International Economic Instability and US Imperial Decline* (Monthly Review Press, New York).

McFarlane, B. (1988), *Yugoslavia: Politics, Economics, Society* (Pinter, London).

Machin, H. (1990) 'Changing Patterns of Party Competition' in Hall, P, Hayward, J. & Machin, H.,(eds), *Developments in French Politics* (Macmillan,

Basingstoke).

Machin, H. (1990), 'Changing Patterns of Party Competition' in Hall, P, Hayward, J. & Machin, H.,(eds), *Developments in French Politics* (Macmillan, Basingstoke).

Macridis, R. (1984), *Greek Politics at the Crossroads: What Kind of Socialism?* (Hoover Institution Press, Stanford).

MacShane, D. (1986), *French Lessons for Labour* (Fabian Tract 512).

Magri, L. (1982), 'The Peace Movement and European Socialism' in *New Left Review* 131.

Mahon, E., (1987), 'Women's Rights and Catholicism in Ireland' in *New Left Review* 166.

Mahon, R. (1991), 'From Solidaristic Wages to Solidaristic Work: A Post-Fordist Historic Compromise for Sweden' in *Economic and Industrial Democracy* 12 (3).

Malone, S. (1992), 'Abortion Rights in Poland' in *Labour Focus on Eastern Europe* (1).

Mandel, D. (1990), 'The Social Basis of Perestroika' in White, S., Pravda, A. & Getelman, Z., (eds), *Developments in Soviet Politics* (Macmillan, Basingstoke).

Mandel, E. (1974), *Marxist Economic Theory*, (Merlin, London).

Mandel, E. (1979), *Trotsky: A Study in the Dynamic of His Thought* (New Left Books, London).

Mandel, E. (1987), *Late Capitalism* (Verso, London).

Mandel, E. (1989), *Beyond Perestroika: The Future of Gorbachev's USSR,* (Verso, London).

Marcuse, H. (1969), *An Essay in Liberation* (Allen Lane Penguin, London).

Marcuse, H. (1970a), *Five Lectures* (Allen Lane Penguin, London).

Marcuse, H. (1970b), 'On The New Left' in M. Teodori (ed) *The New Left* (Cape, London).

Marcuse, H. (1972), *Counterrevolution and Revolt* (Beacon, Boston).

Marcuse, H. (1974), *One Dimensional Man* (Sphere, London).

Marcuse (1989), 'The Reification of the Proletariat' in Bronner, S. & Kellner, D., (eds), *Critical Theory and Society: A Reader* (Routledge, New York).

Markovic, M. (1982), *Democratic Socialism: Theory and Practice* (Harvester, Sussex).

Markovic, M. & Petrovic, G. (1979), (eds), *Praxis* (Reidel, Dordrecht).

Markovits, A. & Reich, S. (1991), 'Modell Deutschland and the New Europe' in *Telos*, 89.

Marsh, D. (1992), *The Bundesbank* (Heinemann, London).

Martinez–Alier, J. & Roca, R. (1988), 'Spain After Franco: From Corporatist Ideology to Coporatist Reality' in Cox, A. & O'Sullivan, N., (eds), *The Corporate State: Corporatism and the State Tradition in Western Europe*

(Edward Elgar, Aldershot).

Marx, K. (1969), *Preface to A Contribution to the Critique of Political Economy* (Progress, Moscow).

Marx, K. (1974), *The First International And After* (Penguin, Harmondsworth).

Marx, K. & Engels, F. (1973), *Selected Works* – in one volume (Lawrence & Wishart, London).

Marx, K. & Engels, F. (1976), *Collected Works*, volume 5, (Lawrence & Wishart, London).

Marz, E. (1988), 'Austria's Economic Development' in Sweeney, J. & Weidenholzer, J., (eds), *Austria: A Study in Modern Achievement* (Avebury/Gower, Aldershot).

Mazey, S. (1990) 'Power Outside Paris' in Hall, P, Hayward, J. & Machin, H.,(eds), *Developments in French Politics* (Macmillan, Basingstoke).

Meacher, M. (1979), 'Whitehall's Short Way With Democracy' in Coates, K., (ed), *What Went Wrong?* (Spokesman, Nottingham).

Meacher, M. (1982), *Socialism With a Human Face: The Political Economy of Britain in the 1980s* (Allen & Unwin, London).

Medvedev, R. (1976), *Let History Judge* (Spokesman, Nottingham).

Medvedev, R., & Medvedev, Z. (1977), *Khrushchev: The Years in Power* (Oxford University Press, Oxford).

Medvedev, Z. (1971), *The Rise and Fall of T. D. Lysenko* (Doubleday, New York).

Medvedev, Z. (1990), *The Legacy of Chernobyl* (Blackwell, Oxford).

Melucci, A. (1989), *Nomads of the Present: Social Movements and Individual Needs in Contemporary Society* (Hutchinson Radius, London).

Merkel, W. (1992), 'After the Golden Age: Is Social Democracy Doomed to Decline?' Lemke, C. & Marks, G., (eds), *The Crisis of Socialism in Europe* (Duke University Press, Durham & London).

Merkl, P. (1988), 'The SPD After Brandt: Problems of Integration in a Changing Society' in *West European Politics* 11 (1).

Micheletti, M. (1991), 'Swedish Corporatism at the Crossroads: The Impact of New Politics and New Social Movements' in *West European Politics* 14 (3).

Michels, R. (1959), *Political Parties* (Dover, New York).

Mies, M. (1987), *Patriarchy and Accumulation on a World Scale: Women in the International Division of Labour* (Zed, London).

Miliband, R. (1969), *The State in Capitalist Society* (Weidenfeld & Nicolson, London).

Miliband, R. (1973), *Parliamentary Socialism* (Merlin, London).

Millar, J. (1976), 'What's Wrong With the "Standard Story"' in *Problems of Communism*, July – August.

Millett, K. (1971), *Sexual Politics* (Sphere, London).

Milner, H. (1989), *Sweden: Social Democracy in Practice* (Oxford University Press, Oxford).

Minkin, L. (1991), *The Contentious Alliance – Trade Unions and the Labour Party* (Edinburgh University Press, Edinburgh).

Minnerup, G. (1989), 'The October Revolution in East Germany' in *Labour Focus on Eastern Europe*, (3).

Mitterand, F. (1982), *The Wheat and the Chaff* (Weidenfeld & Nicolson, London).

Mlynar, Z. (1980), *Night Frost in Prague: The End of Humane Socialism,* (Hurst, London).

Mlynar, Z. (1988), 'The Lessons of the Prague Spring' in *Labour Focus on Eastern Europe* 10 (2).

Molnar, M. (1990), *From Bela Kun to Janos Kadar* (Berg, Oxford).

Molyneux, M. (1990), 'The "Woman Question" in the Age of Perestroika' in *New Left Review* 183.

Morgan, K. O. (1987), *Labour in Power, 1945–1951* (Oxford University Press, Oxford).

Mortimer, E. (1984), *The Rise of the Communist Party, 1920–1947* (Faber & Faber, London).

Moses, J. (1987), 'Socialist Trade Unionism in Imperial Germany, 1871–1914' in Fletcher, R. (ed) *Bernstein to Brandt: A Short History of German Social Democracy* (Edward Arnold, London).

Muller–Rommel, F. (1990), 'New Political Movements and New Politics Parties in Western Europe' in Dalton, R. & Kuechler, M., (eds)., *Challenging the Political Order* (Polity, Cambridge).

Munting, R. (1982), *The Economic Development of the USSR* (Croom Helm, London).

Myant, M. R. (1981), *Socialism and Democracy in Czechoslovakia, 1945–48* (Cambridge University Press, Cambridge).

Narkiewicz, O. (1990), *The End of the Bolshevik Dream: Western European Communist Parties in the Late Twentieth Centuries* (Routledge, London).

Nay, C. (1987), *The Black and the Red: Francois Mitterand, The Story of An Ambition* (Harcourt Brace Jovanovich, San Diego).

Newman, M., (1983), *Socialism and European Unity: The Dilemma of the Left in Britain and France* (Junction, London).

Nove, A. (1972), *An Economic History of the USSR* (Penguin, Harmondsworth).

Nove, A. (1978), 'Agriculture' in Brown, A. & Kaser, M., (eds), *The Soviet Union Since the Fall of Khrushchev* (Macmillan, London).

Nove, A. (1983), *The Economics of Feasible Socialism* (Allen and Unwin, London).

Nove, A. (1989), *Glasnost in Action: Cultural Renaissance in Russia* (Unwin

Hyman, London).

Nugent, N. & Lowe, D. (1982), *The Left in France* (Macmillan, London).

Odom, W. (1991), 'Alternative Perspectives on the August Coup' in *Problems of Communism* 40 (6).

Offe, C. (1984), *Contradictions of the Welfare State* (Hutchinson, London).

Olsson, A., (1990), *The Swedish Wage Negotiation System* (Dartmouth, Aldershot).

Ossman–Dorent, S. (1988), 'SOS Racisme: Studies Disorder in France' in *Socialist Review* 18 (2).

Padgett, S. (1987), 'The West German Social Democrats in Opposition, 1982–86' in *West European Politics* 10 (3).

Padgett, S. (1993), 'The German Social Democrats: A Redefinition of Social Democracy or Bad Godesberg Mark 2?' in *West European Politics* 16 (1).

Padgett, S. & Paterson, W. (1991a), 'The Rise and Fall of the West German Left' in *New Left Review*, 186.

Padgett, S. & Paterson, W. (1991b), *A History of Social Democracy in Postwar Europe* (Longman, London).

Palan, R. & Gills, B. (1993), (eds), *Transcending the Global–State Divide* (Lynne Reinner, Boulder).

Palmer, J. (1988), *Europe Without America? The Crisis in Atlantic Relations* (Oxford University Press, Oxford).

Panitch, L. (1986), *Working Class Politics in Crisis: Essays on Labour and the State* (Verso, London).

Parkin, S. (1989), *Green Parties: An International Guide* (Heretic Books, London).

Pasquinelli, C. (1984), 'Beyond the Longest Revolution: The Impact of the Italian Women's Movement on Cultural and Social Change' in *Praxis International* 4 (2).

Pasquino, G. (1980), 'From Togliatti to the Compromesso Storico' in Serfaty, S. & Gray, L., (eds), *The Italian Communist Party* (Aldwych, London).

Pasquino, G. (1993), 'Programmatic Renewal and Much More: From PCI to PDS' in *West European Politics* 16 (1).

Pasquino, G. (1988) 'Mid–Stream and Under Stress: The Italian Communist Party' in Waller, M. & Fennema, Meindert, (eds), *Communist Parties in Western Europe* (Blackwell, Oxford).

Pateman, C., *Participation and Democratic Theory* (Cambridge University Press, Cambridge, 1970).

Pateman, C. (1989), *The Disorder of Women: Democracy, Feminism and Political Theory* (Polity, Cambridge).

Paterson, W. (1989), 'Foreign and Security Policy' in Smith, G., Paterson, W. & Merkl, P., (eds), Developments in *West German Politics* (Macmillan,

Basingstoke).

Paterson, W. (1993), 'Germany and Europe' in Story, J. (ed) *The New Europe* (Blackwell, Oxford).

Paterson, W. & Thomas, A. (1977), (eds), *Social Democratic Parties in Western Europe* (Croom Helm, London).

Pavlowitch, S. (1988), *The Improbable Survivor: Yugoslavia and its Problems, 1918-1988* (Hurst, London).

Pelikan, J. (1972), 'The Struggle for Socialism in Czechoslovakia' in *New Left Review* 71.

Pelikan, J. (1971), (ed), *The Secret Vysocany Congress* (Allen Lane Penguin, London).

Pethybridge, R. (1974), *The Social Prelude to Stalinism,* (Macmillan, London).

Phillips, A. (1991), *Engendering Democracy* (Polity, Cambridge).

Picciotto, S. (1991), 'The Internationalisation of the State' in *Capital and Class* 43.

Piekalkiewicz, J. (1972), *Public Opinion Polling in Czechoslovakia, 1968-69* (Praeger, New York).

Pierson, C. (1986), *Marxist Theory and Democratic Politics* (Polity, Cambridge).

Pierson, C. (1991), *Beyond the Welfare State* (Polity, Cambridge).

Poguntke, T. (1992a), 'The Resurrection of the Christian Democratic Party State?' in *Politics* 12 (1).

Poguntke, T. (1992b), 'Unconventional Participation in Party Politics: The Experience of the German Greens' in *Political Studies* 40 (2).

Poguntke, T. (1993), *Alternative Politics: The German Green Party* (Edinburgh University Press, Edinburgh).

Pollard, S. (1982), *The Wasting of the British Economy* (Croom Helm, London).

Ponting, C. (1989), *Breach of Promise: Labour in Power, 1964-70* (Hamish Hamilton, London).

Pontusson, J. (1984), 'Behind and Beyond Social Democracy in Sweden' in *New Left Review* 143.

Porrit, J. (1988) *Seeing Green* (Blackwell, Oxford).

Potel, J-Y, (1982), *The Summer Before the Frost,* (Pluto, London).

Poulantzas, N. (1978), *State, Power, Socialism* (New Left Books, London).

Pravda, A. (1973), *Reform and Change in the Czechoslovak Political System, January – August 1968* (Sage Research Papers in the Social Sciences, Beverly Hills and London).

Preston, P. (1981), 'The PCE's Long Road to Democracy, 1954-77' in Kindersley, R. (ed) *In Search of Eurocommunism* (Macmillan, London).

Pridham, G. (1989), 'Southern European Socialists and the State' in Gallagher, T. & Williams, A., (eds), *Southern European Socialism* (Manchester University Press, Manchester).

Prittie, T. (1974), *Willy Brandt: Portrait of a Statesman* (Weidenfeld & Nicolson, London).

Radice, G. & Radice, L. (1986), *Socialists in the Recession* (Macmillan, London).

Radice, H. & Swain, N. (1981), (eds), *Hungary: A Decade of Economic Reform* (Allen & Unwin, London).

Rehn, G. & Viklund, B. (1990), 'Changes in the Swedish Model' in G. Baglioni & C. Crouch, (eds), *European Industrial Relations: The Challenge of Flexibility* (Sage, London, 1990).

Reich, J. (1990), 'Reflections on Becoming an East German Dissident, On Losing the Wall and a Country' in Gwyn Prins (ed), *Spring in Winter: The 1989 Revolution* (Manchester University Press).

Richet, X. (1981), 'Is There An Hungarian Model of Planning?' in Hare, P., Robert Wood (1989), 'The IMF and the World Bank in A Changing World Economy' in Arthur MacEwan & William Tabb, (eds), *Instability and Change in the World Economy* (Monthly Review Press, New York).

Rocard, M. (1992), 'Socialist Action Today' in *Socialism of the Future* 1 (1).

Rodriguez–Ibanez, J. (1980) 'Spanish Communism in Transition' in Boggs, C. & Plotke, D., (eds), *The Politics of Eurocommunism: Socialism in Transition* (Macmillan, London).

Rootes, C. A. (1991), 'Environmentalism and Party Competition: British Greens in the 1989 Elections to the European Parliament' in *Politics* 11 (2).

Ross, G & Jenson, J. (1985), 'Political Pluralism and Economic Policy' in John Ambler (ed) *The French Socialist Experiment* (Institute for the Study of Human Issues, Philadelphia).

Ross, G. & Jenson, J. (1988). 'The Tragedy of the French Left' in *New Left Review* 171.

Rowbotham, S. (1972), *Women, Resistance and Revolution* (Allen Lane, London).

Rowbotham, S., Segal, L., Wainwright, H., (1979) *Beyond The Fragments: Feminism and the Making of Socialism* (Merlin, London).

Rowthorn, B. (1980), *Capitalism, Conflict and Inflation* (Lawrence & Wishart, London).

Ruane, K. (1982), *The Polish Challenge* (BBC, London).

Rutland, P. (1990), 'Economic Management and Reform' in White, S., Pravda, A. & Getelman, Z., (eds), *Developments in Soviet Politics* (Macmillan, Basingstoke).

Ryle, M. (1988), *Ecology and Socialism* (Rodins, London).

Sainsbury, D. (1991), 'Swedish Social Democracy in Transition: The Party's Record in the 1980s and the Challenge of the 1990s' in *West European Politics* 14 (3).

Sainsbury, D. (1993), 'The Swedish Social Democrats and the Legacy of Continuous Reform: Asset or Dilemma:' in *West European Politics* 16 (1).

Sakwa, R. (1990), *Gorbachev and His Reforms, 1985–1990* (Philip Allan, Hemel Hempstead).

Sakwa, R. (1989), *Soviet Politics: An Introduction* (Routledge, London).

Sanford, G. (1983), *Polish Communism in Crisis* (Croom Helm, Beckenham).

Sanford, G. (1986), *Military Rule in Poland; The Rebuilding of Communist Power, 1981–1983* (Croom Helm, London).

Sanford, G. (1990) (ed), *The Solidarity Congress, 1981* (Macmillan, Basingstoke, 1990).

Sartre, J–P. (1974), *Between Existentialism and Marxism*, (New Left Books, London).

Sassoon, D. (1981), *The Strategy of the Italian Communist Party: From the Resistance to the Historic Compromise* (Pinter, London).

Sassoon, D. (1989), *Contemporary Italy: Politics, Economy and Society Since 1945* (Longman, London)

Schumacher, E. F. (1973), *Small is Beautiful: A Study of Economics as If People Mattered* (Blond and Briggs, London).

Scott, R. (1993), 'Reforming Working Lifetimes' in Coates, K. & Barrett Brown, M., *A European Recovery Programme* (Spokesman, Nottingham).

Scott, A. (1990), *Ideology and New Social Movements* (Unwin Hyman, London).

Segal, L. (1991), 'Whose Left? Socialism, Feminism and the Future' in *New Left Review* 185.

Selucky, R. (1979), *Marxism, Socialism, Freedom* (Macmillan, London).

Seroka, J. (1988), 'The Interdependence of Institutional Revitalisation and Intra–Party Reform in Yugoslavia' in *Soviet Studies* 40 (1).

Seyd, P. (1987), The Rise and Fall of the Labour Left (Macmillan, London).

Share, D. (1989), *Dilemmas of Social Democracy: The Spanish Socialist Workers Party in the 1980s* (Greenwood Press, Westport).

Shaw, E. (1988), *Discipline and Discord in the Labour Party* (Manchester University Press, Manchester).

Shoup, P. (1989), 'Crisis and Reform in Yugoslavia' in *Telos*, (Spring).

Sik, O. (1976), *The Third Way* (Wildwood House, London).

Simecka, M. (1984), *The Restoration of Order: The Normalisation of Czechoslovakia, 1969–1976* (Verso, London).

Simmons, M. (1991), *The Reluctant President: A Political Life of Vaclav Havel* (Methuen, London).

Simon, R. (1990), 'Group Influence in the Gorbachev Era: The Law of the State Enterprise', M.A. thesis, Nottingham Polytechnic.

Singer, D. (1988), *Is Socialism Doomed?: The Meaning of Mitterand* (Oxford

University Press, Oxford).

Singer, D. (1970), *Prelude to Revolution* (Jonathan Cape, London).

Sirianni, C. (1982), *Workers Control and Socialist Democracy: The Soviet Experience* (Verso, London).

Sked, A. & Cook, C. (1979), *Post–War Britain: A Political History* (Penguin, Harmondsworth).

Skilling, H. Gordon (1976), *Czechoslovakia's Interrupted Revolution* (Princeton University Press, Princeton).

Skjeie, H. (1991), 'The Uneven Advance of Norwegian Women' in *New Left Review* 187.

Smith, G., Paterson, W., Merkl, P. (1989), (eds), *Developments in West German Politics* (Macmillan, Basingstoke).

Smith, K. (1989), *The British Economic Crisis: Its Past and Future* (Penguin, Harmondsworth).

Smith, M. & Spear, J. (1992), *The Changing Labour Party* (Routledge, London).

Smrkovsky, J. (1984), 'How They Crushed the Prague Spring of 1968' in Tariq Ali (ed) *The Stalinist Legacy* (Penguin, Harmondsworth).

Socialist International (1985), *Global Challenge: From Crisis to Cooperation: Breaking the North–South Stalemate* (Pan, London).

Solomon, S. (1983), (ed) *Pluralism in the Soviet Union* (Macmillan, London).

Solow, R. (1991), 'Unemployment as a Social and Economic Problem' in J. Cornwall (ed) *The Capitalist Economies: Prospects For the 1990s* (Edward Elgar, Aldershot).

Somers, F. (1991), *European Economics: A Comparative Study* (Longman, London).

Spence, M., (1987), 'After Chernobyl' in *Capital and Class* 32.

Spourdalakis, M. (1988), *The Rise of the Greek Socialist Party* (Routledge, London).

Stalin, J. (1970a), *Selected Writings* (Greenwood Press, Westport).

Stalin, J. (1970b), *The Foundations of Leninism* (Foreign Languages Press, Peking).

Stamiris, E. (1987), 'The Women's Movement in Greece' in *New Left Review* 158.

Staniszkis, J. (1991), *The Dynamics of Breakthrough in Eastern Europe: The Polish Experience,* (University of California Press, Berkeley).

Stephens, J. (1979), *The Transition From Capitalism to Socialism* (Macmillan, London).

Stern, C. (1965), *Ulbricht: A Political Biography* (Pall Mall, London).

Stevens, A. (1990), '"L'Alternance" and the Higher Civil Service' in Hall, P, Hayward, J. & Machin, H.,(eds), *Developments in French Politics* (Macmillan, Basingstoke).

Stoffaes, C. (1985), 'The Nationalisations: An Initial Assessment, 1981–84' in Machin, H. & Wright, V., (eds), *Economic Policy and Policy–Making Under the Mitterand Presidency* (Pinter, London).

Story, J. (1979), 'The Spanish Communist Party' in della Torre et al (eds) *Eurocommunism: Myth or Reality?* (Penguin, Harmondsworth).

Story, J. (1993), `Spain's Transition to Democracy' in Story, J., (ed) *The New Europe* (Blackwell, Oxford).

Story, J. & De Cecco, M. (1993), `The Politics and Diplomacy of Monetary Union' in Story, J. (ed) *The New Europe* (Blackwell, Oxford).

Story, J. & de Carmoy, G. (1993), `France and Europe' in Story, J. (ed) *The New Europe* (Blackwell, Oxford).

Strange, S. (1988), *States and Markets: An Introduction to International Political Economy* (Pinter, London).

Sully, M. (1981), *Political Parties and Elections in Austria* (Hurst, London).

Sully, M. (1988), 'The Socialist Party of Austria' in Sweeney, J. & Weidenholzer, J., (eds), *Austria: A Study in Modern Achievement* (Avebury/Gower, Aldershot).

Supek, R. (1979), 'Some Contradictions and Insufficiencies of Yugoslav Self–Managing Socialism' in M. Markovic & G. Petrovic, (eds), *Praxis* (Reidel, Dordrecht).

Svenson, P. (1991), 'Labour and the Limits of the Welfare State' in *Comparative Politics* 23 (4).

Swain, N. (1989), 'Hungary's Socialist Project in Crisis' in *New Left Review* 176.

Swidlicki, A. (1988), *Political Trials in Poland, 1981–1986* (Croom Helm, London).

Sword, K. (1990) (ed), *The Times Guide to Eastern Europe* (Times Books, London).

Syrop, K. (1976), *Spring in October: The Story of the Polish Revolution, 1956* (Greenwood, Westport).

Tariq Ali (1984), (ed) *The Stalinist Legacy* (Penguin, Harmondsworth).

Taylor, A. (1993), 'Trade Unions and the Politics of Social Democracy' in *West European Politics* 16 (1).

Taylor, R. (1976) 'The Uneasy Alliance – Labour and the Unions' in *Political Quarterly*, 47.

Tegel, S. (1987), 'The SPD in Imperial Germany, 1871–1914' in Fletcher, R. (ed) *Bernstein to Brandt: A Short History of German Social Democracy* (Edward Arnold, London, 1987).

Telo, M. (1991), 'The SPD; Between Europe and Modell Deutschland in *Telos*, 80.

Therborn, G. (1977), 'The Rule of Capital and the Rise of Democracy' in *New*

Left Review 103.

Therborn, G. (1991), 'Swedish Social Democracy and the Transition from Industrial to Post–Industrial Politics' in Frances Fox–Piven (ed) *Labor Parties in Post–Industrial Societies* (Polity, Cambridge).

Therborn, Goran, (1992) 'The Life and Times of Socialism' in *New Left Review* 194.

Threlfall, M. (1989), 'Social Policy Towards Women in Spain, Greece and Portugal' in Gallagher, T. & Williams, A., (eds), *Southern European Socialism* (Manchester University Press, Manchester).

Ticktin, H. (1991), 'The International Road to Chaos' in *Critique* 23.

Tigrid, P. (1971), *Why Dubcek Fell* (Macdonald, London).

Tilton, T. (1990), *The Political Theory of Swedish Social Democracy* (Clarendon Press, Oxford).

Tompson, W. (1991), 'The Fall of Nikita Khrushchev' in *Soviet Studies* 43 (6).

Touraine, A. (1983), *Solidarity: Poland 1980–81* (Cambridge University Press, Cambridge).

Touraine, A. (1974), *The Post–Industrial Society* (Wildwood House, London).

Trotsky, L. (1965), *The New Course* (University of Michigan Press, Ann Arbor).

Trotsky, L. (1967), *History of the Russian Revolution*, volume three (Sphere Books, London).

Trotsky, L. (1972), *The Revolution Betrayed: What is the Soviet Union and Where is it Going?* (Pathfinder Press, New York).

Trotsky, L. et al (1973), *The Platform of the Joint Opposition* (1927), (New Park, London).

Trotsky, L. (1975), *Results and Prospects* (New Park, London).

Urban, J. (1990), 'The Power and Politics of Humiliation' in Gwyn Prins (ed) *Spring in Winter: The 1989 Revolutions* (Manchester University Press, Manchester).

Ure, J. (1989), 'Democracy in China' in *Capital and Class* 38.

Vajda, M. (1982), 'Realism and Seeing the Essentials' in *Praxis International* 2 (2).

Van Parijs, P. (1992), (ed), *Arguing for Basic Income: Ethical Foundations for a Radical Reform* (Verso, London).

Van der Pijl, K. (1984), *The Making of an Atlantic Ruling Class* (Verso, London).

Vanek, J. (1990), 'On the Transition from Centrally Planned to Democratic Socialist Economies' in *Economic and Industrial Democracy* 11 (2).

Wainwright, H. (1987), *Labour: A Tale of Two Parties* (Hogarth, London).

Walesa, L. (1987), *A Path of Hope* (Collins, London).

Waller, M. & Fennema, M. (1988), (eds), *Communist Parties in Western Europe: Decline or Adaptation* (Basil Blackwell, Oxford).

Waller, M. & Szajkowski, B. (1986), 'The Communist Movement; From Monolith to Polymorph' in S. White & D. Nelson, (eds), *Communist Politics; A Reader* (Macmillan, Basingstoke).

Waller, M. (1981), *Democratic Centralism: An Historical Commentary* (Manchester University Press, Manchester).

Wallerstein, I. (1983), *Historical Capitalism*, (Verso, London).

Wallerstein, I. (1984), *The Politics of the World Economy: The States, The Movements and The Civilisations* (Cambridge University Press, Cambridge).

Wallerstein, I. (1991), 'The Ideological Tensions of Capitalism: Universalism versus Racism and Sexism' in Balibar, E. & Wallerstein, E., *Race, Nation, Class: Ambiguous Identities* (Verso, London)

Warner, M. (1990), 'Yugoslav Self–Management and Industrial Relations in Transition' in *Industrial Relations Journal* 21 (3).

Webb, Sidney (1987) *Socialism in England* (Dartmouth, Aldershot).

Weir, A. & Wilson, E. (1984), 'The British Women's Movement' in *New Left Review* 148.

White, S. (1986), 'The Supreme Soviet and Budgetary Politics in the USSR' in White, S. & Nelson, D., (eds), *Communist Politics: A Reader* (Macmillan, Basingstoke).

White, S. (1990), *Gorbachev in Power* (Cambridge University Press).

White, S. (1991), 'Rise and Fall of a Party Pooper' in *The Times Higher Educational Supplement*, August 30.

Whiteley, P. (1983), *The Labour Party in Crisis* (Methuen, London).

Whyte, M. (1992) 'Prospects for Democratisation in China' in *Problems of Communism,* May–June.

Wightman, G. (1991) 'The Collapse of Communist Rule in Czechoslovakia and the June 1990 Parliamentary Elections' in *Parliamentary Affairs* 44 (1).

Wilde, L. (1990), 'Class Analysis and the Politics of New Social Movements' in *Capital and Class* 42.

Wilde, L. (1991), 'Poles Apart' and 'Women Against the Church' in *Catalyst* 8.

Wilde, L. (1992), 'The Left in Czechoslovakia' in *Catalyst* 9.

Williams, R. (1976), *Keywords: A Vocabulary of Culture and Society* (Fontana/Croom Helm, London).

Williams, P. (1979), *Gaitskell* (Jonathan Cape, London).

Williams, R., *Socialism and Ecology* (Socialist Environment and Resources Association, London, n.d.).

Wilson, H. (1964), *Purpose in Politics* (Weidenfeld & Nicolson, London).

Wilson, H. (1971), *The Labour Government, 1964–70: A Personal Record* (Weidenfeld & Nicolson, London).

Wilson, H. (1979), *Final Term: The Labour Government, 1974–76* (Weidenfeld & Nicolson, London).

Wilson, F. (1985), 'Trade Unions and Economic Policy' in Machin, H. & Wright, V., (eds), *Economic Policy and Policy–Making Under the Mitterand Presidency* (Polity, Cambridge).

Wilson, D. (1980), *Tito's Yugoslavia* (Cambridge University Press).

Wohl, R. (1966), *French Communism in the Making, 1914–1924* (Stanford University Press, California).

Wolchik, S. (1992) 'The Crisis of Socialism in Central and Eastern Europe and Socialism's Future' in Lemke, C. & Marks, G., (eds), *The Crisis of Socialism in Europe* (Duke University Press, Durham and London).

Wolf, F. O. (1986), 'Eco–Socialist Transition on the Threshold of the 21st Century' in *New Left Review* 158.

Wollstonecraft, M. (1992), *A Vindication of the Rights of Woman* (Penguin, Harmondsworth).

Woods, R. (1986), *Opposition in the GDR Under Honecker, 1971–85: An Introduction and Documentation* (Macmillan, Basingstoke).

World Commission on Environment and Development (1987), *Our Common Future* (Oxford University Press, Oxford).

Wright, P. (1987), with Greengrass, P., *Spycatcher* (Heinemann, Australia).

Wright, V. (1990) 'The Administrative Machine: Old Problems and New Dilemmas' in Hall, P, Hayward, J. & Machin, H.,(eds), *Developments in French Politics* (Macmillan, Basingstoke).

Yevtushenko, Y. (1991), *Fatal Half Measures: The Culture of Democracy in the Soviet Union* (Little, Brown & Co., Boston).

Zielonka, J. (1989), *Political Ideas in Contemporary Poland* (Gower, Aldershot).

Index